CW00643362

THE CAMBRIDGE COMPANION TO
LAW AND LITERAT

Despite an unprecedented level of interest in th
literature over the past two decades, readers have had no accessible introduction
to this rich engagement in medieval and early Tudor England. *The Cambridge
Companion to Medieval English Law and Literature* addresses this need by
combining an authoritative guide through the bewildering maze of medieval
law with concise examples illustrating how the law infiltrated literary texts
during this period. Foundational chapters written by leading specialists in legal
history prepare readers to be guided by noted literary scholars through
unexpected conversations with the law found in numerous medieval texts,
including major works by Chaucer, Langland, Gower and Malory. Part
I contains detailed introductions to legal concepts, practices and institutions in
medieval England, and Part II covers medieval texts and authors whose verse and
prose can be understood as engaging with the law.

Candace Barrington is a Professor in the English Department of Central
Connecticut State University. She has written multiple articles for journals and
edited volumes and is the co-editor of *Letter of the Law: Legal Practice and
Literary Production in Medieval England* (with Emily Steiner, 2002).

Sebastian Sobecki is Professor of Medieval English Literature at Groningen
University. He is the author of *The Sea and Medieval English Literature* (2008)
and *Unwritten Verities: The Making of England's Vernacular Legal Culture,
1463–1549* (2015).

THE CAMBRIDGE
COMPANION TO
MEDIEVAL ENGLISH LAW
AND LITERATURE

EDITED BY
CANDACE BARRINGTON
Central Connecticut State University

SEBASTIAN SOBECKI
University of Groningen, The Netherlands

CAMBRIDGE
UNIVERSITY PRESS

CAMBRIDGE
UNIVERSITY PRESS

University Printing House, Cambridge CB2 8BS, United Kingdom

One Liberty Plaza, 20th Floor, New York, NY 10006, USA

477 Williamstown Road, Port Melbourne, VIC 3207, Australia

314–321, 3rd Floor, Plot 3, Splendor Forum, Jasola District Centre,
New Delhi – 110025, India

79 Anson Road, #06–04/06, Singapore 079906

Cambridge University Press is part of the University of Cambridge.

It furthers the University's mission by disseminating knowledge in the pursuit of
education, learning, and research at the highest international levels of excellence.

www.cambridge.org
Information on this title: www.cambridge.org/9781107180789
DOI: 10.1017/9781316848296

First published 2019

Printed and bound in Great Britain by Clays Ltd, Elcograf S.p.A.

A catalogue record for this publication is available from the British Library.

ISBN 978-1-107-18078-9 Hardback
ISBN 978-1-316-63234-5 Paperback

CONTENTS

Contents

ILLUSTRATIONS

CONTRIBUTORS

CANDACE BARRINGTON is Professor of English at Central Connecticut State University

NEIL CARTLIDGE is Professor of English at Durham University

PETER D. CLARKE is Professor of Ecclesiastical History at the University of Southampton

GWILYM DODD is Associate Professor of History at Nottingham University

ANDREW GALLOWAY is Professor of English at Cornell University

STEFAN JURASINSKI is Associate Professor of English at SUNY Brockport

EMMA LIPTON is Associate Professor of English at the University of Missouri

ANTHONY MUSSON is Head of Research at Royal Palaces

PAUL RAFFIELD is Professor of Law at the University of Warwick

WENDY SCASE is the Geoffrey Shepherd Professor of Medieval English Literature at the University of Birmingham

DON C. SKEMER is Curator of Manuscripts at Princeton University Library

SEBASTIAN SOBECKI is Professor of Medieval English Literature and Culture at the University of Groningen

FIONA SOMERSET is Professor of English at the University of Connecticut

EMILY STEINER is Professor of English at the University of Pennsylvania

CORINNE SAUNDERS is Professor of English at Durham University

R.F. YEAGER is Professor of Medieval and Renaissance Studies at the University of West Florida

ABBREVIATIONS

AND: S. Gregory, W. Rothwell, D. A. Trotter, and M. Beddow (eds.), *Anglo-Norman Dictionary* (London: Maney Publishing for the Modern Humanities Research Association, 2005) www.anglo-norman.net/.

DIMEV: L. R. Mooney, D. W. Mosser, with E. Solopova, D. Thorpe and D. H. Radcliffe (eds.), The *DIMEV: An Open-Access, Digital Edition of the Index of Middle English Verse* www.dimev.net.

MED: H. Kurath, S. M. Kuhn and R. E. Lewis (eds.), *Middle English Dictionary* (Ann Arbor: University of Michigan Press, 1954–) http://quod.lib.umich.edu/m/med/.

TNA: The National Archives, Kew.

PREFACE

The last fifteen years have seen an unprecedented surge of interest in law and literature, particularly in medieval and early modern treatments. Despite this considerable interest, there exists no convenient introduction to this topic. Ever since the publication of Richard Firth Green's seminal study, *A Crisis of Truth: Literature and the Law in Ricardian England* (1999), the law has been recognised as central to the field of medieval English literature, not least because many leading late medieval writers were themselves trained in the law. Virtually all canonical writers of the period such as Geoffrey Chaucer, John Gower, William Langland, Thomas Hoccleve, John Lydgate, John Skelton, Thomas Wyatt and John Rastell engage with the law and legal forms in their texts, yet the arcane nature of much medieval and early modern law restricts access to specialists. Illuminating the connections between law and literature in late medieval England requires the reader to be familiar with the esoteric world of early English legal systems and to recognise the open-ended routes Middle English literary texts make through that legal world.

The challenges of late medieval English scholarship are familiar enough; those with the study of the contemporaneous legal system are less so. For instance, dealing with late medieval English courts means understanding, at least, three systems (ecclesiastical, royal and manorial) and three traditions (canon, civil and common law) whose interconnections remain understudied. It also means reading primary texts in three languages – Latin, Anglo-Norman (eventually known as Law French) and Middle English. And, most frustratingly, it means coming to grips with immense gaps in the documentary record (due to fires in the Inns of Court in the early fifteenth century) by working forward from the early thirteenth century and back from the mid-fifteenth century.

The Cambridge Companion to Medieval English Law and Literature addresses the need for an authoritative guide through the bewildering maze of late medieval law as well as the need for concise examples of how the law infiltrated contemporaneous literary texts. The *Companion* combines accessible chapters written by leading specialists in legal history with chapters exploring literary conversations with the law in the works of later medieval authors. Most of the literary chapters will cluster authors and texts by topics and genres; however, three chapters each focus exclusively on a canonical author: Langland, Chaucer and Gower. Our choice of the later medieval period captures not only the richness of literary uses of legal material, but also reflects the teaching curricula of many university programmes.

Our organising principle for this *Companion* addresses the need for detailed introductions to legal concepts, practices and institutions in post-Conquest England geared for literary scholars. Thus, Part I, 'Legal Contexts', provides a series of chapters that bring together recent scholarship on the most pertinent aspects of legal history: 'English Law before the Conquest', 'Languages and Law', 'Canon and Civil Law', 'Custom and Common Law', 'Magna Carta and Statutory Law' and, finally, 'Treatises, Tracts and Compilations'. Each of these chapters covers a broad field and assumes no prior knowledge of English legal history. Although our literary focus is the vibrant Middle English period, the legal background chapters in Part I also draw on much of the post-Conquest period to provide readers with a historical understanding of some of England's legal institutions. Where relevant, these chapters will also refer to pre-Conquest Anglo-Saxon institutions and traditions such as the *Leges Edwardi Confessoris*, royal charters, and continuities in ecclesiastical traditions.

Part II, 'Literary Texts', contains chapters on ten families of texts and authors from across the later medieval period whose verse and prose can be understood as engaging with legal discourse at several points of contact: 'Treason', 'Complaint Literature', 'Political Literature and Political Law', 'William Langland', 'Geoffrey Chaucer', 'John Gower', 'Lollards and Religious Writings', 'Lancastrian Literature', 'Middle English Romance and Malory's *Morte Darthur*' and 'Marriage and the Legal Culture of Witnessing'. These chapters refer to and employ the legal terms and concepts introduced in Part I. In this way, *The Cambridge Companion to Medieval English Law and Literature* forms the basis for students wishing to explore this rich area or for scholars to familiarise themselves with literary uses of the law.

Linda Bree at Cambridge University Press supported our project from its very inception, and we wish to express our sincere gratitude to her. We would also like to thank our contributors for their authoritative and finely crafted chapters and for their patience with our interventions during the copy-editing process. Work on this *Companion* has a been a pleasure, and we hope that our book will guide students and researchers through the bewildering maze of early English law and assist them in opening up the rich treasures still locked away in the field of medieval law and literature.

Candace Barrington and Sebastian Sobecki

Legal Contexts

PART 1

Legal Contexts

I

STEFAN JURASINSKI

English Law before the Conquest

Royal legislation issued in English between the baptism of Æthelberht of Kent (*c.* 600 AD) and the reign of Cnut (r. 1016–35) comprises one of Europe's more remarkable records of early political and legal thought. In it we see the transformation of England from a collection of disputing kingdoms to a nation united under the rule of Wessex in resistance to Viking incursions – all before one such Viking, Cnut (or 'Canute the Great'), overcame Æthelred II ('Ethelred the Unready') and then made full use of the laws maintained by Æthelred and his ancestors, thereby easing the shock of alien rule. No polity of early Western Europe (save Ireland) left such a lengthy record of its reflections on matters of law in its own language. As we will see, this corpus encompasses a range of prose genres beyond those issuing from the royal court; most were read and copied long after the Norman Conquest.

The most immediately striking aspect of Anglo-Saxon law is its having been written in the vernacular even as Latin was preferred for such purposes elsewhere in Europe. Why England favoured its own language for official use defies easy explanation. Poor Latinity does not account for it, as the kingdoms of Northumbria and Kent were pre-eminent centres of Latin learning until the arrival of Viking armies at the close of the eighth century.[1] When seen in a wider context, the advent of vernacular law-making in England may not even be as extraordinary as it now seems. In Einhard's *Vita Karoli Magni*, we learn of Charlemagne's wish to have in writing the most ancient heroic verse (*antiquissima carmina*) of the Franks and of his attempt to prepare a grammar of his own tongue (*grammaticam patrii sermonis*).[2] Poems such as the *Hêliand* and the fragmentary *Hildebrandslied* give some sense of the vigour of Francia's native verse tradition and suggest why its preservation interested the royal palace of Aachen. But not much of the literature to which Einhard referred is now extant, and one wonders if Anglo-Saxon England would occupy so central a place in the history of vernacular writing had more such texts from the continent survived.

King Alfred the Great (r. 871–99), whose book of laws (*domboc*) is the most complex to have been issued in the Anglo-Saxon period, was perhaps inspired to reinvigorate writing in English as much by Charlemagne's example as by the pressure of native tradition. (Ties between the house of Wessex and the Carolingian court had earlier been established when Alfred's father Æthelwulf married the daughter of Charles the Bald.) But Alfred's ambitions for the vernacular surpassed those of Charlemagne and subsequent Frankish monarchs. A number of Old English versions of Latin texts (among them Boethius's *Consolation of Philosophy*, Gregory the Great's *Pastoral Care*, and Augustine's *Soliloquies*) seem indebted to Alfred's initiative and perhaps to his own efforts as translator. Alfred also established schools where young aristocrats learned to read and write in their own language. In the decades after Alfred's death, such efforts allowed the West-Saxon dialect of Old English to serve (until the Norman Conquest) as the standard language for writing new texts and copying older ones.

While use of the vernacular must have advantaged the Anglo-Saxon state in countless ways, post-Conquest ignorance of Old English rendered its legislative achievements effectively mute during the later Middle Ages. The situation was hardly better in the early age of print. Anglo-Saxon law did not attract the enthusiasm of early modern antiquarians nearly as much as continental materials, a contrast evident in the reception of Charlemagne's *Admonitio generalis* (789) and Alfred's *domboc*, both of comparable importance to their respective polities. While no fewer than four editions of the *Admonitio* appeared between 1543 and 1557, Alfred's laws were not printed until 1568 (when they were edited by William Lambarde alongside other known works of Anglo-Saxon legislation), and not again until 1644, when Lambarde's edition was revised by the Cambridge orientalist Abraham Wheelocke.[3]

Another reworking of Lambarde's edition in 1721 by David Wilkins (also an orientalist) formed the basis of all commentary for well over a century. Inevitably, however, editing the Old English legal corpus came to be influenced by comparative philology, a movement then ascendant in some German universities. Its most famous exponent was Jakob Grimm, whose pioneering studies of historical grammar, mythology, folklore and law shaped the field for generations. (More will be said about comparative philology and its uncertain outcomes later in the present chapter.) To the chagrin of Frederic William Maitland, the pre-eminent legal historian of his day, scholarly writing on Anglo-Saxon law became a largely German affair by the end of the nineteenth century.[4] Felix Liebermann's *Die Gesetze der Angelsachsen* (1903–16), a forbidding monument to the methods then dominant in German scholarship, remains the most reliable edition of the

Anglo-Saxon laws, building upon the earlier efforts of Reinhold Schmid (1832; rev. edn 1858) and Benjamin Thorpe (1840). Not until Patrick Wormald's *Making of English Law* (1999) did the work of returning these texts to Anglophone audiences begin in earnest. Due in part to Wormald's achievement, specialists in the literature of pre-Conquest England have come to recognise that Anglo-Saxon law constitutes an important subgenre of Old English prose whose origins and generic conventions demand the sort of attention long lavished on the homily and the chronicle. The present chapter is meant to help readers approach this corpus of legal prose with a minimum of confusion, particularly those aspects that would endure beyond the Norman Conquest.

The Texts of Anglo-Saxon Law

Identifying Anglo-Saxon legal texts is not as straightforward as it might initially seem. Sticking to laws issued in the names of various kings places us on deceptively safe ground, as a fair number of the materials so categorised are mere royal proclamations of national penance prompted by the renewal of Viking activities. Only the laws of Ine, Alfred and Cnut systematically attempt to establish norms governing disputes and transactions. Thus looking beyond texts issued from the royal court may reveal much about Anglo-Saxon England's legal machinery. The English Church, the great purveyor of literacy at this time, produced a regulatory literature outstripping Old English legislation in scope, volubility and sophistication. Because the Church existed to furnish remedies against sin, it engaged with ineffable problems of juristic casuistry in ways secular authorities might not. The medicine it offered guilty consciences was prescribed in Latin and Old English texts that seemingly recognised few boundaries between questions of pastoral care and those of secular law. This literature, with its refined thinking on matters of culpability, anticipated by centuries the doctrine of *mens rea* (the notion that one's state of mind in performing an act, and not the act itself, rendered one culpable); in time, its provisions would find their way into pre-Conquest royal legislation. Though penitentials and secular laws are customarily considered distinct bodies of normative writing, both literatures were composed by elite clergy and consequently manifest overlapping concerns. Extant manuscripts frequently blur these lines as well: both in England and on the Continent, laws and penitentials sometimes appear in the same codex.[5]

However voluminous, the secular and ecclesiastical laws of Anglo-Saxon England still furnish meager evidence for the workings of governance when compared with what is available in later periods. Such scarcity makes even the briefest statements important. Our knowledge of the law of marriage, for example, would be impoverished without the short tract *Wifmannes beweddung*. Similar texts enumerate the duties of bishops and procedures for administering ordeals and oaths. That clergy seem more concerned to regulate ordeals than marriages is an effect of the period in which these texts appeared. Marriage would not become a sacrament for a century or more, while the support of the Church for ordeals would not be withdrawn until the Fourth Lateran Council (1215).

Establishing the ambit of legal prose is further complicated by the vast, unwieldy and protean corpus known as 'diplomatic' literature: wills, writs and charters. All three legal instruments demonstrate the importance of writing to the practice of law (a matter to be taken up later). Though the debt is not always certain, these three subtypes of diplomatic texts owe something to Roman practice – as did written legislation itself according to Bede.[6] Old English diplomatic texts were of enduring interest in subsequent periods: the fifteenth-century *Liber Abbatiae*, for example, gives Old English wills and charters with translations into Middle English and Latin.

Wills show one way the encroachment of literacy might facilitate legal change. Prior to the widespread use of these written instruments, more rigid strictures encumbered the disposition of land. These new instruments occasioned a new term, *bocland* ('bookland'), to describe parcels not governed by traditional rules of descent; those distributed by older unwritten customs were designated *folcland*. Yet the changes effected by these instruments were less profound than might be imagined, with testamentary disposition (for example) retaining its predominantly oral character through the pre-Conquest era, traces of which are evident in contemporaneous wills.[7] And even *bocland*, as Alfred's laws assert (§41), might fall under the same rules of hereditary descent that governed *folcland* in spite of having been alienated in writing.

Charters – essentially, records of transactions in land – form the bulk of extant Old English writing, and the work of situating them in reliable editions is ongoing. Along with their inherent importance to the history of tenurial law and custom, charters are useful for the incidental light they shed on aspects of procedure left obscure by legislative and other sources. One charter, the 'Fonthill Letter', narrates how a recidivist thief (whose case reached King Alfred) lost all his holdings in land. Another describes a significant council convoked in 824 by the Mercian king Beornwulf. Including 'nearly all the southern English bishops' and a 'papal legate', the council's proceedings were preserved because it considered the descent of 'the minster at Westbury and its endowments'.[8]

Writs – a standard term for sealed letters issued by the royal chancery having a wider range of functions than in later periods – also survive in relative abundance. Their aims were probably more varied than the extant witnesses suggest, which predominately confirm 'grants of lands and liberties to ecclesiastics and religious houses'.[9] Because they were concerned with the descent of property and privileges, both charters and (to a lesser extent) writs were sometimes forged both before and after the Conquest.

Law and Oral Culture

While they are known primarily for establishing the discipline of comparative philology, Jakob Grimm and his followers also emphasised the relationship between law and the spoken word. Influenced by the emergence of modern nation-states and attendant attempts to reclaim indigenous legal practices, Grimm and his generation found oral tradition a more trustworthy vehicle for preserving the law than writing. The former, of course, is accessible only through the latter, and so arose the concomitant assumption that traces of unwritten custom are most conspicuous in aphorisms, often poetic in nature, either embedded in literary and legislative texts or circulating independent of them. However hoary the rhetoric in which these assumptions come down to us, they should not be dismissed outright. One cannot read *Beowulf* without being struck by its admonitory style and legal formulae, some enduring into the present. Hrothgar temporarily transfers ownership of Heorot to Beowulf with an alliterative phrase – *Hafa nu ond geheald husa selest* ('Have now and hold the best of houses') – familiar from the Book of Common Prayer's rite for the solemnisation of matrimony. Other works employ a distinctly legal register pointing back to a shared Germanic past. Wulfstan, for example, admonishes those guilty of grave sins to *þingian* ('negotiate, settle') with God, likening thereby penitential acts to the compensations for wounds and slights characteristic of secular law from England to Iceland (where the proceeding was labelled a 'thing'). Those seeking a full sense of Anglo-Saxon law cannot neglect literary texts, though scholars so engaged are now more cautious than was the norm generations ago.

Another reason not to discount the views of Grimm and his generation is that law-giving kings of the Anglo-Saxon period seem to have been aware of the tensions between their ordinances and oral tradition. One way to negotiate the problems that ensued from issuing laws in writing was assuring audiences that nothing was really changing. We find such efforts in one of the earliest works of royal legislation we possess, the laws of Hloþhere and Eadric (679x686), which survive in one manuscript, the *Textus Roffensis* (about which more will be said later). It begins with the following proclamation:

> Hloþhære 7 Eadric, Cantwara cyningas, ecton þa ǽ þa ðe heora aldoras ær geworhton ðyssum domum, þe her efter sægeþ.[10]
>
> (Hloþhere and Eadric, kings of the people of Kent, added to the laws that their ancestors made before with these decrees, which are stated hereafter.)

The prologue's implicit argument, whose language would be repeated in prefaces to the legislation of Wihtred and Ine, is that written laws (*domas*) were suitable means for preserving and expanding upon the customary laws (*ǽ*) that had earlier existed independent of writing. That it was said at all – not once but three times from the seventh to the ninth century – suggests that some in the Kentish and West-Saxon elite still looked wistfully on the period prior to the arrival of written law, which presumably conferred disproportionate advantages on the literate. The resentments of these slighted magnates may well have required soothing each time new laws were issued.

While the belief of Grimm and his descendants that one might glimpse behind laws and poems of this period a uniform 'Germanic law' now enjoys little support, their sense of traditional law as indifferent to the machinations of the royal court continues to shape present-day commentary. Wormald is the most prominent scholar to claim that works of royal legislation were of more symbolic than practical significance. Yet underestimating the importance of royal law is as much a hindrance to grasping the political life of Anglo-Saxon England as the tendency, prevalent among scholars of earlier generations, to assume complacently that legislation in this period functioned in the same manner as modern statutes. While citations of royal law are virtually absent from Anglo-Saxon records of litigation (in marked contrast to what is found in Francia), one charter issued by Wihtred in 699 appears to back provisions for ecclesiastical immunities earlier set forth in his laws of 695.[11] On top of this, ample evidence suggests the longest of the royal lawbooks – King Alfred the Great's *domboc* – was at least *intended* to be read and applied. The circumstances giving rise to the *domboc* are suggested by a passage in Asser's biography of the king (§106), where we are told that Alfred scolded his judges for their ignorance; they responded by devoting themselves to reading and writing.

Allusions to '*seo domboc*' in the subsequent laws of Edward the Elder and Æthelstan (Alfred's son and grandson, respectively) suggest that Alfred's admonitions were of lasting effect. Moreover, provisions of the *domboc* and the earlier laws of Kent resurface in the legislation authored by Wulfstan for Æthelred II and Cnut. The Anglo-Saxon laws were not merely paper boats floating on a sea of oral tradition. Rather, pre-Conquest England established a tradition of legal literacy that pervaded most aspects of dispute resolution by the end of Anglo-Saxon period.

How long written law remained in a state of tension with oral tradition is uncertain. The persistence of such a climate into the ninth century is suggested by the fact that *æ* and *domas* are used in the prologue to Alfred's laws much as they were in the seventh century. The terms are not found in later materials, so Alfred's *dombóc* may mark one of the last occasions in which an Anglo-Saxon king felt obliged to justify writing laws down. By the later Anglo-Saxon period, both terms would be eclipsed by the ancestor of our Modern English word 'law', Old English *lagu*, a term borrowed from the Danes and related etymologically to the Norse verb *leggja*, 'to lay down'.[12] Once adopted by the English, the term may have designated enactments issuing from the royal court and *witan* (a body of elite counsellors) rather than the informal 'law' of unwritten custom.[13]

Prior to the introduction of *lagu*, Old English was developing its own inventory of terms to designate written law. The words *riht* ('what is in accordance with law, human or divine') and *asetnysse* ('what is set or fixed, a statute, law'), which have some rough correspondence in meaning to *æ* and *dom*, respectively, were favoured in the post-Alfredian period but not unknown before it.[14] Though *æ* (meaning 'customary law') survives into the later period and should not be confused with 'marriage', another sense of the same word, its meaning eventually edges closer to *asetnysse* than *riht*; by the time of Alfred, *æ* is being used to refer to divine law as set forth in Scripture.[15] For its part, *riht* begins its drift towards denoting personal liberties (and thus, perhaps, the space once occupied by *æ*) in the sermons of Wulfstan, leaving the Old English lexicon with no word to designate 'custom' save *þeaw*, a term infrequently used in a legal register.

Law in Practice

Scholarship on Anglo-Saxon legal procedure remains scant: the sole book-length treatment remains an 1876 volume published by Henry Adams and his group of Harvard students.[16] In part, research on this question has been hindered by earlier historians' tendency to view the pre-Conquest legal order as governed by inflexible, arbitrary rules and mindless superstition. Such modern perceptions contributed to the consensus that Anglo-Saxon law relied on self-help and feuding, with an effective state apparatus emerging only during the reign of Henry II (r. 1154–89).[17] (Earlier generations of scholars had mistakenly credited King Alfred with inventing trial by jury and much else besides.) The genuine innovations in Alfred's laws, however, make it difficult to assume a wholly ineffectual Anglo-Saxon state.

Above all, Alfred's *domboc* is an imposing monument to the notion of written law itself. Nearly half the text reproduces Ine's laws, the fullest representation available of royal law in the seventh century. Alfred's contributions begin with an eccentric translation of the Ten Commandments and subsequent legal clauses in Exodus before narrating (in compressed and highly distorted fashion) the Council of Jerusalem recorded in Acts 15. Alfred then claims nameless English 'synods' as the sources of his own laws while also acknowledging debts to those of his predecessors Æthelberht, Ine and Offa.

Alfred's implicit argument for making the written text the basis for legitimate law was perhaps meant to render his magnates and bishops more amenable to legislative reforms. One of these is a reliance upon confession and penance for correcting wrongs not evident in prior laws. Traditionally, scholars have assumed that incorporating these religious practices indicates the state's weakness during Alfred's reign. But whether these new clauses show the church acting as the agent of the state, or the state of the church, is in fact difficult to determine, and perhaps misses the point. Anglo-Saxon kings and bishops were not in the habit of thinking of themselves as occupying distinct spheres of action. Not until the reign of William I would clear lines between secular and ecclesiastical jurisdictions emerge.[18]

In spite of such apparent novelties, Alfred's laws offer a calculated impression of continuity amid change. As in prior legislation, wrongs are principally remedied by self-help, with the king assuming when necessary the role of peacemaker and mediator. Compensations for injuries are carefully tabulated, much as they had been in Æthelberht's laws. Looming over these provisions are the two mainstays of pre-Conquest proof: the oath and (arguably) the ordeal, two legal rituals not as distinct in this period as our nomenclature suggests. Both permitted litigants to invoke divine witness in support of their testimony with the understanding that subsequent misfortunes (illness, infection, falling from a horse, or choking on Eucharistic bread) would show forth their guilt. Alfred emphasises the importance of honouring one's oath and pledge (*wedd*), a legal feature perhaps motivated, as Wormald maintained, by his introduction of oaths of loyalty to the king.[19] Stressing the oath also ensured clerics remained central to the disputing process. Alfred's principal 'innovations' thus rest upon elements of litigation – the oath and the role of clergy as mediators of legal rituals – present in written English law from its inception but newly emphasised in the *domboc*.

The ambitions underlying Alfred's *domboc* had deep roots in the West-Saxon past, as seen in Ine's earlier laws. By beginning his laws with a concern for ecclesiastical disciplines such as abstention from 'servile work' on Sunday as well as the prompt baptism of infants, Ine established himself as a protector of the church and its interests. Similarly, Ine recognised the royal court's entitlement to be part of negotiations between wrongdoers and the aggrieved. Resolving disputes privately, without involving official justices, is accorded harsh penalties, presumably for the first time. With the help of these precedents, law at the time of Alfred's death was set on a path towards becoming centralised and bureaucratic, a development not fully realised until the late twelfth century.

Manuscripts and Later Witnesses

The surviving manuscripts containing Anglo-Saxon legislation constitute a fraction of what circulated prior to the Conquest. None is earlier than the tenth century, which means that all extant texts reach us somewhat distorted by their manuscript setting. Nevertheless, the manuscripts show these texts were often consulted and thus anything but idle acts of royal self-aggrandisement. Whereas most Old English poems have a single manuscript witness, the major compilations of Old English law – those of Alfred and Cnut – survive in six and three, respectively.

A few manuscripts illustrate how Old English legislative prose was used before and after the Norman Conquest. Cambridge, Corpus Christi College 173 (also known as the 'Parker Manuscript') is the earliest witness to both the *domboc* and the *Anglo-Saxon Chronicle* (a collection of annals initiated during the lifetime of King Alfred). That these texts share space in one manuscript says much about how the *domboc* was viewed during the reign of Æthelstan. Even as Alfred's descendants asserted the lingering authority of his *domboc*, the importance of the document probably resided in its status as a monument to the ambitions of the West-Saxon kingdom, no longer the minor polity which Bede had practically ignored.

In all likelihood, other manuscripts shared the organisation of Corpus 173. This is almost certain to have been the case with British Library, Cotton Otho B.xi, which was largely destroyed in a fire at Ashburnham House in 1731 – the same fire responsible for the extensive *lacunae* towards the end of our sole manuscript copy of *Beowulf*. We know the contents of Cotton Otho B.xi only through transcripts Laurence Nowell made in 1562 and a later eighteenth-century description. Another manuscript prepared in roughly the same period as Cotton Otho B.xi, BL Burney MS 277, was destroyed much earlier. Those who used it for penmanship exercises in the thirteenth century probably had no sense of its importance; nor did those who, not long thereafter, unbound its leaves and used the one leaf that remains to us as 'a wrapper'.[20]

Such was the fate of much Anglo-Saxon material during the later Middle Ages. But one event that would seem to have boded ill for the Anglo-Saxon laws acted contrary to expectation. The Norman Conquest brought with it the demolition of Anglo-Saxon churches and cathedrals as well as the replacement of local bishops and abbots by French speakers loyal to Duke William. It also initiated an extraordinary attempt to come to terms with the legal traditions of a now-subjugated kingdom. What we owe to preservation efforts during the reign of Henry I is made clear by Wormald, who identifies them as the primary vehicle for transmitting Old English law for the next half millennium.[21] For example, without the *Textus Roffensis*, prepared in Rochester in 1124, we would know nothing of early Kentish legislation, including the laws of Æthelberht, probably the oldest text we possess in Old English, antedating even *Cædmon's Hymn*. That the scribe often modernises the text shows that these laws were still being read. His substitutions of newer for more archaic terms indicate its status as a text intended for regular use.

A less celebrated member of this post-Conquest tradition is Cambridge, Corpus Christi College 383, a codex probably originating at St Paul's in London. Although the manuscript is no longer assumed to be contemporary with *Textus Roffensis*, its copies of the laws of Alfred and Cnut do exhibit the deteriorating knowledge of the Old English language often characteristic of the post-Conquest era. In common with *Textus Roffensis*, its extensive twelfth-century marginalia show the scribe supplying text from other manuscripts for his own emendations, and his work reflects eager if often misguided study of Anglo-Saxon laws. Uniquely, it introduces each chapter of the *domboc* with rubrics loosely based on the list of chapter titles found in Corpus Christi 173.

Another stream of this post-Conquest tradition was of more enduring relevance than those just described. For most of the later Middle Ages, Anglo-Saxon legislation was known only through twelfth-century Latin translations. Two of these, the *Consiliatio* and *Instituta Cnuti*, show the particular interest of Anglo-Norman clerics in Cnut's legislation. More ambitious texts of this sort were *Quadripartitus* and the *Leges Henrici Primi*, both traceable to the same anonymous author. The former assembles most Anglo-Saxon legislation, whereas the latter, in spite of its title, represents a *catena* of Anglo-Saxon legal sources, Old English penitential canons, clauses of Frankish legislation and quotations from patristic writings. Together, these translations provided a rough sense of the pre-Conquest legal tradition.

Some of the specialised terms of Anglo-Saxon pleading survived into later periods, perhaps through these texts' influence. Old English *morð* became *murdrum* (in time losing its original association with secret homicide); *mund*

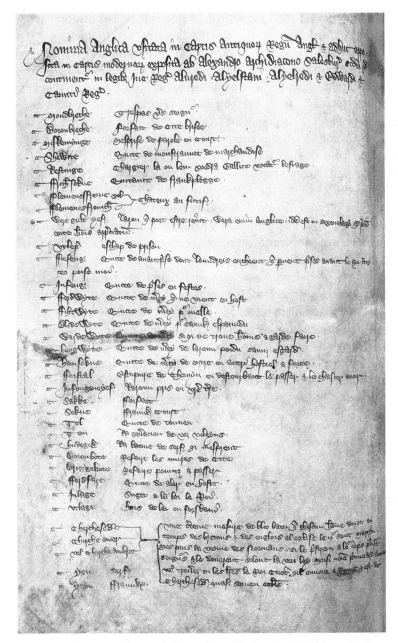

Figure 1.1 The *Expositio vocabulorum* from The National Archives, London, MS E 164/2, f. 302v. By permission of The National Archives, London.

became *mundium*. Other terms less susceptible to Latinisation were still regarded as furnishing knowledge of English custom that might prove indispensable to the lord of a manor. Their persistence well beyond the Conquest is evidenced by a legal glossary (the *Expositio vocabulorum*; Figure 1.1) that began circulating after the Norman Conquest and survives in manuscripts as late as the thirteenth century. Some witnesses to the *Expositio* include a prologue asserting that its list of *nomina Anglica* are given 'according to what is contained in the laws of King Ine, of Alfred, of Æthelstan, of Æthelred and of kings Edward and Cnut'.[22]

Despite such efforts, knowledge of the Anglo-Saxon legal tradition became scarce by the close of the fourteenth century. That French became the language of pleading in English courts from the twelfth century onwards did little to improve its fortunes. If Chaucer's Sergeant at Law may be taken as representative of his profession, legal memory was not expected to extend to a time before the Norman Conquest.

Yet ghosts of the pre-Conquest past haunt even Chaucer's text. The Sergeant at Law, we are told, knows well the 'doomes alle / that from the tyme of kyng Willam were falle' (I.323–4). And he is adept at preparing the sort of document that we now call a 'contract', but that Chaucer refers to, with all the older associations of the word seemingly intact, as a 'thyng' (I.325).[23] By the close of the fourteenth century, these terms had formed part of the vocabulary of written English law for nearly 800 years. Not for another two centuries would the precocious and intellectually formidable tradition from which they descend be widely known again.

Notes

1. Nicholas Brooks, *The Early History of the Church of Canterbury* (Leicester: Leicester University Press, 1984), 171–4.
2. *Einhardi vita Karoli Magni*, SS rer. Germ. 25, ed. G. Waitz et al. (Hanover: Hahnsche Buchhandlung, 1911), 29, ch. 29.
3. *Die Admonitio generalis Karls des Großen*, MGH Fontes 16, ed. H. Mordek et al. (Wiesbaden: Harrasowitz, 2013), 148–9; William Lambarde, ed. Αρχαιονομια (London: John Day, 1568); and, Abraham Wheelocke, ed. Αρχαιονομια (Cambridge: Roger Daniel, 1644).
4. Patrick Wormald, 'Frederic William Maitland and the Earliest English Law', *Law and History Review* 16 (1998), 1–25 at 9.
5. Abigail Firey, *A Contrite Heart* (Leiden: Brill, 2009), 194–5; Patrick Wormald, *The Making of English Law*, vol. 1 (Oxford: Blackwell, 1999), 210–24.
6. F. E. Harmer, *Anglo-Saxon Writs* (Manchester: University of Manchester Press, 1952), 25–6; Bede, *Ecclesiastical History*, II, 5.
7. H. D. Hazeltine, 'General Preface', in *Anglo-Saxon Wills*, ed. Dorothy Whitelock (Cambridge: Cambridge University Press, 1930), xxii–iii.

8. Patrick Wormald, 'Charters, Law and the Settlement of Disputes in Anglo-Saxon England', in *The Settlement of Disputes in Early Medieval Europe*, ed. Wendy Davies and Paul Fouracre (Cambridge: Cambridge University Press, 1986), 152 and 262.
9. Harmer, *Writs*, 105.
10. *The Beginnings of English Law*, ed. and trans. Lisi Oliver (Toronto: University of Toronto Press, 2002), 126–7.
11. Catalogue number 20, 'Electronic Sawyer' database, an updated version of Peter Sawyer, in *Anglo-Saxon Charters: An Annotated List and Bibliography* (London: Royal Historical Society, 1968); Simon Keynes, 'England, 700–900', in *The New Cambridge Medieval History*, ed. Rosamond McKitterick (Cambridge: Cambridge University Press, 1995), 26.
12. Angelika Lutz, 'Language Contact in the Scandinavian Period', in *The Oxford Handbook of the History of English*, ed. Terttu Nevalainen and Elizabeth Closs Traugott (Oxford: Oxford University Press, 2012), 511.
13. Stefan Jurasinski, *The Old English Penitentials and Anglo-Saxon Law* (Cambridge: Cambridge University Press, 2015), 10.
14. *An Anglo-Saxon Dictionary*, ed. Joseph Bosworth, rev. T. Northcote Toller (Oxford: Clarendon, 1898), s.v.
15. Wormald, *Making*, 95 n. 330.
16. Henry Adams, Henry Cabot Lodge, Ernest Young and J. Laurence Laughlin, *Essays in Anglo-Saxon Law* (Boston: Little, Brown and Co., 1876).
17. Wormald, 'Charters', 149–50.
18. See C. H. Haskins, *Norman Institutions* (New York: Frederick Ungar, 1918; repr. 1960), 30–8.
19. David Pratt, *The Political Thought of King Alfred the Great* (Cambridge: Cambridge University Press, 2007), 233–4.
20. N. R. Ker, *Catalogue of Manuscripts Containing Anglo-Saxon* (Oxford: Clarendon, 1957), 172 (no. 136).
21. Wormald, *Making*, 228.
22. *The Red Book of the Exchequer, part III*, ed. Hubert Hall (London: Eyre and Spottiswoode, 1896), 1032 (my translation); Bruce O'Brien, *God's Peace and King's Peace* (Philadelphia: University of Pennsylvania Press, 1998), 55.
23. Hazeltine, 'General Preface', xxii.

Further Reading

Hough, Carole, *An Ald Reht: Essays on Anglo-Saxon Law*, Newcastle upon Tyne: Cambridge Scholars, 2014.
Jurasinski, Stefan, Lisi Oliver and Andrew Rabin (eds.), *English Law before Magna Carta: Felix Liebermann and Die Gesetze der Angelsachsen*, Leiden: Brill, 2010.
Lambert, Tom, *Law and Order in Anglo-Saxon England*, Oxford: Oxford University Press, 2017.
Liebermann, Felix (ed.), *Die Gesetze der Angelsachsen*, 3 vols., Halle: Niemeyer, 1903–16.
McNeill, John T. and Helena M. Gamer (trans.), *Medieval Handbooks of Penance*, New York: Columbia University Press, 1938.

Munske, Horst Haider, *Der germanische Rechtswortschatz im Bereich der Missetaten*, Berlin: De Gruyter, 1973.
Oliver, Lisi, *The Body Legal in Barbarian Law*, Toronto: University of Toronto Press, 2011.
Robertson, Agnes Jane (ed.), *Anglo-Saxon Charters*, Cambridge: Cambridge University Press, 1956.

2

GWILYM DODD

Languages and Law in Late Medieval England: English, French and Latin

There are inherent complications involved in discerning how the English, French and Latin languages were used to facilitate legal process in late medieval England. These problems relate, for the most part, to the vernacular languages – English and French – for reasons that will become clear in due course. Latin is more straightforward. This is because it was employed principally as a language of the formal written record and its impact is plain to see in the reams of legal records held in The National Archives and in print. Latin was used to compile the main records of the royal courts – the plea rolls – from their very first appearance in the mid-1190s. It was also used in the writs which initiated legal proceedings ('original' writs) and in the writs subsequently issued to control these proceedings ('judicial' writs). It predominated in other branches of central government, particularly within the main administrative offices of the royal bureaucracy: the exchequer and the chancery. The status Latin enjoyed as the foremost language of the legal written record remained undiminished throughout the Middle Ages and it was not until 1731 that it was finally replaced by English. It occupied this position because it was considered a prestige language and a universal language of learning and culture. It was also understood to be the most effective language to convey meaning with precision and exactitude, and to preserve this meaning for posterity. Some of the earliest law manuals, written by Glanvill, Bracton and Hengham, were written in Latin for these reasons. French, and to a much lesser extent English, could also be used for the written record, but it was their employment as *spoken* languages which has, above all, created complications for historians. A key point to note is that the language chosen to record what was said in court did not always indicate the language that had actually been verbalised. This is what makes measuring the respective shares of English and French in the oral/aural legal culture of late medieval England so problematic. In what follows, I explore how historians have approached this particular conundrum. I also consider more generally how languages were used and how a trilingual legal culture determined the way contemporaries both experienced and accessed late medieval law.

A consensus has long existed that in Edward I's reign (1272–1307), and projecting well into the fourteenth century until at least 1362 (the significance of this date will become clear in due course), French was the principal language of pleading in the royal courts. Pleading is the catchall term given to the formal oral proceedings of a court. It required a high level of legal expertise and was conducted as a matter of course by professional men of law; that is to say, serjeants-at-law and attorneys. It involved the initial statement outlining the details of the case (sometimes described as the 'count'), as well as all subsequent legal arguments. The historiographical consensus is founded on an indisputable body of evidence. For instance, from the mid-thirteenth century French began to be used, alongside Latin, in didactic legal texts, many of which provided instruction in pleading. The transcripts of lectures delivered to students studying law in the reign of Edward I were also written in French. More importantly, French was mainly used in the compilation of law reports, which first appeared in c. 1270, and acted as training manuals for law students. Unlike the plea rolls, which noted speech indirectly, they recorded what was actually said in court. It has quite reasonably been argued that law students would hardly have compiled records of this nature, for the purposes of instruction, in a language different from that which had been spoken. Also of importance is the written plaint – or bill. The first surviving bills addressed to the justices of the General Eyre – the main agency of royal justice in the provinces in the thirteenth century – date to 1286. They are brief statements of the litigant's grievance and a plea for assistance. Bills presented to sessions of the General Eyre, along with petitions presented in parliament, and bills presented later in King's Bench and chancery, constituted what has been described as a 'bill revolution' in legal culture and process. The principal language of the written complaint – variously called plaints, bills, petitions or supplications – was, until the fifteenth century, French. The choice of this language was probably a deliberate attempt to emulate common-law procedure by offering, in effect, a written substitute for oral pleading.[1]

The prominence of French in late medieval English legal culture reflected its importance as the preferred vernacular language of the political and educated elites of the twelfth and thirteenth centuries. Research into the languages spoken more generally in this period is fraught with as many methodological difficulties as a more narrow investigation into language-use in a legal context, but there is a general consensus that French would have been learnt from an early age by the men who made careers in the legal profession, as well as those of higher social status who might have made use of the law for their own purposes, especially in the central royal courts. In these circumstances, it made perfect sense for French to be used in courtroom dialogue. The proliferation of French-language legal texts was symptomatic of the growth of this legal profession, as royal justice expanded and demand from litigants for legal representation grew. With the production of legal texts came a tighter definition of legal concepts and processes, and with it the emergence of a new technical vocabulary, which has come to be known as Law French.[2] Common legal terms such as 'tort', 'trespass', 'deceit', 'debt', 'to allege', 'to assert', 'to deny' and 'to prove' were French in origin and carried specific legal meaning. This signalled the synonymy of the French language with legal process. The development of specialist Law French required greater levels of expertise on the part of the men who made law their profession, and this in turn helped foster a sense of professional identity and an *espirit de corps*. It also made the French language virtually indispensable to the implementation of legal process in the medieval period, a crucial factor explaining why its use persisted into the fifteenth century. It was a measure of the status of French as the foremost language of the law that by the early fourteenth century it had superseded Latin as the record of formal statutory legislation. French had been used informally well before this to draft new statutes – underlining the point that this was the language lawyers and royal justices routinely spoke to each other – but the fact that it was now used for the most solemn and definitive of all legal documents shows how vital it had become in shaping the legal life of the kingdom.

While this broad historical narrative has received general acceptance, in two specific areas there has been disagreement. First, although historians are generally agreed that by Edward I's reign the French language was pre-eminent in legal process, assessing the status of French before Edward I's reign has proved less straightforward. In his groundbreaking essay on the subject, George Woodbine argues that French only acquired its prominence in the late thirteenth century, and that before this time English was probably the language used for pleading in the law courts, while Latin was employed for the written record.[3] His arguments are based partly on the delayed emergence of French in the written records. If French had been the dominant language of the law from the outset, he reasons, why was it not until the late thirteenth century that its pre-eminent position becomes clear in surviving documentation? For Woodbine, the shift from Latin to French in legal writing indicated a shift to French *from English* in legal discourse. He notes that when Latin proved incapable of adequately conveying meaning in the legal treatises of the thirteenth century, such as *Bracton*, it was English words rather than French that were routinely substituted for translation. At the very least, he remarks, this indicated 'a wide general knowledge and use of English among the higher classes of Englishmen'.[4] For Woodbine, the impetus for the spread of French was the 'French invasion of the thirteenth century'; that is to say, the influx into government, and the king's circle, of high-ranking courtiers and administrators from Poitou and other parts of France.

More recently, his views have been challenged, and to a great extent superseded, by Paul Brand.[5] Brand points out that the English words found in *Bracton* are of a very limited nature, mostly relating to criminal justice which had its roots in the Anglo-Saxon past. Brand also notes evidence dating to 1210 which indicates that the oath taken by the jurors of a grand assize was spoken in French: 'it is difficult to believe', Brand argues, 'that this would have been the case if the rest of the court's proceedings were being conducted in English'.[6] For Brand the emergence of French legal writing in the late thirteenth century was not a symptom of a shift in the language spoken in the courts, but indicative of the growth of the legal profession and an emerging market for instructional and training legal texts.[7] On balance, he concludes that French was very likely to have been 'the [spoken] language of the royal courts from the very beginning of the system of central royal courts established by Henry II [in the late twelfth century]'.[8]

The other area of contention concerns the extent to which French dominated all discussion that took place in court. Some historians have made a point of distinguishing between the more formulaic opening stages of a trial, on the one hand, and the debates and arguments that took place subsequently as part of the legal process, on the other hand. According to Michael Clanchy, 'the language of the formal pleadings was not necessarily that of cross-examinations and forensic dialogue'.[9] He cites a case dating to the 1270s, from the law manual *Placita Corone*, which recorded the cross-examination of a man called Hugh who was accused of stealing a horse. The dialogue is in French. Are we to conclude that Hugh – a 'poor villager' – spoke and understood French? Common sense, Clanchy argues, would suggest not: English was the language of the lower social orders. There is thus a strong case for assuming that the record of this case was compiled primarily to serve the didactic and Francophone needs of its readers (i.e., law students) rather than to record the words actually spoken by the defendant. In another example cited by Clanchy, dating to 1313–14, it is clear that jurors presenting their responses to the 'articles of the Eyre' in Kent were required to submit orally in English through their foreman, and that the use of Latin and French was primarily restricted to the class of legal and clerical professionals.

Against this, however, are examples used by Brand that suggest that French was rather more pervasive. Brand cites a case brought before the King's Bench in 1291 in which the defendant disavowed the arguments made by his serjeants, only to have it pointed out that the presence of his attorney during the pleading of the trial signified consent, and he – the attorney – was fully appraised of his client's position because, as the plea roll noted, he 'understood French'.[10] Similarly, in a case dating to 1295 between the prior of Lewes and the bishop of Gravesend, it was noted that the arguments of Henry Spigurnel, serjeant-at-law, had to be conveyed to the bishop's representative in English because 'he did not understand French'.[11] The clear implication is that French was usually used for the forensic dialogue of the court. In fact, it is not clear how far the views of Brand and Clanchy are incompatible. It is noticeable that while Clanchy's examples involve individuals who were not professional men of law – jurors, defendants and litigants – Brand's examples involve trained legal experts – attorneys and serjeants-at-law – who would have been at least bilingual, possibly even trilingual. Perhaps a solution to the conundrum is to acknowledge that the language of court proceedings was flexible, and determined above all by pragmatism, so that the forensic dialogue of legal proceedings might actually have involved French *or* English, depending on who was party to that dialogue. On balance, while cross-examination of witnesses and other parties to a suit was probably mostly done in English, legal argumentation is likely – at this stage – to have been conducted in French.

What was true of the central royal courts may not necessarily, of course, have applied locally. The growth of the legal profession was strongly associated with the emergence of the royal courts at Westminster, and especially the Common Pleas (essentially a court of civil law, used for the recovery of debt or property), which attracted comparatively wealthy litigants who depended on trained French-speaking professionals to represent their interests. It might be assumed, therefore, that in other contexts the French language was less important. In fact, the indications point in the opposite direction. In the example above, of the case brought before the Eyre of Kent in 1313–14, it is noticeable that French was used by the chief clerk when he was reading out the enrolled presentments to the justices; this was clearly the language that lawyers expected to be spoken even in the provinces. It was in itinerant sessions of the General Eyre, as we have seen, that bills began to be presented in French, which suggests that locally based attorneys and clerks were just as capable of using French for legal purposes as their London-based counterparts. In the localities, just as at Westminster, a cadre of attorneys and scriveners emerged in the course of the thirteenth century, hired, we might suppose, as much for their linguistic as for their legal expertise.[12] Attorneys were active in the county courts, where French also appears to have been the language of official disputation.[13] In the courts of the principal cities, French similarly predominated in court proceedings (alongside Latin as the language of formal record).[14] It is perhaps not surprising that London's courts should have emulated the linguistic practice of the nearby courts at Westminster, but evidence indicating the prevalence of French further afield shows the ubiquitous nature of this language. How far this applied to less exalted court settings, however, is less clear. Paul Brand suggests that it is only in manorial courts that we might find widespread use of English in proceedings in the thirteenth and early fourteenth centuries. But it is equally likely that English was principally spoken in the borough courts of towns, where low-level crimes and civil disputes such as slander, debt and minor trespass were heard. That professional lawyers and serjeants-at-law were less in evidence in these courts, because it was more common for litigants and defendants to represent themselves or else to use prominent and well-placed local men to act as their attorneys, may be an important factor to indicate that English rather than French was the preferred vernacular. It stands to reason, of course, that where legal proceedings rested on the personal testimony of litigants or witnesses, these depositions would have been spoken in English.[15]

Perhaps the clearest indication of the supremacy of French in the proceedings of the royal courts comes in 1362 when, ironically, Edward III enacted legislation which banned the use of the language in legal pleading. It is hard to account for this statute had French not been widely used in legal disputation until this point. The wording of the statute directly points to the problems of comprehension which use of the French language was apparently now creating. It states that

> the laws, customs, and statutes of the said realm are not commonly known in the same realm, since they are pleaded, counted and judged in the French language, which very much unknown in the said realm, so that the people who plead or are pleaded in the king's courts and the courts of others have no understanding or knowledge of what is said for them or against them by their serjeants and other pleaders.[16]

The legislation then ordains that henceforth all pleas are to be 'pleaded and counted in the English language'.[17] The fact that a parliamentary statute was deemed necessary to change the linguistic customs of the king's courts suggests that the impetus for change did not come from within the legal profession. Had the justices, attorneys and serjeants viewed the use of French as an impediment to the proper implementation of law and justice – as the statute implied – one assumes that they might have initiated reform themselves. Indeed, they might also have thought to change the language in which the statute was articulated, for there is acute irony in the fact that legislation which lamented the limitations of the French language for the comprehension of legal process should itself have been drawn up and promulgated in French! In fact, the statute was said to have been prompted by the 'prelates, dukes, earls, barons and all the commons'; that is to say, by the whole political community gathered in parliament. The men attending parliament may have looked to the precedent set by London in 1356 when the mayor and aldermen had decreed that henceforth all pleading in the city's courts should be conducted in English.[18]

In his analysis of the Statute of Pleading, Mark Ormrod suggests that its enactment reflected the Crown's desire to respond to growing unease within the political community about the inaccessibility of the legal process.[19] The statute was in response to broader developments in the legal structure and the growing influence of central court justices and serjeants-at-law in the implementation of justice locally; that is to say, in the courts of assize, in gaol delivery sessions and, crucially, in the commissions of the peace. From 1344 the Crown allowed the keepers of the peace (i.e., local men) to hear and determine the cases brought before them, but only if the peace commissions were reinforced with professional justices from the central courts. The argument is that this influx of a centralising Westminster judicial elite into the local criminal justice system resulted in a clash of linguistic cultures, as the Francophone preferences of the royal justices came into conflict with the Anglophone preferences of the county-based commissioners. In the short term, the statute may also have responded to the increased prominence of the gentry as agents of royal justice in the localities, as a result of the decision in 1361 to drop the requirement to have a quorum of professional judges on the peace commissions. Thus the gentry were now not only in a position to dictate how court proceedings should be conducted, but they also had a vested interest in shaping the wider legal and linguistic environment to suit their needs.

The enactment of the Statute of Pleading self-evidently demonstrated that although French was still being used in the king's courts in the mid-fourteenth century, its deployment no longer commanded universal support, especially among those who did not belong to the legal profession. By implication, French could no longer be considered a mainstream vernacular language. Indeed, it was around this time that French began to be replaced by English for the purposes of teaching Latin in grammar schools. Thus, whereas previously the use of French in legal proceedings had been broadly acceptable because it was the common idiom of the political elite, now the circumstances had changed, and these same elites had come to regard the language as an impediment to their emerging position as the principal enforcers of the king's peace in the shires, though it is worth noting that the Statute itself was couched in terms of the incomprehension of those people who used the courts. There is, Ormrod further contends, an additional consideration, for if the statute of 1362 was enacted, as he suggests, in reaction to the spread of

French outwards from Westminster into the provincial courts, the implication is that the position of English in these courts was already established and well regarded by the county elites.[20] The Statute may therefore have been seeking to *restore*, rather than to establish, English in the courts. Such a hypothesis throws into question how widely used French had been in earlier periods and underlines the enormous challenges involved in deciphering the complex and often incoherent relationships between orality and written texts in this period.

What impact did the Statute of Pleading have on legal process after 1362? It used to be thought that the legislation made little material difference to court practice and was therefore, in effect, a dead letter.[21] After all, the law reports, those faithful records of what apparently was *said* in court, continued to be penned in French for many decades to come. In fact, the general thrust of more recent scholarship has tended to the view that from about the mid-fourteenth century the close connection between the language of law-reporting and the language of oral pleading began to loosen, and that 1362 did indeed mark an important shift in the oral culture of the king's courts. In 2001 William Rothwell noted that the Statute of Pleading made reference only to what was spoken in court and said nothing about how these proceedings were to be recorded.[22] For Rothwell, what was at issue was not whether English now predominated in legal discourse – he assumes this to be the case – but the continued vitality of French in an increasingly Anglophone oral legal culture. He points to the fact that French had circumscribed legal diction so comprehensively that even if the syntactical framework of the spoken language was now English, the legal vocabulary remained essentially French, so in effect what was spoken in court was a mixture of the two languages – a 'single, amalgamated *Franglais*', as one recent commentator has put it.[23] In his analysis of the impact of the Statute, Mark Ormrod similarly endorses the continued relevance of Law French after 1362, but his arguments centre on an important distinction to be made between the opening stages of pleading, the 'count', on the one hand, which continued to be conducted in French because of the need for absolute precision and accuracy, and the subsequent legal debates and arguments on the other hand, which were now spoken in English to accord with the terms of the legislation.[24] The views of Rothwell and Ormrod, on the survival of French, are supported by the mid-fifteenth-century statement of the royal judge Sir John Fortescue, who notes that 'the English [people] ... were used to pleading [in French], until the custom was much restricted by force of a certain statute; even so, it has been impossible hitherto to abolish custom in its entirety, partly because of certain terms which pleaders express more accurately in French than in English'.[25]

It will be clear, then, that contemporary assumptions about the utility of language in law did not rest on a rudimentary calculation about whether more people understood the English language than they did French. French persisted in an increasingly Anglophone linguistic environment orally, and even more so in a written context, because it had so completely circumscribed legal diction and because of an innate linguistic conservatism within the legal profession. This explains why law students continued to learn their craft in French. Nevertheless, an important change had occurred. Whereas in the thirteenth century French had been used pragmatically in law reports and other legal treatises to reflect the language of legal dialogue, now it was increasingly taking on the characteristics of Latin, as a prestige language employed by a small professional elite primarily to preserve and validate legal process. Thus, statutory legislation remained the preserve of the French language, as did the record of the proceedings of parliament, the parliament roll. Petitions also continued to be written in French well into the fifteenth century. Chancery's equitable jurisdiction came to be known as its 'English side', because of the use of English in its proceedings and records, but it is often forgotten that the first petitions – or bills – presented in chancery at the end of the fourteenth century were not drafted in English, but French. The persistence of French in supplicatory discourse may be explained by the fact that petitions were especially identified with the formal, precise linguistic demands of the 'count' in common-law proceedings, and so naturally leaned towards a Francophone legal context in compilation.[26] In practice, of course, where French articulated words meant for a wider audience, these words would have been translated. As early as 1258 there is evidence that the Crown's proclamations were made in English, to ensure the widest possible dissemination.[27] Likewise, the use of French in supplications indicated above all the linguistic priorities of the clerical and legal classes whose members drafted such documents. Almost certainly, by the early fifteenth century, French-language petitions served as the basis of English-language *oral* proceedings. The tenacity of French in the legal culture of the late fourteenth and fifteenth centuries was thus down to a number of interrelated factors: first, the existence of a different set of linguistic priorities which governed the use of language in the written record, on the one hand, and in oral exchange, on the other; second, a deeply entrenched association of the French language with technical legal process, and the assimilation of French legal terminology into a specific legal discourse, Law French; and finally, its facilitation of elite identity amongst professional lawyers and attorneys, an identity that was enhanced rather than undermined by the contraction in the numbers of people who used French more generally for social exchange.

Nevertheless, in some areas French began to give way to English. The final phase of linguistic development, then, was the gradual appearance of English in some written contexts. This occurred only because a more workable, standardised linguistic form of the English language had begun to emerge in the course of the fourteenth century.[28] Richard Ingham has argued that one important impetus for the shift to English was a general loss of competence in the French language which was driven by various factors including, notably, the disproportionate impact of the Black Death on the clerical teachers of French in the second half of the fourteenth century.[29] The shift towards the production of English-language legal texts occurred in two distinct areas. First, from the late fourteenth century value began to be attached to having certain key aspects of the proceedings of particularly sensitive or high-profile legal cases recorded in English in the formal record. In the case of the trial of Nicholas Louthe in 1402, for example, the English vernacular letter that incriminated him for treason was copied word for word into the otherwise almost exclusively Latinised pleas rolls.[30] Similarly, in 1405, John Stanton's English language confession, in which he admitted to planning the overthrow of the king, was copied out in its original language into the record.[31] These and other instances indicated a new emphasis on the authenticating quality of the English written text, and the belief that having the apparently unmediated words of the accused men set out in writing lent proof to the charges that had been brought against them. In this period, vernacular texts were also produced by those who sought justice for themselves. Adam Usk's appeal of 1384, the Mercers' Petition of 1388 and Thomas Paunfield's personal testimony of 1414 – all the subject of intense scholarly interest – employed the English vernacular as part of a rhetorical strategy to 'speak the language' of those passing judgement on the cases. The very act of writing suggested the newly acquired status and authority of the English language in legal process.

The second context in which English emerged in written form indicates a rather different set of dynamics. Here, we find English beginning to be used in documents which had formerly been the preserve of French. Perhaps because of the close association with pleading, this was most apparent in a supplicatory context where, between 1420 and 1450, English gradually came to dominate both in chancery bills and in parliamentary petitions.[32] In assessing the significance of this development, it is important to remember that decisions about language-use remained, for the most part, the preserve of the clerks and attorneys who wrote the petitions, so the spread of vernacular in the equity courts of parliament and chancery indicated above all an underlying shift in the legal and linguistic culture of the fifteenth-century legal professionals. Nevertheless, the significance of this development lies not so much in the fact that English now began to be used, but that it took so long for this change to take effect. This indicates just how entrenched French had become as the primary language of supplicatory discourse and, concomitantly, how linguistically conservative the legal profession was. The drafting of petitions using the language of the petitioners themselves did not presage a revolution in legal self-help: the technical and legal expertise of lawmen was still required to ensure that bills and petitions adhered to the accepted written forms. The use of English in these contexts may, however, have increased the accessibility of this type of legal process to the participants, and in some instances there are indications that supplicatory narratives reflected the individualised input of the petitioner.[33] But in general, there was no radical shift in the petitionary style. The English language was made to conform to all the epistolary conventions which had been developed in French. Its utility in this respect reflected how far it had come, from a point where it was almost totally invisible in the written record, to a point where it was considered suitable, indeed in some instances more desirable than French, to facilitate formal legal process.

Notes

1. W. Mark Ormrod, 'The Language of Complaint: Multilingualism and Petitioning in Later Medieval England', in *Language and Culture in Medieval Britain: The French of England, c. 1100–c. 1500*, ed. Jocelyn Wogan-Browne et al. (Woodbridge: York Medieval Press, 2009), 31–43(esp. 35–6).
2. J. H. Baker, 'The Three Languages of the Common Law', in idem., *The Common Law Tradition: Lawyers, Books and the Law* (London and Rio Grande: The Hambledon Press, 2000), 225–46.
3. George W. Woodbine, 'The Language of English Law', *Speculum* 18 (1943), 395–436.
4. Ibid., 423.
5. Paul Brand, 'The Languages of the Law in Later Medieval England', in *Multilingualism in Later Medieval Britain*, ed. D. A. Trotter (Cambridge: D. S. Brewer, 2000), 63–76.
6. Ibid., 66.
7. Paul Brand, 'The Language of the English Legal Profession: The Emergence of a Distinctive Legal Lexicon in Insular French', in *The Anglo-Norman Language and Its Contexts*, ed. Richard Ingham (Woodbridge: York Medieval Press, 2010), 94–101.
8. Brand, 'Languages of the Law', 66.
9. M. T. Clanchy, *From Memory to Written Record: England 1066–1307* (Oxford, Blackwell, 1973; repr. 1993), 206–11.
10. Brand, 'Languages of the Law', 64–5.
11. Ibid., 63.

12. Nigel Ramsay, 'Scriveners and Notaries as Legal Intermediaries in Later Medieval England', in *Enterprise and Individuals in Fifteenth-Century England*, ed. Jennifer Kermode (Stroud: Alan Sutton, 1991), 118–31.
13. Robert C. Palmer, 'County Year Book Reports: The Professional Lawyer in the Medieval County Court', *English Historical Review* 91 (1971), 776–801.
14. Brand, 'Languages of the Law', 69.
15. Jeremy Goldberg, 'Echoes, Whispers, Ventriloquisms: On Recovering Women's Voices from the Court of York in the Late Middle Ages', in *Women, Agency and the Law, 1300–1377*, ed. Bronach Kane and Fiona Williamson (London, Pickering & Chatto, 2013), 31–41 (esp. 34).
16. *Statutes of the Realm*, 11 vols. (London, 1810–28), I, 375–6.
17. Ibid.
18. *Calendar of the Letter Books of the City of London*, ed. R. R. Sharpe, 11 vols. (London, 1899–1907), Letter Book G, 73.
19. For this, and what follows, see W. Mark Ormrod, 'The Use of English: Language, Law, and Political Culture in Fourteenth-Century England', *Speculum* 78 (2003), 750–87.
20. Ibid., 770–1.
21. M. Dominica Legge, 'Anglo-Norman and the Historian', *History* 26 (1941), 163–75, esp. 167.
22. W. Rothwell, 'English and French after 1362', *English Studies* 82 (2001), 539–59, esp. 541.
23. Sebastian Sobecki, *Unwritten Verities: The Making of England's Vernacular Legal Culture, 1463–1549* (Notre Dame, IN: University of Notre Dame Press, 2015), 45.
24. Ormrod, 'Use of English', 772–3, developing arguments made by Baker, 'Three Languages of the Common Law', 242–4.
25. Sir John Fortescue, *De laudibus legum Angliae*, ed. and trans. S. B. Chrimes (Cambridge: Cambridge University Press, 1949), 115.
26. See Gwilym Dodd, 'Blood, Brains and Bay-Windows: The Use of English in Fifteenth-Century Parliamentary Petitions', in *Petitions and Strategies of Persuasion in the Middle Ages: The English Crown and the Church, c. 1200 – c. 1550*, ed. Thomas W. Smith and Helen Killick (Woodbridge: York Medieval Press, 2019), 11–39 (esp. 33–35), where I build on suggestions by Mark Ormrod, 'Language of Complaint', 35–8.
27. James A. Doig, 'Political Propaganda and Royal Proclamations in Late Medieval England', *Historical Research* 71 (1998), 253–80 at 264.
28. See Ursula Schäfer, ed., *The Beginnings of Standardization: Language and Culture in Fourteenth-Century England* (Frankfurt am Main: Peter Lang, 2006), esp. 'Introduction' (3–24) and 'Epilogue' (183–200). For an important distinction between a 'standardised language', and a 'standard language', see Tim William Machan, 'Snakes, Ladders, and Standard Language', in *Imagining Medieval English: Language Structures and Theories, 500–1500*, ed. Tim William Machan (Cambridge: Cambridge University Press, 2016), 54–77 (esp. 66–8).
29. Richard Ingham, *The Transmission of Anglo-Norman: Language History and Language Acquisition* (Amsterdam: John Benjamins Publishing Company, 2012), 25.

30. As discussed by E. Amanda McVitty, '"My name of a trewe man": Gender, Vernacularity, and Treasonous Speech in Late Medieval England', *Parergon* 33 (2016), 91–111.
31. *Select Cases in the Court of King's Bench*, vol. VII, ed. G. O. Sayles (London: Bernard Quartich, 1971), 153–4.
32. Gwilym Dodd, 'The Rise of English, the Decline of French: Supplications to the English Crown, c. 1420–1450', *Speculum* 86 (2011), 117–50.
33. Cordelia Beattie, 'Your Oratrice: Women's Petitions to the Late Medieval Court of Chancery', in *Women, Agency and the Law, 1300–1700*, ed. Bronach Kane and Fiona Williamson (London: Pickering and Chatto, 2013), 17–29, 164–9; and see Dodd, 'Blood, Brains and Bay-Windows', 28–31.

Further Reading

Baker, J. H., 'The Three Languages of the Common Law', in idem., *The Common Law Tradition: Lawyers, Books and the Law*, London and Rio Grande, 2000, 225–46.
Brand, P., 'The Languages of the Law in Later Medieval England', in *Multilingualism in Later Medieval Britain*, ed. D. A. Trotter, Cambridge: D. S. Brewer, 2000, 63–76.
'The Language of the English Legal Profession: The Emergence of a Distinctive Legal Lexicon in Insular French', in *The Anglo-Norman Language and Its Contexts*, ed. R. Ingham, Woodbridge: York Medieval Press, 2010, 94–101.
Clanchy, M. T., *From Memory to Written Record: England 1066–1307*, Oxford: Blackwell, 1973, repr. 1993, 206–11.
Dodd, G., 'The Rise of English, the Decline of French: Supplications to the English Crown, c. 1420–1450', *Speculum* 86 (2011), 117–50.
McVitty, E. A., '"My name of a trewe man": Gender, Vernacularity, and Treasonous Speech in Late Medieval England', *Parergon* 33 (2016), 91–111.
Ormrod, W. M., 'The Use of English: Language, Law, and Political Culture in Fourteenth-Century England', *Speculum* 78 (2003), 750–87.
'The Language of Complaint: Multilingualism and Petitioning in Later Medieval England', in *Language and Culture in Medieval Britain: the French of England, c. 1100–c. 1500*, ed. J. Wogan-Browne et al., Woodbridge: York Medieval Press, 2009, 31–43.
Rothwell, W., 'English and French after 1362', *English Studies* 82 (2001), 539–59.
Woodbine, G. W., 'The Language of English Law', *Speculum* 18 (1943), 395–436.

3

PETER D. CLARKE

Canon and Civil Law

The common culture of medieval Europe was derived from two main sources: the shared inheritance of the Roman classical past and the international character of the Western Church. Law was a major element in both these forces shaping European culture. This included civil law, the law of the ancient Roman Empire. It survived the Empire's political collapse in the West through its codification in the Empire's remaining eastern half under Emperor Justinian in the early sixth century. Only parts of this codification were known in the early medieval West, but it was rediscovered there in its entirety by the twelfth century. It became a subject of study in the emerging universities of medieval Europe, and this stimulated its growing international influence. It was an increasingly important source of ideas and rules for other medieval legal systems, notably canon law, the law of the Western Church. Canon law also had a long tradition going back to late antiquity, and the twelfth century was likewise decisive to its international reach and impact. No single collection of canon law enjoyed universal recognition comparable to Justinian's codification till the appearance of Gratian's *Decretum* in c. 1140. This canonical collection was rapidly adopted as the standard textbook for teaching canon law, which emerged as a subject of study alongside civil law in Western universities from the mid-twelfth century. Canon and civil law would remain the only law studied in medieval universities, but their pan-European significance was not limited to the classroom. From the twelfth century the Western Church developed an international system of courts to settle disputes and prosecute crimes under its jurisdiction in accordance with canon law. Civil law also influenced legal practice in these courts since from the late twelfth century it provided the basis for the so-called 'Romano-canonical' procedure followed in them. Canon and civil law thus touched people's lives across later medieval Europe, not least since church courts exercised jurisdiction over major aspects of daily life, notably marriage.

Medieval England was not immune from these developments and indeed formed part of this European culture of the *ius commune*, as canon and civil law were collectively known. Even England's own 'common law', applied through its royal courts, was not as isolated from these continental legal traditions as is often supposed. Two famous medieval common-law treatises, attributed to the royal judges Glanvill and Bracton, respectively, each drew to some extent on civil law, and Richard Helmholz has argued that canon law influenced common law on certain issues, notably defamation, down to the sixteenth and seventeenth centuries.[1] Nevertheless it was mainly through ecclesiastical institutions, notably the church courts, universities and papal curia, that canon and civil law were influential in medieval England, and even the break with Rome did not entirely disrupt their influence in Tudor England. This chapter will hence explore three themes down to the mid-sixteenth century: the application of canon law in English church courts; the teaching and study of canon and civil law in the English universities; and the papal curia as a source of dispensations and other graces relating to canon law. The papacy was also a source of justice and law in the later medieval Church, since cases might be appealed to Rome from lower church courts and papal letters ruling on such cases and instructing local church judges were collected along with papal conciliar decrees as new law supplementing Gratian by the later twelfth century, especially in universities, where they were increasingly studied alongside the *Decretum*. These kinds of papal activity will be treated under the first two themes.

Canon Law and Church Courts

During the 1070s, William the Conqueror ordered the separation of ecclesiastical and secular jurisdictions in his kingdom of England. Before the Norman Conquest of England in 1066 there was no clear distinction between the two. Anglo-Saxon kings as Christian rulers had legislated on ecclesiastical matters often with the advice of their bishops, and cases involving clergy and church affairs were usually heard before secular courts where bishops sat alongside lay judges.[2] William I's decision reflected the contemporary movement of ecclesiastical reform seeking the separation of Church and 'state' but in ruling on ecclesiastical issues it expressed continuing royal influence over the English Church. Indeed the division of church and royal jurisdictions in England became protracted as the Crown sought to control where the boundaries between the two lay. This led to conflict between Henry II of England and Thomas Becket, archbishop of Canterbury. In 1164 Henry II issued the Constitutions of Clarendon, which proposed various reforms in the relationship between ecclesiastical and royal jurisdictions. Henry claimed that these sought to restore ancient royal customs. In opposing them Becket and his supporters cited the rival claims of canon law, which took a different view on the division between ecclesiastical and secular jurisdiction. The most contested issue concerned criminous clergy. Henry proposed that clerks convicted of crimes and deposed from office by their bishops be handed over to royal courts for further trial and punishment as if laymen. Becket resisted this as violating the canonical principle of *privilegium fori*, which required that clergy be cited on criminal charges only before ecclesiastical judges. Becket's murder in his own cathedral in 1170, allegedly on royal orders, forced Henry to renounce jurisdiction over criminous clergy and compromise on other issues in 1172. This did not mark the introduction of canon law into England, as has often been assumed; Henry's Constitutions had reacted to its presence there already and tried to limit its jurisdictional claims. The Becket crisis, nevertheless, resulted in the English Crown's acceptance of many of those claims and an increasing interest among English clergy in canon law, which were fundamental to the development of regular church courts in England.

Another factor promoting this development and the spread of canon law in England was the papacy's growing intervention in disputes in local churches. This was supported by canon law, especially Gratian's *Decretum*, which emphasised the papacy's universal jurisdiction over the Western Church; and the papacy itself had been increasingly assertive of this authority since the late eleventh century and accordingly encouraged greater reference to Rome on legal issues. By the mid-twelfth century the rise in appeals to Rome exceeded the pope's capacity to hear them all in person, thus he referred many back to the provinces where they arose and delegated authority to local ecclesiastical judges there to hear them in his name. The advantage of papal judgements, whether issued by the pope himself or these papal judges delegate, was that backed by the highest ecclesiastical authority they could not easily be ignored or over-turned by lesser church authorities, hence rising numbers of litigants sought to acquire them. The Constitutions of Clarendon tried to restrict such appeals to Rome from England but failed, and the activity of papal judges delegate in England accordingly intensified down to the mid-thirteenth century.[3] The Becket crisis also stimulated English interest in papal judgements as a new source of law, especially on issues Gratian's *Decretum* left unclear. The earliest collections of papal decretals (letters responding to cases referred to Rome or to episcopal requests for legal advice) were indeed compiled in England during the 1170s. Several such collections were produced for English bishops and comprised decretals addressed to them, especially those acting as judges delegate.[4]

The cost and delays involved in seeking papal justice limited its accessibility, but ecclesiastical justice became more widely available in England (and consequently resort to judges delegate decreased) as a structure of local church courts emerged by the thirteenth century. Most bishops delegated their jurisdiction to an official, who presided over the diocesan consistory court, but some bishops retained personal jurisdiction exercised often in parallel through audience courts. Bishops also divided their jurisdiction with lesser clergy, notably archdeacons, who likewise ran courts under their own officials and chiefly dealt with disciplinary cases. Appeals might be made from these lower courts to the local bishop and from his courts to his archbishop. The archbishop of York's consistory court therefore heard appeals from across his northern province as well as diocesan cases, but in the much larger southern province the archbishop of Canterbury had a separate appeal court, the 'Court of Arches', which sat in London; his consistory court at Canterbury only dealt with cases from his diocese. English litigants might still (and did) appeal to Rome and at any stage without first proceeding through this whole hierarchy of local courts.

Apart from appeals, medieval English church courts heard a wide variety of first instance cases. Their business is richly documented in both original case papers, dating as far back as the twelfth century, and act books (which record proceedings in these courts) extant from the fourteenth century onwards.[5] Act books broadly categorise this business as either 'instance' or 'office' cases. Instance cases were so-called for they were brought to court at the instance of the parties and thus amounted to private 'civil' litigation. Office cases concerned canonical crimes which ecclesiastical judges prosecuted by virtue of their office. Some office cases came to court since they were 'promoted' by a specific accuser and thus resemble instance cases, but church courts initiated many themselves on the basis of hearsay evidence. Rumours of alleged offences might be detected at visitations that bishops and archdeacons conducted in parishes by the thirteenth century and reported to church courts. In this and other respects English church courts followed Romano-canonical procedure, in particular its inquisitorial procedure, which admitted the use of hearsay evidence not only in the investigation of heresy but also other canonical crimes.

These courts also broadly followed canon (and civil) law in terms of the kinds of litigation and offences that they dealt with. Canon law defined these on the basis of subject-matter (*ratione materiae*) or depending on personal status (*ratione personae*). The latter mainly concerned the clergy, and accordingly criminal jurisdiction over English clergy was largely reserved to church courts following the Becket crisis till at least the early sixteenth century. English church courts also prosecuted laity for crimes but when their subject-matter made these the Church's concern, notably sexual offences such as adultery and fornication, which contravened its moral doctrine. The subject-matter of instance litigation also normally related to religious concerns, notably marriage, which the Church considered a divine institution and a sacrament. Church courts thus heard virtually all litigation to dissolve or enforce marriages in England, and this became their main category of business in the later Middle Ages. Wills were also the Church's concern since they made provision for the testator's burial and soul, notably through bequests of alms, hence their validity had to be proved in English church courts and any disputes arising from them settled there. Likewise these courts heard litigation regarding 'spiritual goods' of the Church, especially cases of clergy suing to recover unpaid tithes. Less obviously spiritual matters also came under their jurisdiction, notably perjury or 'breach of faith', a charge largely invoked by creditors to recover debts. While seemingly mundane it regarded violation of an oath sworn in God's name or on the Gospels and applied to debtors where they failed to keep sworn promises to repay their creditors by a set deadline. Finally, litigants often sued for defamation before the English church courts, where it was defined as malicious allegation of a crime, such as calling someone a prostitute or a thief. Despite its apparently worldly concern with personal reputation, canon law made defamation the Church's business for it violated the biblical injunction against 'bearing false witness' (as did perjury) and when it imputed canonical crimes, it could give rise to frivolous prosecutions under inquisitorial procedure if unchallenged.

These were the main kinds of cases before the medieval English church courts, and other less recurrent ones, notably usury and assaults on clergy, were likewise rooted in canon law. But these courts did not follow the letter of this law strictly (any more than their continental counterparts). Local custom sometimes caused them to deviate from it, especially where the English Crown restricted its free operation. For example, clergy were notionally immune from temporal justice under *privilegium fori*, but English clergy might still be sued in civil cases before secular courts. And although the Crown recognised the *privilegium fori* in criminal cases after Becket, it limited this immunity in later medieval practice: clergy were arrested and indicted for crimes by royal authorities; if a jury acquitted them, they were released; but if convicted, they had to prove their clerical status and seek transferral to their local bishop's court.[6] Despite occasional clerical protests at royal intrusions into ecclesiastical justice, English church courts largely tolerated such compromises of canonical principles and also often enjoyed royal cooperation. The Church's principal judicial sanction was excommunication, and by the thirteenth century English bishops might invoke 'the aid of the secular arm' in enforcing it. At their request the Crown arrested excommunicates who remained obdurate for forty days or more and held them in custody until they came to terms with the church authorities.[7] The relationship between the English Church and Crown would, however, change dramatically following Henry VIII's break with Rome, and how this affected the operation of canon law and ecclesiastical jurisdiction in Tudor England will be discussed in the conclusion.

Ius commune and the English Universities

The introduction of civil law teaching into England is closely associated with the Italian Master Vacarius. He reputedly studied in the nascent Roman law school at Bologna before coming in *c.* 1144 to England, where he served the archbishop of Canterbury and later that of York.[8] He compiled a textbook, the *Liber pauperum*, an anthology of Justinian's Code and Digest which was designed for students unfamiliar with these and other books in the Justinianic compilation of civil law. He is widely thought to have taught civil law and perhaps devised the textbook for this reason, as his contemporary Gratian compiled the *Decretum* to teach canon law at Bologna. It has been suggested that he taught law at Oxford and as early as 1149 but this is much debated; his teaching has also been linked to Northampton and Lincoln, and there is little hard evidence of civil law studies at Oxford before the 1180s. The *Liber pauperum* is, however, credited with establishing a civil law school at Oxford, and it probably emerged after the book's compilation, once dated to 1149 but now associated with the late 1170s or early 1180s. Certainly the book was used at Oxford from 1190, by when it was studied there alongside the *Decretum*; Simon Sywell (Southwell), John of Tynemouth and Honorius of Kent are known to have taught canon law at Oxford before 1200.[9] This growth of canon and civil law studies in late twelfth-century Oxford has been associated with its importance from the 1170s as a centre of church courts, where law graduates found employment as advocates.

James Brundage has likewise argued that the presence of church courts at Cambridge attracted scholars to settle there in the early thirteenth century, when studies at Oxford were suspended in 1209–14.[10] Whether or not the origins of Cambridge University lie in a consequent migration of Oxford scholars, teaching of canon law was established there early on and its first known chancellor, Richard of Wetheringsett (*c.* 1222), was a canon lawyer. The university had a canon law faculty by *c.* 1250, and its civil law faculty emerged shortly thereafter. Oxford originally had a school of both laws, but separate schools of canon and civil law emerged there after 1234. Leonard Boyle attributes this to the appearance in 1234 of the *Liber extra*, a collection of papal decretals compiled for use in universities and church courts on Pope Gregory IX's orders and so-called as a supplement to Gratian's *Decretum*. It included Pope Honorius III's ruling 'Super specula' forbidding various clergy to study civil law, thus many students might no longer study both laws together. Although originally issued in 1219, this ban seemingly only became known in England after its publication in the *Liber extra*. Another apparent consequence of it was that King Henry III prohibited the teaching of civil law at London in 1234.[11] This meant that civil law and common law were no longer studied together, and the legal profession in royal courts was increasingly reserved to those trained exclusively in common law. Civilians instead sought employment in church courts and ecclesiastical positions.[12] Training in civil law indeed became indispensable to the practice of canon law, notably since procedure in ecclesiastical courts was heavily based on civil law. At Cambridge and Oxford the civil law schools effectively became the undergraduate departments of the canon law schools, as prior study of civil law became an entrance requirement to the latter by the fourteenth century. Clergy affected by 'Super specula' were exempt from this but might still obtain a papal dispensation to study civil law.

From the mid-thirteenth century, civil law students at both universities were expected to attend lectures on the Digest and Code, and canon law students, on the *Decretum* and *Liber extra*. By the mid-fourteenth century both universities expanded their canon law curricula to include new collections of papal legislation, the *Liber sextus* (1298) and *Clementinae* (1317). Law graduates were also expected to perform lecturing duties in order to qualify for a doctorate at Oxford and Cambridge, and as neither university had endowed chairs for law professors and many trained civilians and canonists were quickly lured away from teaching by more lucrative legal practice, the burden of law teaching increasingly fell on graduates.[13] Teachers rented rooms for lecturing and paid the rent out of fees collected from students. At Cambridge law teaching was done in various student hostels, notably the Burden hostel, before the university built a school for each of the two laws in the fifteenth century. Oxford University likewise had a great school of civil law and another of canon law, and law teaching also went on in its student halls. Numbers of law students rose so much in both universities that by the mid-fifteenth century two further law schools opened and some thirty legist halls existed at Oxford, and founders of new colleges at Cambridge restricted their fellowship largely to theologians lest jurists predominated. Earlier founders of Oxford and Cambridge colleges had, however, favoured law studies. At Cambridge Bishop Bateman of Norwich founded Trinity Hall in 1350 to promote 'the growth of canonistic and civilian learning', and the Crown patroned King's Hall (later re-founded as

Trinity College) as a centre of civil law studies from 1317.[14] Such patrons encouraged law studies as they needed trained lawyers in their administrations; civilians being versed in international law especially served the Crown as diplomats. Royal needs would, nevertheless, change following the break with Rome, and this would affect the future of English legal studies as we will later see.

Dispensations and Other Papal Graces

English pilgrims had long visited Rome as an act of penance and sought papal absolution for their sins.[15] By the twelfth century canon law increasingly reserved certain grave sins to papal absolution, such as violent assaults on clergy. Consequently growing numbers of petitioners from across later medieval Europe, clergy and laity, men and women, solicited such absolution and other papal graces from Rome. These other favours mainly comprised dispensations, which relaxed man-made (as opposed to divine) rules of canon law in certain circumstances. Although their origins have been traced back to the early Church, the papacy began granting significant numbers of dispensations only from the late eleventh century. This development (together with the concomitant rise in reserved cases of absolution) can be associated with the growing power of the papacy in this period. Popes indeed claimed that their authority to grant these graces was derived from their 'plenitude of power' in the Western Church; the power of bishops to concede such favours was accordingly limited in canon law. The papacy steadily expanded the range of its favours also in reaction to rising popular demand, which paralleled the contemporary growth of appeals to Rome. As in the latter case the pope was increasingly unable to meet this demand in person and thus progressively delegated his authority to issue graces. By the twelfth century the papal chancery issued many such graces, increasingly authorised by its officials in response to petitions. Popes also conceded 'faculties' empowering other curial personnel to issue graces, notably legates and nuncios, papal emissaries who exercised these faculties on missions to local provinces of the Western Church. By the early thirteenth century the pope appointed a cardinal penitentiary to grant reserved absolution to penitents, and other graces.[16] This cardinal became known as the major penitentiary to differentiate him from the minor penitentiaries subordinate to him, who heard confessions of penitent pilgrims and gave them absolution in various Roman basilicas. By the mid-thirteenth century he headed an office likewise known as the penitentiary; it became one of the major departments of papal government like the chancery but by contrast specialised entirely in papal graces, a measure of their growing popularity.

An increasing number of English petitioners requested papal graces from these various sources before Henry VIII's break with Rome, a further index of canon law's impact in later medieval England. The ongoing calendar of entries relating to Great Britain and Ireland in the chancery registers runs to over twenty volumes for the years 1198–1521, which hint at the scale of petitioning; a recent edition likewise comprises over 4,000 petitions from England and Wales approved by the penitentiary from 1410 to 1503.[17] This evidence shows that the chancery was petitioned for graces largely by clergy, doubtless since it had wider faculties than the penitentiary to grant the kinds of favours that they sought, notably dispensations to hold a plurality of church benefices. Canon law forbade this, especially when these benefices were incompatible, meaning that each had a 'cure of souls' requiring the incumbent to administer the sacraments, notably confession; a 'pluralist' could not be resident in all his benefices at once and thus had to appoint substitutes as a condition of his dispensation to avoid any of his parishioners suffering spiritual neglect.

The penitentiary also had broad faculties and attracted both clerical and lay petitioners by 1410 (its registers survive from this date onwards). According to its fifteenth-century registers, most laity asked the office for marriage dispensations. These mainly permitted marriages within the prohibited degrees; from 1215 canon law forbade marriages between Catholics related within four degrees of kinship through blood or marriage. Other less common marital impediments dispensed by the penitentiary included 'spiritual kinship' (*cognatio spiritualis*) which arose when the parent of one spouse had acted as godparent, or more rarely sponsor at confirmation, for the other. Such dispensations not only affirmed the validity of otherwise illicit marriages but also the legitimacy of their offspring; the latter was a legal prerequisite for inheritance that doubtless often motivated the numerous requests for such graces. Other graces sought by clergy from the penitentiary mainly dealt with legal impediments to receiving ordination or benefices. These included illegitimate birth (*defectus natalium*), which debarred men from holy orders and benefices with cure of souls, and monks or nuns from being head of their monastery or religious order, without a papal dispensation. Another dispensation often requested by clergy dealt with 'defect of age'; without it ordination to the priesthood was forbidden to men under twenty-five, for example. The penitentiary (and chancery) issued various other kinds of graces, too many to list here exhaustively but including favours sought by both clergy and laity, such as licences to eat meat and dairy produce in Lent and other fasting periods when this was normally forbidden. Some graces requested are expressive of personal piety, notably licences to appoint a personal confessor, hold mass at a portable altar, or go on pilgrimage to the Holy Land or Spanish shrine of Santiago (otherwise discouraged lest it involve Christians in illicit contacts with Muslims). The sheer diversity of graces illustrates how canon law touched virtually every aspect of later medieval life, from inter-faith relations to marriage and family.

Conclusion

Just as the UK is now struggling to disentangle itself from five decades of involvement in the European Union's institutions, policies and laws, canon (and civil) law became so embedded in English society over five centuries that its influence was not easily swept away at the break with Rome. Henry VIII prohibited the teaching of canon law at the English universities in 1535, and though his ban took lasting effect, bar a revival of the subject under Catholic Queen Mary, it did not stop private study of canon law. This was partly because Tudor lawyers found little to replace 'Roman' canon law, as Henrician reformers' plans for a new Anglican code of canon law were not immediately realised, and partly because English church courts retained much of their pre-Reformation jurisdiction.[18] Admittedly royal courts took over most of the Church's criminal jurisdiction, notably over clergy, but probate and much civil litigation over issues such as marriage and tithes remained the preserve of English church courts beyond the mid-sixteenth century. Even dispensations did not disappear. In 1533 Henry VIII forbade his subjects to seek those issued on papal authority, but he provided instead for a new Anglican 'Faculty Office' to grant many of those formerly sought from Rome.[19] Cardinal Wolsey's activity as papal legate in the 1520s had prepared the way for this development, for his 'Faculty Office' had established a local source of graces that rivalled the popularity of the papal curia among English petitioners. The Archbishop of Canterbury's Faculty Office founded in 1534 arguably modelled itself on this forerunner and many curial practices.[20] Although the English Reformation brought major radical change, it freighted some remarkable continuities, including many aspects of canon law.

Notes

1. R. H. Helmholz, 'Canon Law and English Common Law', Selden Society Lecture (1983) repr. in his *Canon Law and the Law of England* (London and Ronceverte: Hambledon Press, 1987), ch. 1, esp. 8–19.
2. See Ch. 1 above and R. H. Helmholz, *The Oxford History of the Laws of England*, vol. I: *The Canon Law and Ecclesiastical Jurisdiction from 597 to the 1640s* (Oxford: Oxford University Press, 2004), ch. 1.

3. J. E. Sayers, *Papal Judges Delegate in the Province of Canterbury 1198–1254: A Study in Ecclesiastical Jurisdiction and Administration* (Oxford: Oxford University Press, 1971).

4. C. Duggan, *Twelfth-Century Decretal Collections and Their Importance in English History* (London: Athlone Press, 1963).

5. See *The Records of the Medieval Ecclesiastical Courts*, part II: *England. Reports of the Working Group on Church Court Records*, ed. C. Donahue Jr (Berlin: Duncker & Humblot, 1994).

6. L. C. Gabel, *Benefit of Clergy in England in the Later Middle Ages*, Smith College Studies in History 14 (Northampton, MA, 1929; repr. New York: Octagon Books, 1969), ch. 2.

7. F. D. Logan, *Excommunication and the Secular Arm in Medieval England: A Study in Legal Procedure from the Thirteenth to the Sixteenth Century* (Toronto: Pontifical Institute of Medieval Studies, 1986).

8. J. Taliadoros, *Law and Theology in Twelfth-Century England. The Works of Master Vacarius (c. 1115/1120–c. 1200)* (Turnhout: Brepols, 2006), esp. 2–9, 31–42.

9. L. E. Boyle, 'Canon Law before 1380', in *The History of the University of Oxford*, vol. I: *The Early Oxford Schools*, ed. J. I. Catto (Oxford: Clarendon Press, 1984), 531–64.

10. J. A. Brundage, 'The Cambridge Faculty of Canon Law and the Ecclesiastical Courts of Ely', in *Medieval Cambridge: Essays on the pre-Reformation University*, ed. P. N. R. Zutshi (Woodbridge: Boydell, 1993), 21–45.

11. J. L. Barton, 'The Study of Civil Law before 1380', in *The History of the University of Oxford*, I, 519–30.

12. T. H. Aston, G. D. Duncan and T. A. R. Evans, 'The Medieval Alumni of the University of Cambridge', *Past and Present* 86 (1980), 9–86, at 66 note that of twenty-nine Cambridge alumni appointed to the English episcopate in the fifteenth century, thirteen were civilians and three trained in canon and civil law.

13. Esp. at Oxford: J. L. Barton, 'The Legal Faculties of Late Medieval Oxford', in *The History of the University of Oxford*, vol. II: *Late Medieval Oxford*, ed. J. I. Catto and R. Evans (Oxford: Clarendon Press, 1992), 281–313. This largely explains why neither university produced any jurist of international significance after the mid-thirteenth century.

14. A. B. Cobban, 'Theology and Law in the Medieval Colleges of Oxford and Cambridge', *Bulletin of the John Rylands Library* 65/1 (1982), 57–77.

15. R. A. Aronstam, 'Penitential Pilgrimages to Rome in the Early Middle Ages', *Archivum historiae pontificiae* 13 (1975), 65–83, esp. 67–70.

16. On his office's activity, see K. Salonen, *The Penitentiary as a Well of Grace in the Late Middle Ages: The Example of the Province of Uppsala 1448–1527*, Annales Academiae Scientiarum Fennicae 313 (Helsinki: Academia Scientiarum Fennica, 2001).

17. *Supplications from England and Wales in the Registers of the Apostolic Penitentiary, 1410–1503*, ed. P. D. Clarke and P. N. R. Zutshi, 3 vols. (Canterbury and York Society, 2013–15), see esp. the introduction in vol. I, xiii–lviii.

18. R. Houlbrooke, *Church Courts and the People during the English Reformation 1520–1570* (Oxford: Oxford University Press, 1979); R. H. Helmholz, *Roman Canon Law in Reformation England* (Cambridge: Cambridge University Press, 1990).

19. D. S. Chambers, *Faculty Office Registers, 1534–1549* (Oxford: Clarendon Press, 1966), esp. the introduction at xi–lxv.

20. P. D. Clarke and M. Questier, eds., *Papal Authority and the Limits of the Law in Tudor England*, Camden Fifth Series, vol. 48: Camden Miscellany XXXVI (Cambridge: Cambridge University Press, 2015), 1–30; P. D. Clarke, 'Canterbury as the New Rome: Dispensations and Henry VIII's Reformation', *Journal of Ecclesiastical History* 64 (2013), 20–44.

Further Reading

Brundage, J. A., *Medieval Canon Law*, London: Longmans, 1995.

Helmholz, R. H., *The Oxford History of the Laws of England*, vol. I: *The Canon Law and Ecclesiastical Jurisdiction from 597 to the 1640s*, Oxford: Oxford University Press, 2004.

Roman Canon Law in Reformation England, Cambridge: Cambridge University Press, 1990.

Owen, D. M., *The Medieval Canon Law. Teaching, Literature and Transmission*, Sandars Lectures in Bibliography, Cambridge: Cambridge University Press, 1990.

Stein, P., *Roman Law in European History*, Cambridge: Cambridge University Press, 1999.

4

PAUL RAFFIELD

Custom and Common Law

Introduction

[N]or the laws of any Christian kingdom, are so rooted in antiquity.
Hence there is no gainsaying nor legitimate doubt but that the customs of
the English are not only good but the best.[1]

For Sir John Fortescue, Chief Justice of the King's Bench between 1442 and
1460, nominal Lord Chancellor to Henry VI following the deposition of the
Lancastrian king in 1461, and author of *De laudibus legum Angliae* (from
which the above quotation is taken), the laws and customs of England were
coextensive and indivisible. Fortescue identified three separate forms of
human or municipal law: these were 'either law of nature, customs, or
statutes', and when customs and the law of nature 'have been reduced to
writing' and received royal approval, then they 'are changed into
a constitution or something of the nature of statutes'.[2] Of these three (supposedly indisputable) sources of English law, custom was arguably the least
susceptible to irrefutable definition, and it is therefore something of
a paradox that Fortescue was an exemplar of late medieval judicial authority
expressing the opinion that custom was the singular, defining and unique
feature of the common law.

It is the purpose of this chapter to examine and analyse the juridical notion
of custom in relation to the institutional foundations of common law.
I concentrate primarily on juristic ideas of custom attendant on the theories
espoused by Fortescue in *De laudibus* (written *c.* 1470) and developed in the
first half of the sixteenth century, notably by the barrister and jurist
Christopher St German, author of *Dialogus de fundamentis legum Anglie
et de conscientia*, more commonly known as *Doctor and Student*, published
in English in 1530. In passing, I consider the gradual change in juridical
meaning of *consuetudo*, from that intended by Chief Justiciar of England
Ranulf de Glanvill and cleric, justice and jurist Henry de Bracton,[3] to its
meaning as recorded in the decisions of judges, handed down in the courts of
common law. The judiciary adopted for themselves a didactic and rabbinical
role, in accordance with the description of them by Fortescue as *sacerdotes*
(priests): 'For a priest is by etymology said to be one who gives or teaches

holy things.'[4] Like Fortescue, they were trained in the arcane practices of the English legal system at the Inns of Court and practised their calling as serjeants-at-law in the law courts at Westminster prior to their elevation to the ranks of the judiciary.

Custom, Kings and *Lex regia*

There is compelling documentary evidence that from the end of the sixth century to the middle of the eleventh (starting with the reign of Æthelbert of Kent in *c.* 589 and ending with the reign of Cnut, 1016–35) laws and ordinances were introduced by successive kings.[5] During the seventh and eighth centuries affirmation was provided of forms of communal justice based upon regional customs: folk-rights or *folcriht*. Contemporaneous documents refer to the Kentish *gemot* (or moot) of the eighth century: a folk-assembly at which local grievances were aired; but this could hardly be termed a formal court of law (Pollock and Maitland describe the *folc-gemot* as 'any public court whatever, greater or less').[6] Similar in form and informality was the feudal manorial court, presided over by the lord of the manor or his steward, at which minor disputes were resolved and rural customs effected.[7] The king's justice or *lex regia* was dispensed by means of the hundred courts and county courts, the former sitting every four weeks and the latter biannually.[8] These courts were often controlled by lords, but were subject to supervision by the king's officials, known as reeves. The court of the hundred was regulated at county level by the king's representative, the shire-reeve (sheriff).[9]

Following the Danish invasion of the ninth century, there were three systems of law extant in England: the laws of Wessex, Mercia and Danelaw.[10] But as noted above, by the tenth century England was a single kingdom, and as J. H. Baker has suggested, when the Norman invaders arrived in 1066 they found a relatively sophisticated legal and governmental system, 'as well developed as anything they had left in Normandy'.[11] Despite the irrefutable fact of the Norman Conquest, Fortescue claimed that 'the realm has been continuously ruled by the same customs as it is now'.[12] These customs prevailed, he argued, because their antiquity was guarantor of their legitimate authority: 'if they had not been the best, some of those kings would have changed for the sake of justice or by the impulse of caprice, and totally abolished them'.[13]

Central to the development of custom as a recognisable feature of English law was the increased concentration of power in the person of the king under the Norman monarchs and (especially) their Angevin successors, beginning with the reign of Henry II in 1154.[14] Near the start of the twelfth century (*c.* 1118), the compiler of *Leges Henrici Primi* emphasised the importance of the royal court in preserving 'the use and custom of its law at all times and in all places and with constant uniformity',[15] lending credibility to the thesis that, before the establishment of an independent legal profession, the custom of the realm was defined and determined by the king and his court. At the latter end of the twelfth century stood Glanvill and his insistence that common law was essentially the king's law (*lex regia*), which custom or *consuetudo* supplemented and resembled. The king was 'guided by those of his subjects most learned in the laws *and* customs of the realm whom he knows to excel all others in sobriety, wisdom and eloquence'.[16] Some fifty years after the completion of Glanvill's *Treatise*, Henry de Bracton's *On the Laws and Customs of England* was completed, *c.* 1235. The exact contribution made by Bracton to this work is uncertain: his main input was probably to update text compiled and written by the justice William de Raley (Raleigh), whom Bracton served as a clerk.[17] Like his predecessor Glanvill, Bracton associated common law with *lex regia*. At the start of Book I of *On the Laws*, Bracton stated that English law was unwritten, but that despite the absence of codification, common law had 'the force of law' because it had 'the authority of the king or the prince preceding'.[18] The influence of Roman law is immediately apparent above in Bracton's claim that unwritten law was legitimated by the tacit command of the monarch. *The Institutes* of the Byzantine emperor Justinian expounded the principle that the will or pronouncement of the prince had 'legislative force', because the populace yielded all its authority to him through its acceptance of *lex regia*.[19] This was not to say that, for Bracton, the king was above the law. He explicitly states that 'the king himself ought not to be subject to man, but subject to God and to the law, for the law makes the king';[20] but the subjection of the king to law and not to man had the inevitable juridical consequence that the monarch (and his delegates) remained the ultimate arbiter of what constituted custom.

As far as custom is concerned, for Bracton (as for Glanvill) it was synonymous with local or regional practices and mores: 'There are also in England several and divers customs according to the diversity of places.'[21] In Bracton's juridical scheme (as in Glanvill's), custom supplemented *lex regia*, although it might also on occasion be taken for law itself: 'Custom, also, is sometimes observed for law in parts, where it has been approved by habitual usage, and it fills the place of law, for the authority of long usage and custom is not slight.'[22] It was during the period in which Glanvill was active in shrieval and judicial office (he was Sheriff of Yorkshire and one of the royal justices in the north of England during the reign of Henry II, 1154–89) that the royal court started to play a major role in regulating local activities on a regional basis. If *lex regia* was to extend over the whole of the realm, then its successful administration and enforcement could not depend solely on the person of the king. The writ system was instrumental in enforcing commands of the king throughout the realm, and judicial delegates or deputies of the king were appointed to the role of justiciar (Glanvill became chief justiciar in 1180) to ensure that the king retained control of justice across the entire country. Itinerant justices were sent from the royal household to dispense justice in the shires. 'Wandering justices' (*justiciae errantes*) were organised into circuits and became known as 'justices in eyre' (*justiciae in itinere*) or the 'general eyre'. As well as exercising the functions of a court of law (in civil and criminal matters), the eyre served as an itinerant form of central government, exercising a supervisory and regulatory role over local government and local customs.[23]

The justices of the eyre during this period were politicians and servants of the Crown, often members of the clergy (like Bracton) or knights of the shires (like Glanvill). Although known by the title *justiciarii*, these men were not professional judges (in the sense of having trained and practised as pleaders prior to holding judicial office), and complaints about the arbitrary nature of justice dispensed by the eyre led to the creation by Henry II of a permanent *curia regis* at the Palace of Westminster. The first of these courts, the Exchequer (dealing with control of the king's revenue), had been established at Westminster in 1130, during the reign of Henry I. Of great importance to the centralisation of the legal institution and the gradual emergence of an independent legal profession was the decision of Henry II towards the end of his reign that, although itinerant justices would continue to judge cases on circuit around the realm, at any time five of his judges should remain stationary and sit in *curia regis* at Westminster. Hence foundations were laid for the emergence of the courts of King's Bench and Common Pleas, the former dealing with pleas of the Crown (such as treason and felonies) and the latter with private litigation.[24] Coextensive with the centralisation of the legal institution at Westminster was the emergence of a secular legal profession. The chronicler Matthew Paris recorded that as early as 1230 there was a class of 'forespeakers of the bench', commonly known as *narratores*.[25] The Latin noun *narratores* referred to the recitation by the pleader of the plaintiff's count or *narratio*, but it has inevitable connotations also of a storyteller, chronicler or historian, relating and narrating the supposedly immemorial customs of common law.

Custom, Common Law and the Legal Profession

An ordinance of Edward I in 1292 (20 Edward I) was at least partly responsible for the emergence of the Inns of Court as the physical and spiritual home of the legal community. The ordinance prohibited members of the clergy from acting as pleaders in temporal actions, thus enabling the development of a secular profession. In the same year, Edward I ordered the Chief Justice of the Common Pleas (John of Mettingham) and his fellow justices to 'provide and ordain, from every County, certain Attorneys and Lawyers, of the best and most apt for their learning and skill, who might do service to his Court and people'.[26] This decision, together with the establishment of a permanent *curia regis* at Westminster, prompted the 'Attorneys and Lawyers' to congregate as members of unincorporated associations in London, in close proximity to the royal court, the City, and the courts of common law. By the time Fortescue had written *De laudibus*, the oldest of the four Inns of Court had been in existence for approximately 130 years, the Inner Temple and Middle Temple having been inhabited by lawyers from the 1340s onwards. Gray's Inn was leased to the apprentices of law during the same period. There is no record extant that Lincoln's Inn served as an honourable society of lawyers prior to 1417 (Fortescue was a member of Lincoln's Inn by 1420, and served the Inn as a Bencher from 1425). The parallel Inns of Chancery, where attorneys acquired rudimentary principles of common law, mainly through study of the writ system, were established in the same period: when *De laudibus* was written there were ten Inns of Chancery in existence, each of which was affiliated to one of the Inns of Court.

The primary contribution of the Inns of Court to the development of English law during this period was their role as autonomous educational institutions, where the technicalities and procedures of common law were disseminated to and assimilated by law students (inner-barristers) through a variety of disputatious oral exercises. These consisted of readings (cases presented by senior utter-barristers to members of their particular Inn, and subsequently argued by utter-barristers, Benchers and judges), moots (formal arguments between rival inner-barristers over points of law),[27] and less orthodox oral disputations, known as bolts. As self-governing, municipal authorities, the governing bodies of the Inns thereby ensured that the common law was systemised and rationalised solely through the agency of the legal profession. Decisions of the courts, recorded on the Plea Rolls and collated in the Year Books (prior to the mass publication of law reports from the mid-sixteenth century onward), were no longer in the charge of clerics such as Bracton. These decisions formed the basis for the system of precedent (*stare decisis*), which developed in the sixteenth and early seventeenth century. Interpretation of law became the exclusive domain of judges and serjeants-at-law, all skilled practitioners in and knowledgeable guardians of the arcane, technical procedures of common law. These men were the new custodians and arbiters of common law and legal practice. Consequently, custom in its juridical context became associated with the pronouncements of judges in their capacity as independent interpreters of law. As far as the evolution of common law was concerned, *lex regia*, which (according to Glanvill) custom had merely resembled or supplemented, was of diminished importance.

I refer above to the description by Fortescue of the judges as *sacerdotes* or priests, giving and teaching 'holy things', and noteworthy in this respect is the claim made by him that law students not only studied the technical aspects of common law, but also 'after the divine services' applied themselves to the study 'of Holy Scripture and of chronicles'.[28] Of course, as its title indicates, *De laudibus* was a panegyric in praise of English secular law, but the relevance of religion to the evolution of common law cannot be ignored. In *De laudibus*, the idealised description of judges as *sacerdotes* follows the assertion of Fortescue that, according to *the Book of Deuteronomy*, Moses 'invites you [the Prince of Wales] to strive zealously in the study of the law'. A few lines earlier he notes the injunction of Justinian that an emperor should be '*armed with laws*'.[29] The reference to Justinian (and throughout *De laudibus* to Roman law) marks a significant revision in political and juridical thought from the days of Glanvill and Bracton.

These two medieval jurists stood on either side of the Great Charter of 1215, which symbolised both the restricted powers of the Crown and the inalienable liberties of the subject. Insofar as *Magna Carta* was a statement of privileges made available under the Angevin kings, as well as a statement of principles concerning organisation of the feudal state, it may be argued that the Charter had recourse to local customs, common (with some regional variations) to the whole of Western Europe. Despite its iconic status as a symbol of fundamental liberties, which accrued largely in the early seventeenth century as a response by common lawyers to the threat of Stuart absolutism, to a great extent Magna Carta represented the will and self-interest of the barons. This group of nobles was asserting contended rights in a feudal society, such as those over title to property, the correct form of judgement, and the rightful conduct of a king. Bracton reaffirmed the principle of the limited powers of kingship by stating that the king was under God and law; but, as I have noted above, Book I of *On the Laws* starts with a rehearsal of the (apparently contradictory) principle of Roman law that the will of the prince has the force of law.

The invocation by Fortescue of Justinian in the above passage from *De laudibus* is highly significant, as the central constitutional argument of his treatise (and a signal development from Bracton) is precisely that the will of the prince does not have the force of law, unless it is compliant with the principles of common law. Fortescue was emphatic that the nature of government under an English king was 'not only regal but also political' (a thesis which he was to develop in *On the Governance of England*), by which he meant that the king may not create, alter or otherwise subvert any laws 'without the assent of his subjects',[30] because England was *dominium politicum et regale*.[31] In the context of Fortescue's republican political thought ('republican' in the sense of the best interests of *res publica* or the commonweal), 'assent of his subjects' referred to 'the concession or assent' of the three estates of the realm: nobility, clergy and commonalty, as represented in parliament.[32] In other words, the king must govern in accordance with English law and its customs. Under an 'entirely regal' legal system, it would be permissible for a king to make whatsoever alterations he wished because, as under French civil law (Fortescue was at pains to point out), '*What pleased the prince has the force of law.*' For the avoidance of doubt, Fortescue stated unequivocally that 'The laws of England do not sanction any such maxim.'[33] Given that *De laudibus* was written at least partly in France, while Fortescue was accompanying the exiled wife of Henry VI, Queen Margaret, and acting as tutor to the Prince of Wales, it should come as no surprise that he compared the customs of France with those of England. Nor, given the polemical nature of the work, is it surprising that he should have attributed the hardship suffered by French subjects to the oppressive nature of civil law, as enforced by the absolute monarch Louis XI: 'Exasperated by these and other calamities, the people live in no little misery'; while in England (so Fortescue claimed), due to observance of law by the king, 'the inhabitants of that land are rich, abounding in gold and silver and all the necessaries of life'.[34]

John Selden noted in the 1616 edition of *De laudibus* that Louis XI 'governed, not according to the Ancient Constitution of *France*, by a General Assembly of the three Estates ... They were ruled by Armies and Councils of Power, in which Royal Will and Pleasure only presided.'[35] The phrase 'Ancient Constitution' is closely associated with resistance by English common lawyers and parliamentarians such as Selden to excessive, unconstitutional and (arguably) unlawful exercise of the royal prerogative by the monarch. Indeed, the eulogistic title *De laudibus legum Angliae* was given to Fortescue's work by Selden, presumably to imply the superiority of English common law to rival jurisdictions (as Fortescue had made clear in his comparison between the English and the French legal systems). Its first publication in English (in a translation by Robert Mulcaster) was in 1567 under the title *A Learned Commendation of the Politique Lawes of England*, although as early as 1513 John Rastell had referred in descriptive (rather than titular) terms to it as 'de laudibus

48

legum Anglie'. For Selden (and his contemporary Sir Edward Coke), the 'Ancient Constitution' was a succinct formulation of the principle that unwritten or customary law was of greater authority than statute or imperial edict, because of its immemorial origins. Where Selden and Coke were responding to the burgeoning constitutional conflict between Crown and common law, Fortescue was writing at a time of immense political upheaval and uncertainty, during the dynastic struggle between the Houses of York and Lancaster, popularly known as the Wars of the Roses. As indicated above, in *On the Governance of England* Fortescue developed the theory of political and regal dominion, under which a 'king may not rule his people by other laws than such as they assent to',[36] and the fact that a version of the work was presented to the Yorkist King Edward IV after his restoration to the throne in 1471, following the death of Henry VI, suggests that it may have been intended as a practical guide to kingship rather than a theoretical work solely of academic interest.

Authority for the claim made by Fortescue for the juridical and constitutional sovereignty of common law derived from its antique origins and immutable nature, more ancient even than 'the civil laws of the Romans' and 'the laws of the Venetians, which are renowned above others for their antiquity – though their island was uninhabited, and Rome unbuilt at the time of the origin of the Britons'.[37] According to Fortescue, the professed sources of this much-lauded antiquity were to be found in an eclectic collection of Judaeo-Christian, classical and medieval texts, including the Bible, the theological works of St Augustine and St Thomas Aquinas, *The Politics* and *The Nicomachean Ethics* of Aristotle, and *Historia Regum Britanniae* by Geoffrey of Monmouth. Fortescue thereby forged a link between the custom of common law and the historiography of the ancient and medieval worlds. It was to the *First Book of Samuel* (1 Samuel 8), as interpreted by Aquinas in *On Princely Government*,[38] that Fortescue turned for validation of the proposition that God ruled his people 'under Judges "royally and politically"', until such time as they offended the Almighty Father by desiring to be ruled by a king 'who reigned upon them "only royally"'.[39] The impression created by Fortescue is one of a legal system in which judges played a suprajudicial role as counsellors or *amici principis*, constantly reminding the king of the primacy of custom in shaping the law. Hence, in Chapter II of *On the Governance of England*, when Fortescue states that '*rex* is so-called from *regendo* or ruling',[40] he is alluding to St Augustine, who notes that when the Romans 'found the domination of kings intolerable', they established authority in the form of 'two men, who were called "consuls", from *consulere* (to take counsel), not "kings" (*reges*), a word derived from *regnare* (to reign), or "lords" (*domini*), derived from *dominare* (to dominate)'.[41]

Custom and the Tudor Inheritance

The fusion of classical literature and philosophy with the tenets of Augustinian and Thomist political theology was a notable feature of *De laudibus*. Fortescue reinterpreted the legend of the Trojan Brutus landing in Britain and founding the city of *Troynovant* (as narrated by Geoffrey of Monmouth in *Historia Regum Britanniae*),[42] to depict the descendant of Aeneas as an archetype of English nationhood and a symbolic originary of English law: 'the kingdom of England blossomed forth into a dominion regal and political out of Brutus's band of Trojans, whom he led out of the territories of Italy and of the Greeks'.[43] Fortescue presents Brutus as the iconic embodiment of *dominium politicum et regale*, a form of polity which Fortescue was to analyse and propound in *On the Governance of England*. It is arguable that Fortescue blurred such distinctions as existed between mythology and history, and between literature and law; but undeniable is the significance of Aristotelian civic republicanism both to *De laudibus* and to *The Governance of England*, and its subsequent influence over jurists in the first half of the sixteenth century. Such was the importance of Aristotle to the political thought of Fortescue that he referred to him throughout *De laudibus* as 'the *Philosopher*'; and, in support of the argument that English law was derived from natural law (rather than from statute), he quotes approvingly from Book V of *The Nicomachean Ethics*: '*Natural law is that which has the same force among all men.*'[44] Similar emphasis on the relevance of *ordo naturae* to municipal order was made by Sir Thomas Elyot in *The boke named the Governour* (published in 1531), in which the author claims that the state 'is disposed by the ordre of equite and governed by the rule and moderation of reason'.[45]

The publication of Elyot's *Governour* was roughly contemporaneous with the publication in English of the Second Dialogue of St German's *Doctor and Student* in 1530 (the Latin version of the First Dialogue was published in 1523), a central theme of which was 'the ordre of equite' and the role of the court of Chancery in applying the Aristotelian principle of *epieikeia* or natural equity to the interpretation of English law. St German developed the theory espoused by Fortescue of a pre-existing customary law, related to the law of God and the law of reason, which demanded the exercise of conscience by all subjects of the English legal institution. Conscience was founded in the law of God and the law of nature, and a human law was bad in conscience if it contradicted either of these laws. According to St German, the customs of the realm had been accepted by king and subject alike because they were necessary for the good governance of the state, and were synonymous with common law itself. St German explains that the first ground of

English law was the law of reason, the second ground was the law of God, and 'The thyrde grounde of the lawe of Englande standeth upon dyverse generall Customes of olde tyme used through all the realme: which have ben acceptyd and approvyd by our soveraygne lorde the kynge and his progenytours and all theyr subgettes.'[46] The role of statute or *leges scriptae* in the English legal system described by St German was merely to affirm customs, and not to repeal them. Like Fortescue, St German argues for the sovereign authority of the judiciary in determining whether a custom was law: 'it shall alway be determyned by the Iustyces whether there be any suche *law or generall custome as alleged*, or not'. To this end, in the Coronation oath, the king swore his allegiance and subjection to law: 'that he shal cause all the customes of his realme faythfully to be observyd'.[47] At a time when the Crown was seeking to establish a sovereign, national jurisprudence, independent from and no longer subject to papal jurisdiction, St German was rehearsing the Bractonian principle that a king was subject to God and law (and by extension, to the customs of the realm), because law made the king.

Notes

1. J. Fortescue, *De Laudibus Legum Angliae*, ed. S. B. Chrimes (Cambridge: Cambridge University Press, 1949), 41, ch. XVII.
2. Ibid., 37, ch. XV.
3. See *The Treatise on the Laws and Customs of the Kingdom of England*, completed *c.* 1189, of which Glanvill was the attributed, albeit disputed, author; and H. de Bracton, *On the Laws and Customs of England*, completed *c.* 1235.
4. Fortescue, *De Laudibus*, 8, 9, ch. III.
5. F. Pollock and F. W. Maitland, *The History of English Law before the Time of Edward I*, 2 vols. (Cambridge: Cambridge University Press, 1911), I, 27.
6. Ibid., I, 40.
7. J. H. Baker, *An Introduction to English Legal History* (London: Butterworths, 2002), 4, 8–9.
8. See W. Dugdale, *Origines Juridiciales, or Historical Memorials of the English Laws* (London: F. and T. Warren, 1666), 26.
9. Pollock and Maitland, *History of English Law*, I, 42; Baker, *Introduction to English Legal History*, 9.
10. Ibid., 13.
11. Ibid., 12.
12. Fortescue, *De Laudibus*, 39, ch. XVII.
13. Ibid.
14. P. Brand, '*Multis Vigiliis Excogitatam et Inventum*: Henry II and the Creation of the English Common Law', *Haskins Society Journal* 2 (1990), 197–222; C. Harper-Bill and N. Vincent (eds.), *Henry II: New Interpretations* (Woodbridge: Boydell Press, 2007).
15. *Leges Henrici Primi*, ed. L. J. Downer (Oxford: Clarendon Press, 1972), p. 109.

16. *Tractatus de legibus et consuetudinibus regni Anglie qui Glanvilla vocatur*, ed. G. D. G. Hall (London: T. Nelson, 1965), 2b, 'Prologue', emphasis added.

17. See H. de Bracton, *De legibus et consuetudinibus Angliae*, vol. I: *Introduction*, ed. T. Twiss, 6 vols. (London: Longman et al., 1878–83; repr. Cambridge: Cambridge University Press, 2012), xxiv–xxv; J. L. Barton, 'The Mystery of Bracton', *Journal of Legal History* 14 (1993), 1–142.

18. Bracton, *De legibus*, I, 3, Bk I.I.

19. *Justinian's Institutes*, trans. P. Birks and G. McLeod (London: Duckworth & Co., 1987), 37, Bk I.II ('*De Iure Naturali et Gentium et Civili*').

20. Bracton, *De legibus*, I, 39, Bk I.VIII.

21. Ibid., I, 3, Bk I.I.

22. Ibid., I, 13, Bk I.III.

23. Baker, *Introduction to English Legal History*, 15–16.

24. E. Coke, *The Fourth Part of the Institutes of the Laws of England, Concerning the Jurisdiction of the Courts* (London: E. and R. Brooke, 1797), 73, 98.

25. Matthew Paris, *Chronica majora*, ed. H. R. Luard, 7 vols. (London: Longman & Co., 1876), III,619.

26. *Rotuli Parliamentorum*, I.84, in Dugdale, *Origines Juridiciales*, 141.

27. Ibid., 159.

28. Fortescue, *De Laudibus*, 119, ch. XLIX.

29. Ibid., 5, ch. I.

30. Ibid., 25, ch. IX.

31. J. Fortescue, 'The Governance of England', in *On the Laws and Governance of England*, ed. S. Lockwood (Cambridge: Cambridge University Press, 1997), 83, ch. I.

32. Fortescue, *De Laudibus*, 87, ch. XXXVI.

33. Ibid., 25, ch. IX; 79, ch. XXXIV.

34. Ibid., 83, ch. XXXV; 87, ch. XXXVI.

35. J. Fortescue, *De Laudibus Legum Angliae*, ed. J. Selden (London: R. Gosling, 1737), 77, n. (a), ch. XXXV.

36. Fortescue, 'Governance of England', 83, ch. I.

37. Fortescue, *De Laudibus*, 39, 41, ch. XVII.

38. Aquinas probably wrote only the first book of *On Princely Government* and the first four chapters of the second book; Ptolemy of Lucca is supposed to have completed the work.

39. Fortescue, 'Governance of England', 84, ch. I.

40. Ibid., 85, ch. II.

41. St Augustine, *City of God*, trans. H. Bettenson (London: Penguin, 2003), 197, Bk V, ch.12.

42. Geoffrey of Monmouth, *The History of the Kings of Britain*, trans. L. Thorpe (London: Penguin, 1966), 71–4, Pt I.15–18.

43. Fortescue, *De Laudibus*, 33, ch. XIII.

44. Ibid., 39, ch. XVI.

45. T. Elyot, *The boke named the Governour* (London: T. Bertheleti, 1531), sig. Ar.

46. C. St German, *Doctor and Student*, ed. T. F. T. Plucknett and J. L. Barton (London: Selden Society, 1974), 45, 'First Dialogue', ch. VII.

47. Ibid., 47.

Further Reading

Abbott, L. W., *Law Reporting in England 1485–1585*, London: Athlone Press, 1973.

Barnes, T. G., *Shaping the Common Law: From Glanvill to Hale, 1188–1688*, ed. A. D. Boyer, Stanford: Stanford University Press, 2008.

Brand, P., *The Origins of the English Legal Profession*, Oxford: Blackwell, 1992.

Burns, J. H., 'Fortescue and the Political Theory of Dominium', *The Historical Journal* 28(4) (1985), 777–97.

Cromartie, A., *The Constitutionalist Revolution: An Essay on the History of England, 1450–1642*, Cambridge: Cambridge University Press, 2006.

Fox, A. and Guy, J., *Reassessing the Henrician Age: Humanism, Politics and Reform, 1500–1550*, Oxford: Blackwell, 1986.

Guy, J., *Christopher St German on Chancery and Statute*, London: Selden Society, 1985.

Holt, J. C., *Magna Carta*, 3rd edn, Cambridge: Cambridge University Press, 2015.

Klinck, D. R., *Conscience, Equity and the Court of Chancery in Early Modern England*, Farnham: Ashgate, 2010.

Megarry, R., *Inns Ancient and Modern*, London: Selden Society, 1972.

Milsom, S. F. C., *Historical Foundations of the Common Law*, 2nd edn, London: Butterworths, 1981.

Plucknett, T. F. T., *A Concise History of the Common Law*, London: Butterworth, 1956.

Pocock, J. G. A., *The Ancient Constitution and the Feudal Law: A Study of English Historical Thought in the Seventeenth Century*, 2nd edn, Cambridge: Cambridge University Press, 1987.

5

ANTHONY MUSSON

Magna Carta and Statutory Law

The Nature of Legislation

Traditionally the impetus for legislation came from the sovereign. The law-codes attributed to Anglo-Saxon and Anglo-Norman kings exemplified the monarch's apparent lead in promulgating laws for the good of his subjects. Royal confirmation of the laws of the realm (especially the laws of St Edward the Confessor) was expected of a monarch at his coronation. The experience during the thirteenth century of calling extraordinary assemblies of representatives to discuss the affairs of the realm and approve royal edicts was reflected in Edward II's coronation oath (1308), which included an obligation on the king to uphold 'the laws and rightful customs which the community of your realm shall have chosen'.[1] The consensual element to royal legislation developed further during the fourteenth century with the frequent summoning of parliaments and general recognition that this was where adjustments to the law of the land should be deliberated and enunciated. The commons' request for remedy of specific matters deemed to be for the welfare to the realm in return for their assent to taxation became an established part of parliamentary procedure. The common petitions in which the knights and burgesses attending parliament articulated their demands were frequently used as a basis for legislation. By Richard II's reign it could be declared that 'the law of the land was made in parliament by the king and the lords spiritual and temporal and all the commons of the kingdom'.[2] As Bishop Alcock expressed in his sermon at the opening of parliament in 1485, it was a cooperative enterprise uniting the sovereign and his people in pursuit of 'good governance'.[3]

Royal law, however, was not solely dependent upon an influx of petitions, nor was the Crown's role in promoting or amending legislation necessarily diminished. Even if Edward I was not personally responsible for a legislative code worthy of Sir Edward Coke's accolade 'our Justinian', edicts (such as the Statute of Westminster of 1275) were couched in such a way as 'to suggest not just the king's formal involvement, but also his positive personal interest, in its making':

> Because our lord the king has a great wish and desire to redress the condition of his kingdom in such matters as need amendment … the king has ordained and established the things here written because he believes that they will be beneficial and well-adapted to the needs of the whole kingdom.[4]

In practice, legal experts and other members of the king's council played a decisive role in formulating law. The oft-quoted retort of one of the senior royal judges under Edward I, Chief Justice Ralph Hengham, issued to a fellow lawyer pleading in court before him, bears witness to this: 'Do not gloss the statute; we understand it better than you do, for we made it.'[5] Yet there remained a fundamental belief in the king's constitutional authority to do so and his overriding power to decide what was good and just for the country. Asserting the royal prerogative, he could refuse his assent or make provisos or claim (as did Edward II in respect of the Ordinances of 1311 and Edward III with regard to the revoked statute of 1341) that certain enactments were contrary to the laws and customs of the realm. Nevertheless, as the various constitutional crises requiring confirmation of Magna Carta exemplify, the exercise of royal will required a fine balance to be observed. Accusations of absolutism were levelled against Richard II (in the deposition articles of 1399) for apparently espousing the Roman law maxims 'what pleases the prince has the force of law' and 'the prince has all the laws in the shrine of his breast', maxims that contentiously underpinned Continental jurisprudence on kingship.[6]

Royal legislation was not generally referred to as a 'statute' until the later thirteenth century. As a body of provisions, Magna Carta (1215, 1225) provided a forerunner in character and quality to the later model of legislation, though it was not initially regarded in that vein and the 'unwritten' tradition of English law espoused by the influential twelfth-century treatise, *Glanvill*, perpetuated, despite the fact laws were often written down. They were not always remembered perfectly, however, and miscellaneous material was often included in a single enactment. The council of Merton of 1236, for instance, issued significant 'provisions' in relation to widows, landlords and minors, but was credited (even in the eminent treatise *Bracton*) with additional unrelated legislative points. Indeed, it is only from the legislative initiatives of 1258–9, which served as a basis for the Statute of Marlborough (1267),[7] that a distinction between earlier conceptions of law-making can be drawn.

A more systematic collecting together of legal provisions (codifying judicial decisions and the results of comprehensive local inquiries) took place under Edward I.

Edward I's statutes not only gave rise to a distinct tier of law (*ley especial* or *novel ley*) that could be contrasted with the common law (*ancien ley*), but also engendered an appreciation of the formal expression of royal authority behind it. The direction of legislative thinking also gradually altered and thus the purpose behind formulations of statutes. By Edward III's reign, no longer were they simply judicial interpretations or declarations of the existing common law, but enactments that were often based on a distinct political agenda and brought many hitherto unregulated areas of human life and behaviour within the purview of government regulation. Modifications and adjustments to the law could also be made through legislation, while statutes offered new opportunities for the provision of legal remedies and amending mischief in the common law. Such was the acceptance of the legislative supremacy of parliament that by the 1360s a statute was considered binding on everybody from the moment it was made, regardless of proclamation. By the sixteenth century, contemporaries distinguished 'acts of parliament' according to whether they were special, general or particular. The former, provisions that benefitted individuals or distinct entities, were regarded as private acts. Those addressing broader legal, economic or social matters constituted public acts, while some legislation of a general character affected particular interest groups rather than the population as a whole.

The introduction or preamble to a statute set out the reasoning behind the legislative action and became an increasingly important device. By prefacing significant pieces of legislation with rhetoric that highlighted the inadequacy of the system in times past, rulers were able to point to novel solutions and thus present themselves as reformers addressing the needs of their subjects. Magna Carta, for example, begins with a justificatory preamble that uses language of correction and reform. The trend was again perhaps set by Edward I's legislation, notably the Statute of Winchester (1285), which provided a swingeing denunciation of the state of the peace – complaining that daily there were more crimes committed than formerly – and then proceeded to offer a combination of measures designed to rectify the problem. The tradition was extended and utilised particularly effectively under Edward III and Richard II, during whose reigns the preambles tended to increase in length and verbosity. The prolonged passage preceding the statute of 1378, for example, not only maintained that the 'people ... who conspire' did so without 'consideration to God, the laws of Holy Church, or of the land, or to right, or justice ... refusing and setting apart all processes of law', but stressed their actions were to the 'great mischief and grievance of the people and the hurt of the king's majesty and against the king's crown'.[8] Acknowledging the different hierarchies of law and need for due process, this preamble also unites the interests of Crown and people. Preambles to numerous statutes strategically employ the discourse of amending the law for the 'common profit of the realm', suggesting the phrase had not only become standardised in form, but also a necessary tag in the minds of legislative draftsmen. It was a phraseology which equally gained currency outside royal circles. From the early fourteenth century it was adopted by the parliamentary commons in petitions (particularly those relating to fiscal and economic matters), thereby demonstrating an appreciation of the textual precedents as well as asserting their moral right to speak for the welfare of the kingdom.[9]

From 1297 a special place in the legislative canon was reserved for Magna Carta. Following Edward I's confirmation of the charters, the 'Great Charter of Liberties' was formally absorbed into the common law and however ambiguous technically, took on the mantle of the pre-eminent statute of the realm.[10] Magna Carta continued to receive endorsement in parliamentary legislation up to Henry VI's reign, though it was so firmly recognised as having statutory authority that confirmation (whether explicit or implicitly in the language used) had become routine. Indeed, it was so embedded that until at least 1435 a formula was included in the chancellor's (or chief justice's) opening speech to parliament. Confirmation of the liberties of the church 'by authority of parliament' continued into the sixteenth century, even if endorsement of the full import of Magna Carta was no longer considered necessary.[11]

Sources and Dissemination

Royal government and the judiciary frequently had need to refer to past legislation and could review in council or call into court registers and rolls in which royal edicts had been set down as a permanent record. In 1299, the chancery started compiling what was known as 'the Great Roll of the Statutes'. Initially, this roll was itself neither complete nor authoritative owing to 'errors and deficiencies' both in the pre-1299 legislation and in what was included on the roll. It began to be accorded special authority, however, when (around the mid-fourteenth century) chancery assumed responsibility for the rolls of parliament. Since legislation was emerging more consistently from common petitions presented in parliamentary sessions, it was thus regularly read out and enrolled at their conclusion. Such was the refinement of parliamentary business that by the later fifteenth century the clerks were recording on their rolls only matters that resulted in new legislation.

Not surprisingly, Magna Carta and the statutes played an important part in legal education. Surviving moot questions (problems drawn from particular statutes) indicate that disputation on areas of law, especially those

ANTHONY MUSSON

espoused by the Great Charter, was a theme favoured by lawyers, probably members of the emergent Inns of Court, as early as the 1340s. The earliest surviving manuscripts show that the statute book formed the basis for these exercises and that the interpretation of at least seventeen clauses of Magna Carta were debated before the earliest 'Readings' (lectures) on the subject were held in the fifteenth century. Readings on a particular chapter of a key statute were delivered at both the Inns of Court and the Inns of Chancery by a bencher (senior member) of the Inn over dinner during one of the law term vacations. Surviving authors' texts and students' notes of these lectures reveal they focused predominantly on Magna Carta and the core statutes of Edward I's reign with very few readings given on the legislation of 1300–1485.[12]

In addition to being a feature of legal training, volumes of statutes (containing Magna Carta and other legal material) were produced from the late thirteenth century onwards not just for lawyers and administrators, but also clergy, merchants, nobility, gentry and civic and ecclesiastical institutions, all of whom had a stake in the justice system. Symbolically placed at the head of these volumes, Magna Carta precedes the collections known as *statuta antiqua*, which proceed chronologically with legislative provisions from Henry III's reign, followed by the great canon promulgated by Edward I and enactments dated to Edward II's reign.[13] Magna Carta occasionally precedes collections of *nova statuta*. These comprise legislation from the reigns of individual monarchs (depending upon their date of compilation) and thus provide a more or less comprehensive source of contemporary statutory law up to the reign of Henry VII. The perceived importance of the Great Charter was such that it was included by late thirteenth- and early fourteenth-century copyists in manuscript collections of much earlier legal texts. Here it was intended either as the apotheosis of a tradition of early English laws – one that included early twelfth-century compilations such as the *Consilatio Cnuti*, comprising his 'Winchester code' and other pre-conquest texts, and the *Leges Edwardi Confessoris* – or as an extension of that tradition.[14]

Those without bespoke compilations interested in obtaining chapter and verse of the latest statutory law had access to the sheriff's office where copies of the Great Charter and other legislation were deposited. Copies of relevant statutes were also made available upon request to justices of the peace.[15] The advent of printed editions of statutes increased the accessibility of legislation beyond the legal profession and enhanced textual reliability.[16] Ownership of, or at least access to, these books, thus enabled both a personal and (where there was multiple ownership) a collective form of engagement with political and legal matters.[17] Chronicles, too, were repositories of legislation and

58

provide accounts of legislative activity which otherwise might be lost, indicating their perceived importance to contemporaries: Matthew Paris frequently draws the reader's attention to different pieces of legislation proclaimed orally during Henry III's reign,[18] while fourteenth-century chronicler Adam Murimuth, for instance, included in his account the text of the Ordinance of Justices (1346).[19]

The church played an important role, too, in the dissemination of Magna Carta and other legislative provisions. At a council held at Reading in 1279, the newly appointed archbishop of Canterbury, John Pecham, ordered Magna Carta to be read out and posted up in churches and cathedrals. Even though not long after this Edward I ordered the removal of all copies from display, there is evidence that it continued to be read out publicly in all cathedrals twice a year. It also became common practice for bishops to issue a formal decree annually declaring that any person who violated the Great Charter would be excommunicated. The clergy, it appears, were generally enthusiastic about disseminating the provisions of Magna Carta, preserving versions in bishop's registers and clergy instruction manuals, thereby enabling them to familiarise the laity with the key points. Far from being the preserve of the literate elite, 'every parishioner was kept, or supposed to be kept conscious of Magna Carta'.[20]

Access to legislative provisions was enhanced by oral proclamation. Under the Articles on the Charters (1300), transcripts of the Great Charter were to be sent to sheriffs so it could be read out 'before the people four times a year' at Michaelmas, Christmas, Easter and Midsummer.[21] Regular recitation of Magna Carta and the Statute of Winchester of 1285 (measures for local policing) in the county court, the shire's prime meeting point, thus afforded attendees a firm basis of the key tenets of English justice. Following parliamentary assent, new legislation was also proclaimed in towns and cities, at fairs and markets, and in the countryside at important crossroads. Occasionally, Magna Carta was recited for particular effect or in order to underscore its provisions: in 1318, it was confirmed and read out before the assembled clergy, earls and barons,[22] while in 1404 the bishop of Rochester produced a copy and read it during a parliamentary debate on what he considered were unlawful royal plans for clerical taxation.[23]

Magna Carta's accessibility and absorption was equally assisted by the language of its dissemination and proclamation. It was issued to the barons in Anglo-Norman French, as a contemporary 1215 version implies, and other copies in vernacular French were circulated during the thirteenth century through their inclusion in chronicles, cartularies and legal collections.[24] It is clear from chronicles and instructions sent out to sheriffs that not only was a French text of Magna Carta (and other statutes) prepared for recitation, but also the provisions were translated by the crier himself and proclaimed in English for the benefit of those for whom it was their mother tongue. Comprehension of royal legislation was thus considerably advanced by this linguistic inclusivity, backed up by the printed publication of French and, by the late fifteenth century (purportedly at the insistence of Henry VII), English versions of royal statutes.[25]

Evidence of Contextualisation

An appreciation of the value of citing the import of a statute or employing the appropriate language of the legislation is demonstrated by the way suppliants at all levels of society cited Magna Carta or specific statutes back to the Crown in their petitions or in litigation. William de Boys, for example, demanded delivery of the issues and rents that were due him from the manors not held of the king that he had inherited from his brother, basing his right on Magna Carta and the Statute of Marlborough.[26] Joan, the widow of Ralph Basset of Drayton, claimed that commissions of special oyer and terminer issued to Hugh Meynill to 'hear and determine' complaints against her and her servants contravened 'the statutes providing that an oyer and terminer should only be granted in cases of serious trespass and before justices of king's bench or common pleas'.[27] Isabel, the widow of Richard de Cleterne, complained that in Edward III's reign charters of pardon were too commonly given regardless of recent legislation.[28] These petitioners do not offer precise chapter and verse, yet their claims do have a firm grounding in real statutes: they were not just making a vague allusion to legislation in the hope that they would be taken seriously. However, even lawyers occasionally bluffed their way. The serjeant-at-law Thomas Littleton is mentioned in the law reports as smiling when he cited a statute which he thought would assist his client. Since Littleton's argument was dismissed by the court, the description of him smiling might indicate an attempt to bolster a weak line of argument, in this instance one based on a statute which did not apply in the circumstances.[29]

Chroniclers referenced statutory law (and Magna Carta in particular) both as a yardstick for lawful behaviour and to exemplify guarantees as to royal conduct. According to the anonymous Worcester Annalist, the consensus amongst the leading barons gathered in parliament in 1300 was that they would only consent to taxation if their 'liberties' as enshrined in the Great Charter and Forest Charter were confirmed ('when we have secure possession of our forests and of our liberties, often promised to us, then we will willingly give a twentieth, so that the folly of the Scots may be dealt with').[30] Recounting the political crisis of 1340–1, another chronicler, Roger of

Avesbury, pointed to the arrests of officials during Edward III's purge of his administration as behaviour contrary to the law of the land and Magna Carta.[31]

Perceptions of the law could be affected by an inaccurately rendered point or imperfect comprehension. Hearing it proclaimed, albeit at regular intervals, rather than reading it personally at leisure brought the possibility of inaccuracies and misunderstandings. In 1290 Robert of Tilbury used Magna Carta (c.17) as authority that he did not have to answer in the court *coram rege* (king's bench) on a plea of warranty by equating the prohibition on common pleas following the king with the notion that 'common pleas should be held in a certain place, that is the [Common] Bench'.[32] For some the capacity to digest it fully may have been limited to certain memorable clauses or the gist of what was presented. The enigmatic demand by the rebels of 1381, for 'no law but the law of Winchester', may exemplify this.[33] The source of this can only be speculated, but was popularly perceived to be a framework of fundamental principles. They may have been referring obliquely to the Statute of Winchester, given its frequent proclamation, but it is just possible they meant Cnut's 'Winchester Code', laws decreed at Winchester in the early eleventh century that like its thirteenth-century counterpart contains many provisions of fundamental importance to the local community and the operation of justice. Alternatively they could have been referring to the Domesday Book, also known as the 'roll of Winchester' or 'book of Winchester' because it originally resided in the royal treasury there. The Domesday Book, the result of William the Conqueror's attempt to provide a written record of property-holding rights, was regarded (erroneously) by many as a statute and was at least quasi-law in the minds of the many litigants who cited it as source of proof in property disputes as well as villeins who used it to assert that their manor had the privileges of 'ancient desmesne' status. In the context of the Peasants' Revolt four years later, therefore, the Domesday Book may have been viewed as an iconic 'law' legitimating claims to freedom. However, if read in conjunction with the rest of Wat Tyler's demands, which included the abolition of outlawry and serfdom so that 'all should be free and of one status', the rebel leaders may equally have been invoking a particular paradigm of values analogous to Magna Carta.[34]

Conclusion

The late medieval period witnessed the development of statutory law as a directly enforceable body of rules adjunct to the common law. The extent to which in practice it was driven by the king's personal engagement as opposed to the internal logic and momentum of government is open to speculation. Certainly, by the fourteenth century the making of legislation was influenced by the concerns of parliamentary representatives, even if these usually reflected the agenda of the privileged classes. In gauging the effect of statutory law no reign should be viewed in isolation, nor should any piece of legislation be necessarily seen as the finished product. While Edward I's reign was significant for its statutes setting out the substantive law, Edward III's reign witnessed a number of 'establishments' in the areas of judicial administration and procedure that were important to contemporaries who were experiencing the law in action. Although Richard III's brief reign is remembered for its conspicuous legislative initiatives, many were reversed or adapted by Henry VII or his successors. Moreover, legislation must adapt to society and so is rarely totally frozen in time: judges sometimes override or attenuate its effect, while legislators may abolish it or tinker with it to suit the prevailing conditions. Labour legislation, first issued in 1349 and still being adjusted in the 1490s, is a remarkable case in point.[35]

The effectiveness of legislation depended entirely upon its interpretation and enforcement by the courts. Texts invoking or referencing Magna Carta and statutory law (the parliament rolls, private petitions, chronicles, readings and moots of the Inns of Court together with the records of cases appearing in the law courts) provide a significant insight into the development and influence of legislation as well as evidence of the law's practical application of it. Such texts also 'help to construct discourses of royal justice and grace that both responded to a particular historical moment and continue to resonate over time'.[36] They are invaluable sources therefore for the diversity of royal law's reception within medieval society. More particularly, they demonstrate the continued applicability of Magna Carta's chapters to a variety of legal, social and economic circumstances, though paradoxically, the Great Charter itself became less overtly visible as supplementary legislation elaborated on its substantive clauses and its principles became absorbed into the fabric of the legal system.

Notes

1. Michael Prestwich, *Plantagenet England 1225–1360* (Oxford: Clarendon Press, 2005), 28–9, 179.
2. *PROME*, Parliament of 1388, Part 3.
3. Paul Cavill, *The Early English Parliaments of Henry VII, 1485–1504* (Oxford: Oxford University Press, 2009), 167.

4. Paul Brand, 'Edward I and Justice', in *La culture judiciaire anglaise au Moyen Âge*, ed. Yves Mausen (Paris: Mare and Martin, 2017), 118–22.

5. *Year Books 33 and 35 Edward I*, ed. Alfred. J. Horwood (London: Longman, 1879), 82.

6. Christopher Given-Wilson, trans., *Chronicles of the Revolution, 1397–1400: The Reign of Richard II* (Manchester: Manchester University Press, 1992), 172–3, 175–8, 180–1.

7. As part of efforts at reconstruction following a period of civil war, the statute of Marlborough incorporated many of the measures which the baronial reformers had proposed in 1258–9.

8. *Statutes of the Realm*, ed. A. Luders et al., 11 vols. (London, 1810–28), II, 9–10 [hereafter, *SR*].

9. W. Mark Ormrod, '"Common Profit" and "The Profit of the King and Kingdom": Parliament and the Development of Political Language in England, 1250–1450', *Viator* 46 (2015), 219–52.

10. *Selected Readings and Commentaries on Magna Carta, 1400–1604*, ed. Sir John Baker, *Selden Society* 132 (London, 2015), xxxix–xl.

11. Cavill, *English Parliaments*, 233–4.

12. *Readings and Moots at the Inns of Court in the Fifteenth Century*, ed. Samuel. E. Thorne and John H. Baker, Selden Society, 105 (London, 1990), cxlii–cxliii.

13. Donald. C. Skemer, 'Sir William Breton's Book: Production of *Statuta Angliae* in the Late Thirteenth Century', in *English Manuscript Studies, 1100–1700*, ed. P. Beal and J. Griffiths (London, 1998), VII, 27–8, 38–42.

14. Bruce O'Brien, 'Pre-Conquest Laws and Legislators in the Twelfth Century', in *The Long Twelfth-Century View of the Anglo-Saxon Past*, ed. Martin Brett and David Woodman (Farnham: Ashgate, 2015), 233–4.

15. John Maddicott, 'The County Community and the Making of Public Opinion in Fourteenth Century England', *Transactions of the Royal Historical Society*, 5th series, 18 (1987), 36–7.

16. John H. Baker, 'Books of the Common Law', in *The Cambridge History of the Book in Britain, 1400–1557*, vol. 3, ed. L. Hellinga and J. B. Trapp (Cambridge: Cambridge University Press, 1999), 422–3.

17. Donald C. Skemer, 'Reading the Law: Statute Books and the Private Transmission of Legal Knowledge in Late Medieval England', in *Learning the Law: Teaching and the Transmission of English Law, 1150–1900*, ed. Jonathan Bush and Alain Wijfels (London: Hambledon, 1999), 113–31.

18. Michael T. Clanchy, *From Memory to Written Record: England 1066 to 1307*, 3rd edn (Oxford: Blackwell, 2013), 266.

19. *Adae Murimuth Continuatio Chronicarum. Robertus de Avesbury de Gestis Mirabilibus Regis Edwardi Tertii*, ed. E. M. Thompson (London, 1889), 193–4.

20. William A. Pantin, *The English Church in the Fourteenth Century* (Cambridge: Cambridge University Press, 1955; new edn, 2010), 198.

21. *SR* I, 136.

22. See Seymour Phillips, *Edward II* (New Haven, CT and London: Yale University Press, 2011), 331.

23. *The St Albans Chronicle II, 1394–1422*, ed. John Taylor, Wendy R. Childs and L. Watkiss (Oxford: Clarendon Press, 2011), 423.
24. Sir James Holt, *Magna Carta*, 3rd edn (Cambridge: Cambridge University Press, 2015), 399.
25. Dean Rowland, 'The End of the Statute Rolls: Manuscript, Print and Language Change in Fifteenth-Century English Statutes', in *The Fifteenth Century IX: Concerns and Preoccupations*, ed. Linda Clark (Woodbridge: Boydell Press, 2012), 107–26.
26. London, The National Archives, Special Collections, Ancient Petitions, SC 8/35/1736 (http://discovery.nationalarchives.gov.uk/details/r/C9061935).
27. SC 8/32/1551 (http://discovery.nationalarchives.gov.uk/details/r/C9061747).
28. SC 8/39/1937 (http://discovery.nationalarchives.gov.uk/details/r/C9062140).
29. Gwen Seabourne, '"Et Subridet etc.": Smiles, Laughter and Levity in the Medieval Year Books', in *Law and Society in Later Medieval England and Ireland*, ed. Travis R. Baker (Abingdon: Routledge, 2018), 205, 218.
30. *Annales Monastici*, ed. H. R. Luard, 4 vols. (London, 1864–9), IV, 544.
31. Thompson, ed., *Adae Murimuth*, 324–9.
32. Michael T. Clanchy, 'Magna Carta and the Common Pleas', in *Studies in Medieval History Presented to R. H. C. Davies*, ed. Henry Mayr-Harting and R. I. Moore (London: Hambledon, 1985), 223–7.
33. *The Anonimalle Chronicle, 1333–1381*, ed. V. H. Galbraith (Manchester: Manchester University Press, 1927), 147.
34. Discussed in A. Musson, *Medieval Law in Context: The Growth of Legal Consciousness from Magna Carta to the Peasants' Revolt* (Manchester: Manchester University Press, 2001), 250–3.
35. Christopher Given-Wilson, 'The Problem of Labour in the Context of English Government, 1350–1450', in *The Problem of Labour in Fourteenth Century England*, ed. James Bothwell, W. Mark Ormrod and Jeremy Goldberg (Woodbridge: York Medieval Press, 2000), 85–100.
36. Rosemarie McGerr, *A Lancastrian Mirror for Princes: The Yale Law School New Statutes of England* (Bloomington, IN, Indiana University Press, 2011), 13.

Further Reading

Brand, P., *Kings, Barons and Justices: The Making and Enforcement of Legislation in Thirteenth-Century England*, Cambridge: Cambridge University Press, 2003.
Cavill, P., *The Early English Parliaments of Henry VII, 1485–1504*, Oxford: Oxford University Press, 2009.
Doig, J. A., 'Political Propaganda and Royal Proclamations in Late Medieval England', *Historical Research* 71 (2002), 253–75.
Hanbury, H. G., 'The Legislation of Richard III', *American Journal of Legal History* 6 (1962), 95–113.
Holt, Sir James, *Magna Carta*, 3rd edn, Cambridge: Cambridge University Press, 2015.
Maddicott, J. R., 'The County Community and the Making of Public Opinion in Fourteenth Century England', *Transactions of the Royal Historical Society* 18 (1987), 27–43.

Musson, A., *Medieval Law in Context: The Growth of Legal Consciousness from Magna Carta to the Peasants' Revolt*, Manchester: Manchester University Press, 2001.

Musson, A. and Ormrod, W. M., *The Evolution of English Justice: Law, Politics and Society in the Fourteenth Century*, Basingstoke: Macmillan, 1999.

Ormrod, W. M., 'On and Off the Record: The Rolls of Parliament, 1337–1377', *Parliamentary History* 23 (2004), 29–56.

'"Common Profit" and "The Profit of the King and Kingdom": Parliament and the Development of Political Language in England, 1250–1450', *Viator* 46 (2015), 219–52.

Richardson, H. G. and Sayles, G. O., 'The Early Statutes', *Law Quarterly Review* 50 (1934), 201–23, 540–71.

Rowland, D., 'The End of the Statute Rolls: Manuscript, Print and Language Change in Fifteenth-Century English Statutes', in *The Fifteenth Century IX: Concerns and Preoccupations*, ed. Linda Clark, Woodbridge: Boydell Press, 2012, 107–26.

Skemer, D. C., 'Reading the Law: Statute Books and the Private Transmission of Legal Knowledge in Late Medieval England', in *Learning the Law: Teaching and the Transmission of English Law, 1150–1900*, ed. Jonathan Bush and Alain Wijfels, London: Hambledon, 1999, 113–31.

Thompson, F., *Magna Carta: Its Role in the Making of the English Constitution, 1300–1629*, Minneapolis, MN: University of Minnesota Press, 1948; repr. 1978.

6

DON C. SKEMER

Treatises, Tracts and Compilations

English law was influenced by many legal traditions: Anglo-Saxon, Danish, Frankish and Norman law and custom; feudal and seignorial law; borough customs, mercantile law and guild regulations; and Roman and canon law taught at English and continental universities. Common law became a recognisable legal system in the twelfth and thirteenth centuries, and the expansion of royal justice created a need for unofficial treatises, tracts and compilations in Latin and Anglo-Norman (Law French). These legal texts served a diverse readership of judges, lawyers, religious houses, prelates, landowners, manorial stewards, urban corporations, merchants and others needing legal knowledge. Commercial book production in Greater London and beyond resulted in a proliferation of legal manuscripts, from plain scribal copies for working lawyers to deluxe illuminated copies for high-status patrons. Supplementing these were manuscripts copied for their own use by lawyers, clerks and law students, especially after the rise of the Inns of Court from the 1340s. Scribal transmission of individually executed copies, usually written on parchment in varying grades of Anglicana script (an English book cursive of documentary origin) gave way from the 1480s to lawbook printing and publishing on paper.

Treatises and Tracts

The Norman and Angevin kings and their administrators needed Latin or Anglo-Norman versions of Anglo-Saxon law-codes and a record of legal changes since 1066. This led to several anonymous compilations and translations from Old English, which were largely impostures. The *Quadripartitus* (*c.* 1113–18) constitutes two parts of a planned four-part Latin digest of Anglo-Saxon law, updated with Henry I's legal provisions. The same compiler was probably responsible for *Leges Henrici I*, a contemporary treatise on laws in force at the time. The *Leges Edwardi Confessoris* (*c.* 1135–50), Anglo-Norman *Leis Willelme*

66

(*c.* 1150) and its Latin translation *Leges Willelmi I* (before 1215) purported to preserve Anglo-Saxon law under Edward the Confessor (r. 1042–66).[1] By the mid-twelfth century, England came to be influenced by the 'learned laws' through the revival of Roman law and codification of canon law, offering conceptual models, terminology and classifications useful in presenting English law.

Royal government and justice expanded rapidly in scope and technical complexity from Henry II (r. 1154–89) to Edward I (r. 1272–1307). People who might otherwise seek legal remedy in seignorial and communal courts were drawn to the king's courts at Westminster and to county courts visited by itinerant justices on general eyre. One could thus avert archaic legal procedures, such as trial by battle in feudal disputes. Chancery clerks prepared fee-based writs in the king's name and issued them to sheriffs and other local officials to initiate specific forms of action, each with its own procedures and remedies, and royal judges could issue judicial writs or quash writs they considered unsuitable.[2] Between the 1220s and 1320s, the work of Chancery and royal courts grew exponentially.[3] This created demand for judges to dispense justice, clerks to prepare writs and keep records, attorneys and serjeants-at-law to advise and represent litigants, and manuscripts to disseminate fundamental law to the Community of the Realm and serve as procedural manuals and formularies.

Ranulf Glanvill (*c.* 1112–90), chief justiciar under Henry II from 1180 to 1189, has been ascribed authorship of the first authoritative common law treatise, *The Treatise on the Laws and Customs of the Kingdom of England* (*c.* 1187–9). Some scholars believe that it might have been the work of a contemporary judge or higher-level clerk, possibly under Glanvill's supervision, or even his nephew Hubert Walter (*c.* 1160–1205), a future justiciar. The pragmatic approach to royal justice was likely influenced by the inside view of Exchequer administration in *Dialogus de scaccario*, probably written in the 1170s by Richard Fitz Neal (*c.* 1130–98), lord treasurer under Henry II. The *Treatise* praises common law as unwritten but accepts the authority of legal enactments of the king in council.[4] The *Treatise* devotes books I–XIII to civil cases in the king's courts and book XIV to criminal cases. The focus on writ-based justice and inclusion of seventy-six writs, perhaps copied from an official Chancery register or file, makes the text more procedural than theoretical. Yet the author was familiar with Roman legal principles, especially Justinian's *Institutes*. At least forty-one Glanvill manuscripts (including a roll) survive from the twelfth to the fourteenth century, in original *alpha* (*c.* 1187–9) and revised *beta* (*c.* 1265) versions.[5] Over time, manuscripts added rubrics, cross-references, marginal notes and numbers for the books and chapters to facilitate use. Glanvill was not printed until 1554.

Far more comprehensive was Henry de Bracton (*c.* 1210–68), *On the Laws and Customs of England*, which F. W. Maitland praised as 'the crown and flower of English medieval jurisprudence'.[6] Bracton was a royal justice in southwestern England, who wrote the treatise around 1250–6, in part as a revision of one or more tracts from the 1220s and 1230s, but left the treatise incomplete and imperfectly organised before it began circulating in the 1270s. He also found inspiration in Roman law, especially Justinian's *Institutes* and Azo of Bologna's *Summa institutionum*. Bracton emphasised writ-based royal justice and incorporated a much larger number of writs, as well as some 500 authoritative judicial decisions, chiefly those of Martin Pateshall (d. 1229) and William Raleigh (d. 1250), royal justices in the southwestern counties (1217–40), in order to counteract abuses of unwritten law by ignorant judges. Bracton had previously assigned his clerks to transcribe some 2,000 judicial decisions from official plea rolls, probably beginning with intermediate copies on separate pieces of parchment. These were then sorted and copied into Bracton's *Note Book* (British Library, Add. MS 12269).[7] Bracton selected a portion of these decisions for his treatise, which was partially a compilation in the medieval and modern sense of a gathering and rearrangement of pre-existing textual or documentary materials to create a new written work.[8]

More than fifty extant manuscripts of the Bracton treatise survive, most being plain copies of the late thirteenth and fourteenth centuries, often bound with other legal texts. Many show evidence of work by multiple scribes, to whom commercial stationers had subcontracted the production of particular quires in a regulated system of providing official parts for scribal copying.[9] Relatively few are illuminated, such as British Library, Add. MS 11353, from Edward I's reign. Many judges and lawyers probably owned Bracton manuscripts. John de Longeville (d. *c.* 1324), a lawyer and public official in Northamptonshire, may have owned one from *c.* 1307 (Cambridge University Library, Dd.7.6). Walter de Langton (1243–1321), bishop of Coventry and Lichfield, as well as royal treasurer, may have owned another (Cambridge University Library, Dd.7.14).[10] Several had an early ecclesiastical provenance: Glastonbury Abbey (British Library, Add. MS 21614); Chertsey Abbey (British Library, Add. MS 24067); Luffield Abbey (Cambridge University Library, Ee.1.1); Worcester Cathedral Library (MS F. 87); and St Augustine Abbey, Canterbury (York Minster Library and Archives, XVI.D.6).[11]

Legal professionals spread Bracton's influence through epitomes and procedural tracts that incorporated new laws and procedures. Derivative works include *Fleta* (1290–1300), a Latin epitome and updating of Bracton by a royal justice or lawyer, possibly Matthew of the Exchequer (fl. *c.* 1285–95), in London's Fleet Prison. *Fleta* survives in a fourteenth-century copy (British Library, Cotton Julius B.viii). Other lawbooks derived from Bracton include *Britton*, an Anglo-Norman treatise (post-1290) attributed to John le Breton (d. 1275), with occasional Middle English words, and the *Summa* of Gilbert de Thornton (d. 1295), Chief Justice of King's Bench. Ralph de Hengham (1235–1311), Chief Justice of King's Bench (1274–90) and of Common Pleas (1301–9), prepared two Latin treatises: *Hengham magna* or *Summa magna*, an unfinished epitome of Bracton; and *Hengham parva* or *Summa parva*, lectures on procedure for law students.

Many anonymous procedural tracts with model forms date from the reigns of Edward I to Edward III, often surviving in one-volume compendia of treatises, tracts and compilations for lawyers. Early tracts making dubious claims to authorship by Ralph de Hengham include *Fet asaver* (*c.* 1267); *Judicium essoniorum* (*c.* 1267–75); and *Modus componendi brevia* and *Exceptiones ad cassandum brevia*, intended probably as two parts of the same tract (after 1285).[12] Procedural tracts on writs and pleadings in royal courts include *Brevia placitata* (*c.* 1260) and *Casus placitorum* (*c.* 1260s–70s). Among other tracts are *Placita corone* (*c.* 1274–6), on criminal law, in Latin and Anglo-Norman versions; and *Old Natura brevium* and *Novae narrationes* (reign of Edward III). Later legal texts include copies of instructional lectures and disputations at the Inns of Court. Readings on Statutes were copies of interpretative lectures, some as early as the 1430s–50s, and copies of pleading exercises at readings and moot courts circulated chiefly from the 1480s and 1490s.[13]

Two late medieval treatises by jurists educated at the Inns of Court would influence common law study for centuries through printed editions: Thomas de Littleton (*c.* 1407–81), *Tenures* (*c.* 1460), originally in Law French, a basic textbook on land law; and John Fortescue, *De laudibus legum Angliae* (*c.* 1468–71), a treatise on constitutional law and government, written in exile by Henry VI's Chief Justice of King's Bench.

Statute Books

The most popular common law compilation was the Statute Book (*Statuta Angliae*), of which more than 400 manuscripts survive. Over half were produced before 1327 and the remainder date from the Edward III to the early Tudors.[14] From around 1225, ecclesiastical archives occasionally retained engrossed copies of statutes dispatched to the counties as sealed rolls for public proclamation (or later transcriptions). Royal officials and lawyers also retained personal copies for reference and were perhaps responsible for assembling prototypes of Statute Books from earlier collections or groups of copies in booklets or rolls circulating among legal professionals. Statute Books assume recognisable form by the 1280s and 1290s (Figure 6.1). Most are codices, but some examples produced around 1300 are in Exchequer-style roll format, which, like small 'pocket' codices, could be carried to court in a satchel.[15]

Statute Books through the reign of Edward II (r. 1307–27) are called *vetera statuta* (Old Statutes). They were non-interpretive collections of enacted law and related texts in Latin and Anglo-Norman. The contents were organised in discernible categories – perhaps as they had circulated earlier – such as fundamental laws; royal government and finance; money, weights and measures; land tenure; and judicial procedures. *Vetera statuta* begin textually (often after tables of contents) with versions of Magna Carta (1215) and the Charter of the Forests (1217), as confirmed and reissued by Henry III (r. 1216–72) and Edward I. These are followed by multi-part enactments of the king in parliament, including the Provisions of Merton (1235/36) and Statutes of Marlborough (1267), Westminster I (1275), Gloucester (1278) and Westminster II (1285); and then by an assortment of genuine statutes, together with royal writs, ordinances and letters patent deemed important enough for inclusion and occasionally even labelled statutes; for example, Edward I's articles of inquest on the Jews and coin-clipping (1290), found in a dozen Statute Books; and brief texts, such as Anglo-Norman versions of *Expositio vocabulorum*, a glossary of archaic and pseudo-archaic Old English legal terms related to land tenure and privileges, useful for reading old charters.[16]

During the reign of Edward III (r. 1327–77), the mixed content of the *vetera statuta* was replaced by the more homogeneous *nova statuta* (New Statutes), which presented authentic statutory enactments of the king in parliament, arranged in chronological order by regnal year to parallel the Chancery's filing order of statute rolls kept in the Tower of London (1278–1430, 1446–68). In the fourteenth century, these official rolls came to enjoy public authority as archival 'record copies' of authentic statutes, and continued to function in this way until they were replaced in 1483 by Chancery enrolments of the Acts of Parliament. While *vetera* and *nova statuta* have differing contents and internal organisation, Statute Books of all periods were designed to facilitate use. Tables of contents in Latin or Anglo-Norman eventually gave way to alphabetical subject indices facilitating access to the growing bulk of statute law. A Middle English alphabetical index (*Accusations–Suerte*) of statutes until the 1440s (Columbia University Library, Plimpton MS Add. 5) was another such effort.[17] The London firm of John Lettou and William de Machlinia printed *Abbreviamentum statutorum* (1481–2),

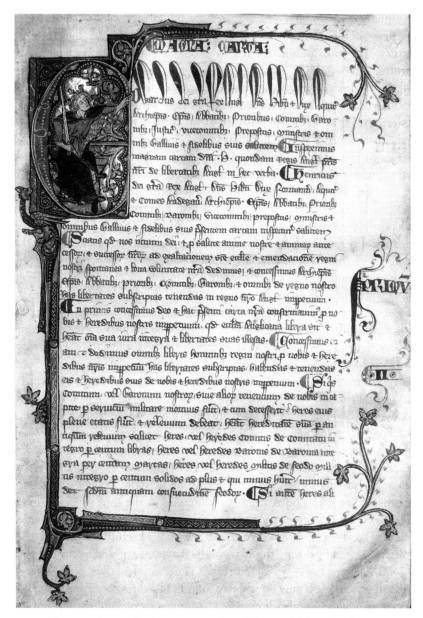

Figure 6.1 Statute Book, *c.* 1300–10 from Princeton University Library, Scheide M30, fol. 1 r. Text opens with an inhabited initial *E* ['Edwardus'], depicting an enthroned Edward I, as 'English Justinian', who holds the sword of justice and points to his *Inspeximus* (1297) of Henry III's reissue of Magna Carta (1265).

an alphabetical summary of statute law by subject, before they printed the first Statute Book (*nova statuta*) around 1484. In the sixteenth century, lawbook publishers began producing authoritative editions of statutes, prepared for press by jurists at the nearby Inns of Court, especially Middle Temple.

Scattered provenance evidence suggests that Statute Books had a varied readership. In 1294, the imprisoned royal official named Matthew of the Exchequer owned a Statute Book and two compilations of Magna Carta and statutes of Henry III and Edward I, bound with legal treatises and tracts, as well as owning standard works of canon and civil law. Another was owned by the London fishmonger, public official and jurist Andrew Horn (*c.* 1275–1328), who compiled the *Liber Horn* (British Library, Cotton Claudius D.ii) and possibly authored the *Le mirroir des justices* (Parker Library, Corpus Christi College, Cambridge, MS 258). Other Statute Books can be traced to members of the royal family, aristocracy and gentry. Isabella de Fortibus (1237–93), countess of Devon, owned a Statute Book (Huntington Library, MS H.M. 25782). William Breton (fl. *c.* 1285–1316), a Lincolnshire knight, owned a Statute Book of *c.* 1300 (Princeton University Library, Garrett MS 146). Deluxe illuminated copies were commissioned as gifts. In 1326, Philippa of Hainault (1314–69) gave one to her betrothed, the future Edward III (Harvard Law School Library, MS 12); and Margaret of Anjou (1430–82), Henry VI's queen consort, may have commissioned one for her son Edward of Lancaster, Prince of Wales (Yale Law School Library, MS G St11/1).[18]

Lawbook ownership and readership cannot be reduced to mutually exclusive classes. Landowners served the Crown in a way aptly described as 'local self-government at the king's command'.[19] The lawbooks of landowners, sometimes bound with Walter of Henley's *Le Dite de Hosebondrie* (*c.* 1280), a manual on estate management, might be used by their stewards and administrators. Book borrowing was common at the Inns of Court in the fifteenth century.[20] After legal practice became professionalised, landowners remained 'end users' of law and found lawbooks useful in defending their property, especially during the Wars of the Roses, as attested by the struggles of John Paston (1421–66) of Norfolk. The Paston Letters often refer to statute law, and the family owned two Statute Books, probably *nova statuta*, as well as Middle English literature.[21] Many sons of landowning families attended the Inns of Court without expecting to pursue legal careers. They remained there long enough to acquire basic legal knowledge, especially about land tenure, and make useful social connections in pursuit of economic self-interest.[22] John Fortescue (*c.* 1394–1479) observed about students at the Inns of Court: 'There is scarcely a man learned in the laws to be found in the realm, who is not noble or sprung of noble lineage. So they care more for their nobility and for the preservation of their honour and reputations than others of like estate.'[23]

Moreover, lawyers were socially mobile and could amass landed estates and substantial personal libraries, including lawbooks. For example, Thomas Kebell (d. 1500) of Leicestershire and Roger Townsend of Norfolk were serjeants-at-law who invested in land and owned standard treatises, tracts and compilations.[24] Statute Books of a church prelate or landowner could thus pass by inheritance or estate sale to a royal judge or professional lawyer, as was the case with an illuminated Statute Book of *c.* 1300–10 (Princeton University Library, Scheide M30). Anthony Bek, bishop of Durham (r. 1283–1311), was the manuscript's first owner. It later passed either to John Markham (d. 1409), Justice of Common Pleas; or his son John Markham (d. 1479), who in 1461 became Chief Justice of King's Bench.[25] In short, patterns of diverse readership helps explain the large number of extant Statute Books.

Registers of Writs

The second major compilation was the Register of Writs (*Registrum brevium*). The earliest registers date from Henry III's reign, but it was not until Edward I's reign that the name *Registrum brevium* became common for these anonymous compilations. At least 100 survive, either bound separately or incorporated into hefty compendia along with other legal texts. Professional lawyers, scribes and clerks were probably responsible for producing most copies, though some originated with Chancery clerks, such as Cambridge University Library, Dd.6.89.[26] Lost Chancery registers or files of writs, separately written on parchment slips or strips to serve as models (*formulae*), perhaps suggested the organisational structure. Registers of Writs varied widely and expanded over the centuries in volume and complexity. Most manuscripts begin with writs of right on land and inheritance, then continue with writs related to personal liberty and status, the person and chattels, crime and judicial procedures, administration and royal prerogatives, and other matters.[27] Fairly typical of the form achieved by the early fifteenth century is Princeton University Library, Garrett MS 147, containing hundreds of writs from the reigns of Edward III to Henry IV, with explanatory *regula* and *notae* (Figure 6.2).

Judges and lawyers no doubt were the prime users of Registers of Writs. But at least ten copies are from religious houses, chiefly Benedictine. The so-called 'Irish Register' (*c.* 1227–35), now part of a larger manuscript (British Library, Cotton Julius D.ii, fols. 143 v–47 v, 150 r), may have originated at the Cathedral Priory of Christ Church, Canterbury, or was owned by a Chancery official connected with the priory.[28] Around 1300, Registers of Writs were at Luffield Priory (Cambridge University Library, Ee.1.1) and

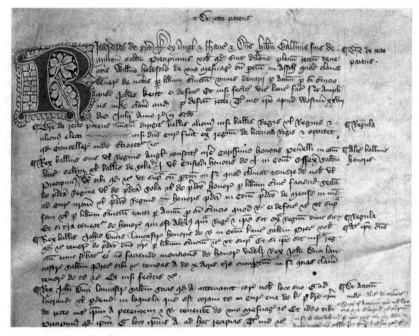

Figure 6.2 Register of Writs, early fifteenth century from Princeton University Library, Princeton MS. 147, fol. 1 r (detail). Text opens with a seven-line initial R ['Ricardus'] for a writ of right tested at Westminster, 28 July 1379 [2 Richard II (1379)], in which the king orders his bailiffs in Milton (probably Milton Regis, Kent) to give full right to William Hodesole in his lawsuit against John Kent for a messuage, with appurtenances, in 'Assche' (Parish of Ash).

Thorney Abbey (Cambridge, Corpus Christi College Library, MS 297).[29] Registers of Writs are occasionally found in baronial libraries, bound or shelved with other lawbooks. For example, Morgan Library, MS M812, contains two documents showing baronial associations: a Register of Writs (c. 1275–1320), illustrated with small marginal drawings of riding and hawking, which suggest aristocratic ownership; and a Statute Book with the arms of the Dinham family (fol. 66 r).[30] Registers of Writs continued to be produced in manuscript until 1531, when William Rastell published the first printed edition with more than 400 folios of original and judicial writs. Revised editions appeared through 1687, but Registers of Writs were largely replaced over time by books of practice and pleading.[31]

Year Books

The third major Common Law compilation was the Year Book, unofficial summary reports on court cases, chiefly in the Court of Common Pleas, from *c.* 1268 to 1535. Year Books recorded pleadings (given orally in Anglo-Norman until around 1475), procedural moves and arguments of serjeants-at-law representing the parties; they also include pithy summaries of the presiding justices' judgements, though the latter did not yet enjoy binding authority as judicial precedent for citation in other cases, as they would in Anglo-American law centuries later. Year Books were practical compilations, offering examples of pleadings and arguments to follow or avoid, and like Statute Books evolved internally over the centuries. Earlier law reports generally had a topical arrangement by actions (such as debt, entry, novel disseisin) and occasionally added side notes or marginal headings to help readers locate particular types of cases. Over time, Year Books came to be organised in chronological order by regnal year, judicial term and jurisdiction. By the 1320s, they include queries about how cases might have turned out if facts had been different, which may suggest instructional use.[32]

Paul Brand has traced thirty-nine early manuscripts containing Common Bench law reports before 1290. Reporters from the bar and bench, anonymous until the mid-fifteenth century, compiled law reports from notes retained for personal use or borrowed from others, occasionally supplemented by transcripts from court rolls. Year Books could be copied by serjeants-at-law for their own use or for other lawyers. Early owners also included lay landowners and ecclesiastical institutions. There is evidence of manuscripts passing between social classes. The early owners of Cambridge University Library, D.7.14 (*c.* 1290–1325), possibly included the landowning Solers family of Gloucestershire and Winchcombe Abbey. The manuscript includes forty-eight reports on cases in Common Pleas, as well as legal treatises, procedural tracts, selected statutes, and other texts and documents.[33] Similarly, British Library, Add. MS 31826, shows evidence of compilation in the early fourteenth century by someone with connections in the counties of Warwick and Leicester, as well as with local landowner William de Bosco (du Boys). In the later fourteenth century, it passed from Edmund of Brantingthorpe to the Merevale Abbey.[34]

Year Books continue to be produced and circulate in manuscript form for centuries. In 1481, John Lettou and William de Machlinia printed the Year Books of 33–37 Henry VI (1454–9), uncritically using available manuscripts as 'setting copy'. Long before Year Book production ceased in 1535, the growing bulk of case law led to the creation of abridgments of the Year Books, offering excerpts of the principal cases within an overall subject. Nicholas Statham's *Abridgement of Cases*, in Anglo-Norman, probably completed soon after 1461, included about 3,633 cases under 253 titles (such as assise, essoin, trespass). Most were names of the writs initiating actions. Guillaume Le Talleur printed Statham's *Abridgement* in Rouen for Richard Pynson, who later printed *The Abridgment of the Book of*

Assises (*c.* 1509/10), with an organisation similar to Statham. More influential was Anthony Fitzherbert (1470–1538), *Graunde Abridgement*, printed in 1514–17, including about 14,000 cases under 263 titles. Robert Brooke (d. 1558) and others published expanded editions of Fitzherbert, until 1586, when it included more than 20,000 cases under 404 titles.[35] In 1553, Richard Tottel (*c.* 1530–94) received an exclusive patent to publish standardised editions of Year Books and other legal texts. The 'accurate officialism' of such editions produced by London-based law publishers would serve the present and future needs of the legal profession.[36]

Notes

1. John Hudson, *The Oxford History of the Laws of England* (Oxford: Oxford University Press, 2012), II (871–1216), 869–72; Patrick Wormald, 'Quadripartitus', in *Legal Culture in the Early Medieval West: Law as Text, Image and Experience* (London: Hambledon, 1998), 81–114; L. J. Downer (ed.), *Leges Henrici Primi* (Oxford: Clarendon Press, 1972), 27–34.
2. Elsa de Haas and G. D. G. Hall, eds., *Early Registers of Writs*, Publications of the Selden Society, 87 (London: Selden Society, 1970), xi–cxxxvi; Alfred J. Horwood, ed., *Year Books of the Reign of King Edward the First*, Rolls Series, no. 31, vol. I (London: Longman, 1863), ix–liv; Paul Brand, 'Henry II and the Creation of English Common Law', in *Henry II: New Interpretations*, ed. Christopher Harper-Bill and Nicholas Vincent (Woodbridge, Suffolk: Boydell & Brewer, 2007), 215–41.
3. M. T. Clanchy, *Memory to Written Record: England, 1066–1307*, 2nd edn (Oxford: Blackwell, 1999), 57–62; David Carpenter, 'The English Royal Chancery in the Thirteenth Century', in *The English Royal Chancery in the Thirteenth Century*, ed. Adrian Jobson (Woodbridge, Suffolk: Boydell & Brewer, 2001), 49–50, 55–6.
4. G. D. G. Hall, ed., *The Treatise on the Laws and Customs of the Realm of England Commonly Called Glanvill*, Oxford Medieval Texts (Oxford: Clarendon Press, 1993), xviii–xxvii, xxx–xxxiii.
5. Hall, *Treatise*, ix–x, lxv–lxviii, 199–201; Sarah Tullis, 'Glanvill after Glanvill: The Afterlife of a Medieval Legal Treatise', in *Laws, Lawyers and Texts: Studies in Medieval Legal History in Honour of Paul Brand*, ed. Paul Brand, Susanne Jenks, Jonathan Rose and Christopher Whittick (Leiden: Brill, 2012), 327–59.
6. Frederick Pollock and F. W. Maitland, *The History of English Law*, 2nd edn, with additions by S. F. C. Milsom (Cambridge: Cambridge University Press, 1968), I, 206.
7. F. W. Maitland, ed., *Bracton's Note Book: A Collection of Cases Decided in the King's Courts during the Reign of Henry the Third* (Cambridge: Cambridge University Press, 1887), I, 61–116; H. G. Richardson, *Bracton: The Problem of his Text*, Selden Society Supplementary Series, 2 (London: Selden Society, 1965), 72–5; F. W. Maitland, *Bracton and Azo*, Publications of the Selden Society, 8 (London: Selden Society, 1894), 5–6.

8. R. E. Latham, *Revised Medieval Latin Word-List from British and Irish Sources* (London: British Academy, 1965), 101; R. E. Latham et al., eds., *The Dictionary of Medieval Latin from British Sources*, fascicule II (Oxford: Oxford University Press for the British Academy, 1981), 406–7.

9. Nigel Ramsay, 'Law', in *The Cambridge History of the Book in Britain*, vol. II: *1100–1400*, ed. Nigel Morgan and Rodney M. Thomson (Cambridge: Cambridge University Press, 2008), 277.

10. J. H. Baker and J. S. Ringrose, *Catalogue of English Legal Manuscripts in Cambridge University Library* (Woodbridge, Suffolk: Boydell Press, 1996), 68, 72; Paul Binski and Patrick Zutshi, *Western Illuminated Manuscripts: A Catalogue of the Collection in Cambridge University Library* (Cambridge: Cambridge University Press, 2011), 126–7, no. 135 (Dd.7.6).

11. *Bracton on the Laws and Customs of England*, ed. George E. Woodbine and trans. with revisions and notes by Samuel E. Thorne (Cambridge, MA: Harvard University Press in association with the Selden Society, 1968), I, 1–20.

12. George E. Woodbine, *Four Thirteenth Century Law Tracts* (New Haven: Yale University Press, 1910), 1–50.

13. Samuel E. Thorne and J. H. Baker, eds., *Readings and Moots at the Inns of Court in the Fifteenth Century*, Selden Society Publications, 74, 105 (London: Selden Society, 1954, 1990), I, ix–xxiii, l–li; vol. II, xlvi–lii.

14. Don C. Skemer, 'Reading the Law: Statute Books and the Private Transmission of Legal Knowledge in Late Medieval England', in *Learning the Law*, ed. Jonathan A. Bush and Alain Wijffels (London: The Hambledon Press, 1999), 113–31. Baker and Ringrose, *Catalogue of English Legal Manuscripts*, xxii–xxiv.

15. Don C. Skemer, 'From Archives to the Book Trade: Private Statute Rolls in England, 1285–1307', *Journal of the Society of Archivists* 16:2 (1995), 193–206.

16. Don C. Skemer, 'King Edward I's Articles of Inquest on the Jews and Coin-Clipping', *Historical Research: The Bulletin of the Institute of Historical Research* 72 [no. 177] (1999), 1–26; Don C. Skemer, '*Expositio vocabulorum*: A Medieval English Glossary as Archival Aid', *Journal of the Society of Archivists* 19:1 (1998), 63–75.

17. J. H. Baker, *English Legal Manuscripts in the United States of America: A Descriptive List*, Part I (London: Selden Society, 1985), 5, no. 12.

18. Robert Jowett Whitwell, 'The Libraries of a Civilian and of a Common Lawyer, AN. 1294', *Law Quarterly Review* 21 (1905), 393–400; V. H. Galbraith, 'Statutes of Edward I: Huntington Library MS H. M. 25782', in *Essays in Medieval History Presented to Bertie Wilkinson*, ed. T. A. Sandquist and M. R. Powicke (Toronto: University of Toronto Press, 1969), 176–87; Don C. Skemer, 'Sir William Breton's Book: Production of the *Statuta Angliae* in the Late Thirteenth Century', *English Manuscript Studies, 1100–1700* 6 (1996), 11–37; M. A. Michael, 'A Manuscript Wedding Present from Philippa of Hainault to Edward III', *Burlington Magazine* 127 (1985), 582–99; Rosemarie P. McGerr, *A Lancastrian Mirror for Princes: The Yale Law School New Statutes of England* (Bloomington, IN: Indiana University Press, 2011), 98, 100–2, 138.

19. Bryce D. Lyon, *A Constitutional and Legal History of Medieval England* (New York: Harper & Row, 1960), 391–407.
20. J. H. Baker, 'The Books of Common Law', in *The Cambridge History of the Book in Britain*, vol. III, ed. Lotte Hellinga and J. B. Trapp (Cambridge: Cambridge University Press, 1999), 415–17.
21. H. S. Bennett, *The Pastons and Their England: Studies in an Age of Transition*, 2nd edn (Cambridge: Cambridge University Press, 1932), 7–9, 139–40, 180–92, 261–2.
22. Margaret McGlynn, *The Royal Prerogative and Learning of the Inns of Court* (Cambridge: Cambridge University Press, 2004), 18–19.
23. John Fortescue, *De laudibus legum Anglie*, ed. and trans. S. B. Chrimes (Cambridge: Cambridge University Press, 1949), 118–19.
24. C. E. Moreton, 'The "Library" of a Late-Fifteenth-Century Lawyer', *The Library* 13:4 (1991), 338–46; E. W. Ives, *The Common Lawyers of Pre-Reformation England: Thomas Kebell, A Case Study*, Cambridge Studies in English Legal History (Cambridge: Cambridge University Press, 1983), 362–3, 365–7.
25. Adelaide Bennett, 'Anthony Bec's Copy of Statuta Angliae', in *England in the Fourteenth Century: Proceedings of the 1985 Harlaxton Symposium*, ed. W. M. Ormrod (Woodbridge, Suffolk: Boydell Press, 1986), 1–17.
26. Baker and Ringrose, *Catalogue of English Legal Manuscripts*, 47.
27. De Haas and Hall, *Early Registers of Writs*, 347–54.
28. De Haas and Hall, *Early Registers of Writs*, xii, xxxiii–xl; Elsa De Haas, 'An Early Thirteenth-Century Register of Writ', *The University of Toronto Law Journal* 7:1 (1947), 196–226. For an earlier date of 1210 for this manuscript register, see Paul Brand, 'Ireland and the Literature of Early Common Law', *Irish Jurist* xvi (1981), 95–113.
29. De Haas and Hall, *Early Registers of Writs*, xliv–lv, xcix–civ.
30. Michael Camille, 'At the Edge of the Law: An Illustrated Register of Writs in the Pierpont Morgan Library', in *England in the Fourteenth Century: Proceedings of the 1991 Harlaxton Symposium*, ed. Nicholas Rogers, Harlaxton Medieval Studies, 3 (Stamford: Paul Watkins, 1993), 1–14.
31. De Haas and Hall, *Early Registers of Writs*, xii.
32. Ramsay, 'Law', 286.
33. Paul Brand, ed., The Earliest English Law Reports. vol. I: Common Bench Reports to 1284 (London: Selden Society, 1996), xxvi–xxxiv; Baker and Ringrose, *Catalogue of English Legal Manuscripts*, 69–83.
34. Brand, *The Earliest English Law Reports*, I, lxi–lxx.
35. Percy H. Winfield, 'Abridgments of the Year Books', *Harvard Law Review* 37:2 (1923), 214–44; J. H. Baker, 'English Law Books and Legal Publishing', in *The Cambridge History of the Book in Britain*, ed. John Barnard and D. F. McKenzie (Cambridge: Cambridge University Press, 2014), IV, 476; David J. Seipp, 'Introduction', *Statham's Abridgment of the Law*, trans. Margaret C. Klingelsmith (Clark, NJ: The Lawbook Exchange, 2007), xiii–xvii.
36. F. W. Maitland, 'History of the Register of Original Writs', in *The Collected Papers of Frederic William Maitland*, ed. H. A. L. Fisher (Cambridge: Cambridge University Press, 1911), II, 119.

Further Reading

Baker, John H., 'The Books of Common Law', in *The Cambridge History of the Book in Britain*, vol. 3: *1400–1557*, ed. Lotte Hellinga and J. B. Trapp, Cambridge: Cambridge University Press, 1999, 411–32.

The Oxford History of the Laws of England, vol. 6: *1483–1558*, Oxford: Oxford University Press, 2003.

Holdsworth, W. S., *Sources and Literature of English Law*, Oxford: Oxford University Press, 1925.

Plucknett, T. F. T., *Early English Legal Literature*, Cambridge: Cambridge University Press, 1958.

Ramsay, Nigel, 'Law', in *The Cambridge History of the Book in Britain*, vol. 2: *1100–1400*, ed. Nigel Morgan and Rodney M. Thomson, Cambridge: Cambridge University Press, 2008, 250–90.

Winfield, Percy H., *The Chief Sources of English Legal History*, Cambridge, MA: Harvard University Press, 1925.

Literary Texts

PART II

Literary Texts

7

NEIL CARTLIDGE

Treason

Attempts to define treason often imply a debate about the very nature and limits of the law, and about the legal authority of governments.[1] Medieval literature reflects such tensions, but also seems to invest imaginatively in the concept of treason to an extent that the history of law alone cannot explain. In this chapter it is argued that treason took on a new shape during the period from the 1260s to the 1340s, and that this was to have a lasting effect on its representation, not just in English law, but also in English culture more generally. This evolution was significantly conditioned by the political turmoils of the period, including the Second Barons' War of 1264–7, Edward I's campaigns in Wales and Scotland, Edward II's conflict with Thomas of Lancaster, and Edward II's eventual deposition in 1327. Literary texts testify to the legal paradigm-shifts provoked by these events, and to the differences of political principle that underlay them; but they themselves seem to have played a part in the very processes that led to the creation of these new paradigms. What we see in several late thirteenth- and early fourteenth-century texts is something of the cultural and political ferment in which new attitudes to treason were formed.

Defining Treason

In the wake of Edward Snowden's unauthorised disclosure of classified information about American government surveillance programmes in 2013, several senior US politicians suggested that he was guilty not only of violations against the Espionage Act and of theft of government property (with which he was eventually charged), but also, much more dramatically, of 'treason'.[2] Compared with the fast-moving news-media agenda which these politicians were trying to influence, and with the virtual world of high-tech espionage exposed by Snowden's revelations, this term might seem inappropriately conservative, if not downright archaic;[3] but it is perhaps precisely the antiquity of 'treason' that explains why the word was used in this context at all. It implies that even in the seemingly transient and insubstantial cyber-world, it nevertheless remains possible for citizens to commit crimes of a gravity which is perennial. Moreover, it is unlikely that those who accused Snowden of 'treason' did so in innocence of the fact that treason is historically associated with 'peculiarly ghastly punishment':[4] not just the death penalty, but also some spectacularly cruel and ingenious means of exacting it. Right into the nineteenth century, the penalties for treason were highly ritualised and expressly symbolic, forming what Michel Foucault calls a 'liturgy of torture and execution' designed to make as manifest as possible 'the physical, material and awesome force of the sovereign'.[5] The pitilessness of these displays of power reflects the fact that treason was often seen as a transgression inherently so serious as to mark the point at which the law is, or should be, completely merciless. In the verse chronicle of Peter Langtoft (d. 1305), it is said that:

> Homme dait mercy aver;
> Mès à traitur ne dait valer,
> Iloke la lay la suspent.

Man ought to have mercy, but this should not avail a traitor: in this case the law suspends mercy.[6]

The historical connotations of the term 'treason' explain to a large extent why its use produced such a frisson in 2013, and why it continues to be a provocative term in discussions of the state's rights and duties in relation to the loyalty and/or security of its citizens. However, it is not a charge that is easy to make stick, certainly not in the USA at least, where the Constitution's definition of this crime is 'deliberately narrow and does not embrace constructive or questionable treason'.[7] The Constitution specifically states that 'treason against the United States shall consist *only* in levying war against them, or in adhering to their enemies, giving them aid and comfort' (my italics). As it happens, the Constitution's language is at this point notably medieval, directly reflecting the wording of the Great Statute of Treasons enacted by Edward III in 1351. This statute declares that it is treason 'if a Man do levy War against our Lord the King in his realm, or be adherent to the King's Enemies in his Realm, giving to them Aid and Comfort'.[8] Yet levying war and adhering to the king's enemies are, in fact, only two of the several ways in which the Great Statute defines treason. It offers a long list of different misdemeanours, including compassing or imagining the death of the king or queen, 'violating' the king's wife, eldest daughter or eldest son, counterfeiting royal seals or 'the Money of England', killing the king's officers or justices, and also 'another manner of Treason' (i.e., 'petty treason'), which refers to such crimes as a servant's murder of his master or a wife's murder of her husband. The framers of the Constitution clearly made very selective use of the Great Statute, and this was entirely deliberate. They were concerned that if treason were allowed to be 'indeterminate' (as one of the Founding Fathers himself put it), then this 'alone is sufficient to make any government degenerate into arbitrary power'.[9] In other words, the US Constitution represents a deliberate attempt at setting a limit on the idea of the treason, precisely in order to provide protection 'against politically vindictive prosecutions or the punishment of those who merely think disloyal thoughts'.[10]

In an English context, treason has never been defined more broadly than it was in the Great Statute of 1351 (certainly in terms of the way it is extended into fields that from a modern perspective seem entirely non-political), but even the Great Statute itself could also be seen as the result of an attempt at limiting the powers of government. It came about as 'a direct result of the royal judges trying to extend the common law of treason';[11] and, in particular, it put an end to the growing tendency on the part of such judges to extend the definition of treason so as to include 'the accroaching of royal power', that is, the usurping or slighting of royal prerogatives.[12] In this respect, it too clearly sets a limit on the extent to which treason law might serve to enforce the authority of the sovereign; and indeed it could be argued that it was a remarkable concession on Edward III's part even to allow such matters to be determined by a parliamentary statute. He may well have been driven to this concession to some extent by his 'pressing need' for parliament's support in raising funds for his French wars;[13] but he was also a pragmatist, and he may well have recognised how dangerous it was for 'divers Opinions to be held' about the definition of treason.[14] He probably understood only too well just how much the regime of his father Edward II had been undermined by what was widely perceived to be his high-handed use of treason law, in particular his summary execution of the greatest of his magnates, Thomas of Lancaster, in 1322. The allegation that Edward II had abrogated the laws of the land by executing the earl 'without just cause' was one of the justifications for the coup against him by Queen Isabella and her supporters that led ultimately to his deposition.[15] Edward III was no doubt not alone in wishing no return to those 'dark days'.[16] Meanwhile, Thomas himself had by the 1340s acquired something of the status of a martyr. In a Latin poem in British Library MS Royal 12 C 12, Thomas is explicitly compared with St Thomas Becket ('per necem imitaris Thomam Cantuariæ'), because he stood up for the peace and security of the citizens of the realm ('pro pace et tranquillitate regnicolarum Angliæ'), was condemned 'without cause' ('sine causa') and was 'beheaded for the sake of the people' ('acephalatur plebis pro juvamine').[17] Whatever Edward III's motivations, his Great Statute brought a degree of stability to the concept of treason. This does not mean that treason law was to be any less hotly contested in the following centuries (and, indeed, it remains contested now, as the Snowden case shows), but the 1351 Statute nevertheless remains the foundation of all treason law since (certainly in the UK, where it remains in force, but also in the various jurisdictions that borrowed from UK law), and all subsequent discussion of treason refers to it to a greater or lesser extent. In effect, this statute 'became the whole law of treason for after times; every word of it was weighed, interpreted and glossed by successive generations'.[18]

The Right to Resist

A hundred years earlier than this, in the middle of the thirteenth century, understandings of treason had been so fluid that there was no consensus even on the two definitions of treason adopted by the US Constitution from the Great Statute, that is, levying war against the sovereign and adhering to his enemies. Many Englishmen would have seen the governance of the realm as a matter for negotiation between the king and his barons, among whom the monarch was for some essentially only *primus inter pares*, first among equals.[19] The Magna Carta of 1215 explicitly recognises that there are circumstances in which the barons can and should take action against the king; for example, by seizing his 'castles, lands and possessions'.[20] Until the 1260s, medieval governments were remarkably slow to apply the penalties for treason even to military action against them; indeed, 'for two centuries after the Conquest, the frank, open rebellions of the great folk were treated with a clemency which, when we look back to it through intervening ages of blood, seems wonderful'.[21] No English earl was formally executed for open rebellion between 1076 and 1306:[22] 'not until the reign of Edward I did the English kings find it necessary to treat rebellion as treason'.[23] A case in point is the baron Fulk FitzWarin who rebelled against King John in 1201-3, but was subsequently pardoned. In the medieval romance based on his life (which, as it happens, is also preserved in BL MS Royal 12 C 12), it is suggested that he effectively forestalled any charge of treason simply by formally renouncing his homage to the king as a preliminary to rebellion, and the romance clearly assumes that he has a right to do this.[24] The high point of the barons' confidence in their right of resistance to the unjust use of royal authority was reached with Simon de Montfort's defeat of Henry III at the Battle of Lewes in 1264, and the subsequent parliamentary settlement, by which the king's powers were subjected to strict control by a council of barons.[25] A detailed justification for the barons' position is provided by the

968-line Latin poem known as *The Song of Lewes*, which survives from the Middle Ages only in British Library MS Harley 978 (a manuscript best known to literary history for the collection of *lais* traditionally ascribed to Marie de France, and for the Middle English song 'Sumer is icumen in').[26] Indeed, *The Song of Lewes* can fairly be described as a poetic manifesto for the baronial party. What it presents, in effect, is a persuasive defence of the subject's rights of resistance against a sovereign who acts unlawfully.

One of the allegations made in this poem is that Prince Edward, the future King Edward I, is so ruthless and dishonest in his own interest that he asserts himself to be above the law:

> Nephas det placencia fasque nominatur;
> Quicquid libet, licitum dicit, et a lege
> Se putat explicitum   (ll. 442–4)

Wrong gives him pleasure and is called right; whatever he likes he says is lawful, and he thinks that he is released from law[27]

Yet, says the poet, every king is, or ought to be, ruled by the laws that he makes ('Nam rex omnis regitur legibus quas legit'); and kings who break the law (such as Saul and David) will be deposed or punished. Edward, suggests the poet, has all the makings of a tyrant, a ruler who has no respect for the law:

> O edwarde! fieri uis rex sine lege;
> Vere forent miseri recti tali rege!
> Nam quid lege rectius qua cuncta reguntur?   (ll. 451–3)

O Edward! thou dost wish to become king without law; verily they would be wretched who were ruled by such a king! For what is more right than law, whereby all things are ruled?

However, the poet is also careful to acknowledge the opposing arguments, to the extent that his work amounts to a substantial and serious debate about the issues, despite its ultimate partisanship:

> Rex cum suis uoluit ita liber esse,
> Et sic esse debuit, fuitque necesse,
> Aut esse desineret rex priuatus iure
> Regis, nisi faceret quicquid uellet ...
> Non intromittentibus se de factis regis
> Anglie baronibus, uim habente legis
> Principis imperio   (ll. 489–92, 501–3)

The King with his party wished to be thus free, and urged that he ought to be so, and was of necessity, or that deprived of a king's right he would cease to be

87

king, unless he should do whatever he might wish ... without the barons of England interfering in the King's acts, as 'the command of the prince has the force of law'

In other words, a king is not properly a king unless he has authority of his own, the 'freedom' to act: a position which is here explicitly supported by reference to a dictum in Roman law, *quod principi placuit, legis habet vigorem* (literally: 'what pleases the prince has the force of law').[28] This whole argument is made all the more complex and provocative, I would suggest, by its theological dimensions: the implicit question of whether God (the ultimate sovereign monarch) is likewise free to act above the law, or is necessarily bound by the law. On the one hand, there can be no limits on God's freedom to act (God is omnipotent), but, on the other hand, God is the very embodiment of justice (and therefore incapable of doing anything this is unjust). This is a tension that is explored elsewhere in medieval literature, as for example in the Middle English poem 'Mercy and Righteousness', where the allegorical figure of Mercy insists that 'Almyȝti God is ouer [above] þe lawe', while her antagonist Righteousness answers that God 'dede neuyr but þat was ryȝte'.[29] *The Song of Lewes* does not hide the complexity of the issues, and the answer that it offers in answer to the arguments of the king and his party is by no means an easy one:

> Set quis uere rex, est liber uere
> Si ne recte rexerit regnumque ...
> A ligando dicitur lex, que libertatis
> Tam perfecte legitur qua seruitur gratis.
>
> (ll. 693–4, 699–700)

But whoever is truly king is truly free, if he rule himself and his kingdom rightly ... Law is so-called from binding [i.e., *lex* 'law' is etymologically derived from *ligando* 'binding'], which is so perfectly described as the law of liberty, as it is freely served.

Thus, freedom resides, paradoxically, in being bound by the law; and a ruler is properly free to rule only when he is a servant of the law. More pragmatically, the poet argues that it is also the barons' duty to 'reform and magnify the kingly state' ('reformare ... statum regium & magnificare'), just as it is their duty to come to the kingdom's aid when it is threatened with devastation by its enemies ('si ab hostibus regnum uastaretur').[30] Treason is only at issue if a baron fails to protect the kingdom: 'him the law would punish as guilty of perjury, as a betrayer of the king ('ipsum lex puniret / Vt reum periurij, regis proditorem').[31] The barons are obliged to act whenever the kingdom needs reform – whenever, that is, it has become terminally '*de*formed' ('Cum uelut in termino regnum deformatur').[32]

In the event, the barons' ascendency over Henry III and his son Edward proved to be very short-lived. The balance of power celebrated in *The Song of Lewes* was decisively shifted in the king's favour by the Battle of Evesham the following year (1265). According to Langtoft, Edward proved himself a 'good son' by rescuing his father on the battlefield ('Sire Eduuard, cum bon fiz, delivera par espeye / Sun pere de prisoun'); the leader of the baronial party, Simon de Montfort, was dismembered on the battlefield, and parts of his body sent off as tokens of his defeat ('Ses membrez sunt tranchez, envayez pur present'); and the surviving rebels were either forced to take to the woods (i.e., to live as outlaws)[33] or were put in gaol ('Les uns sunt al boys, les uns enprisonez'). Never again would English monarchs allow armed rebellion within their realm to be viewed as anything other than treason. Moreover, the brutal treatment of Simon de Montfort's corpse could be seen to augur a new ferocity in the punishment of traitors. Key here perhaps is the personality of the victor at Evesham, the future Edward I, 'in whom some modern writers have detected a brutal and vicious streak', as Bellamy puts it.[34] Whether or not Edward was innately 'brutal and vicious', *The Song of Lewes* clearly suggests that his instincts were already authoritarian even before de Montfort's brief supplanting of his father ('whatever he likes he says is lawful'), but the experience of Lewes and Evesham surely hardened Edward's attitudes. This possibly explains to some extent why 'the reign of Edward I seems to have been the high point of what may be called the royal thesis of treason'.[35] He was certainly determined to make treason law an instrument of royal authority, but he also seems to have been personally responsible for the establishment of the 'peculiarly ghastly' punishments that were to become such a familiar feature of late medieval and early modern political culture.[36]

Punishing Treason

In August 1305, the Scottish rebel William Wallace was brutally executed for treason, and in September of the following year his compatriot Simon Fraser suffered the same fate.[37] These events are gleefully celebrated in a Middle English poem ('Song on the Execution of Sir Simon Fraser') now extant only in a single manuscript, BL MS Harley 2253 (which, as it happens, is in the same hand as BL MS Royal 12 C 12, mentioned earlier).[38] The poem explains how Wallace was drawn (i.e., dragged behind a horse), hanged and then disembowelled, and how this savage treatment of one of Edward's most effective opponents was designed 'To warny alle the gentilmen that bueth [dwell in] in Scotlonde' (l. 17). Here Wallace's death is explicitly read as a public demonstration of 'the physical, material and awesome force of the sovereign'. It is a method of instilling terror, which the poet associates directly with the will and personality of Edward I:

> Sire Edward, oure kyng, that ful ys of piete,
> The Waleis quarters sende to is oune contre,
> On four half to honge, huere myrour to be
> Theropon to thenche, that monie myhten se ant drede. (ll. 25–9)

In other words, Wallace's body was quartered, and the quarters were sent back to Scotland in order to give the Scots 'something to think about', and to provide them with a 'mirror' in which they might look, and be afraid. This, the poet tells us, with unapologetically grim irony, is the work of a king who is full of 'pity'. He goes on to describe the execution of Simon Fraser according to the same ghastly protocol. Fraser too was drawn to the gallows 'for that he wes lord-swyke': because he had betrayed his lord. Then he was hanged and 'al quick by-heveded, thah him thohte longe', a line that depends for its force on a cruel joke; that is, the pun on 'quick' meaning both 'alive' and 'rapid' (i.e., he was beheaded while still 'quick', alive, though it did not seem 'quick', rapid, to him).[39] Finally, 'he wes y-opened, is boweles y-brend' (he was opened up, and his bowels burned). In Peter Langtoft's equally partisan account of the fate of the 'traytours of Scotland', this 'liturgy of torture and execution' is repeatedly described, and with a similar relish. As in the English poem, Langtoft tries to suggest that each of its elements can be rationalised: that it is morally and symbolically appropriate to the crimes of the victim. So, for example, Wallace was drawn on a hurdle because of his treasons ('à fourches fut treyné pur tresouns'); he was hanged because of his robberies and murders ('Pendu pur roberyes et pur occisiouns'); his entrails were burned because he had committed arson ('pur ceo k'il avait ennenty par arsouns / Viles et eglises et religiouns'); and he was beheaded because he had made war ('maintenuz la guere') and seized the lordship of a kingdom belonging to someone else ('Seysye seygnurye ... De altri realme').[40]

The question this immediately raises, of course, is how any of the 'traytours of Scotlond' could really be guilty of treason to a king whom they did not recognise as their own, and to whom they did not believe they owed any allegiance. In fact, this was precisely the defence offered by Wallace, little good though it did him.[41] Edward's use of treason law against his Scottish opponents was not just an assertion of 'the physical, material and awesome force of the sovereign' but also a means of asserting an extension of that sovereignty to a new realm. The same could perhaps be said of his use of treason law against his opponents in Wales, such as Dafydd ap Gruffydd, the last independent ruler of Wales, who died by drawing, hanging and disembowelling in

October 1283,[42] or Rhys ap Maredudd, who was executed by drawing and hanging in June 1292.[43] It is surely no coincidence that the high point of the 'royal thesis of treason' coincides with a war of expansion, and that the worst penalties of treason tended to be directed at those who did not regard themselves as subject to the king's authority at all.[44]

However, what is even more striking is that it was only in this period that this 'liturgy of torture and execution' emerged in the first place. We have become so familiar with the association between treason and the elaborate ritual of drawing, hanging and quartering (which was officially only abolished in England by the Forfeiture Act of 1870), that it is difficult to imagine a time when this ritual was actually an innovation. However, apart from a couple of isolated instances much earlier in the century,[45] Dafydd's execution in 1283 was unprecedented. It marks a turning point in English political culture, and one with long-lasting consequences. Certainly, nobody as high-ranking as Dafydd had previously been subjected to such ruthless and humiliating treatment in the name of 'treason'; and his brutal death was perhaps deliberately intended to announce that, as far as Edward I was concerned, even the 'great folk' were not exempt from its consequences. Ever since then, treason has tended to be defined, more than any other crime, by the nature of its punishment. From this perspective, the repetitive emphasis on the complex ceremony of drawing, hanging and quartering (and on its various political and moral significances), which is found in early fourteenth-century political poems such as the 'Song on the Execution of Sir Simon Fraser', or in Langtoft's *Chronicle*, can be seen as an aspect of the process by which demonstrative state violence of this kind actually came to be normalised in English political culture. Without necessarily reflecting any organised propaganda-campaign, such texts seem designed to canvas and/or to coerce support for this newly red-clawed application of 'the royal thesis of treason'. Not only do they witness to the emergence of drawing, hanging and quartering as the appropriate punishment for betrayal of the sovereign, but they also contribute to the creation of a political climate in which such a horrifying ritual could become accepted.

Notes

1. J. G. Bellamy, *The Law of Treason in England in the Later Middle Ages* (Cambridge: Cambridge University Press, 1970), 9: 'Concepts of treason never flourish in a vacuum. They depend greatly on the prevailing thesis of government.'
2. J. Richard Broughton, 'The Snowden Affair and the Limits of American Treason', *Lincoln Memorial University Law Review* 3 (2015), 5–34, at 6–7.

3. Writing before the Snowden affair, Kristen E. Eichensehr argues that treason is not the dead letter it is sometimes taken to be ('Treason in the Age of Terrorism: An Explanation and Evaluation of Treason's Return in Democratic States', *Vanderbilt Journal of Transnational Law* (November, 2009), 1443–507).

4. Frederick Pollock and F. W. Maitland, *The History of English Law before the Time of Edward I*, 2nd edn, 2 vols. (Cambridge: Cambridge University Press, 1898; repr. with intro. by S. F. C. Milson, Cambridge: Cambridge University Press, 1968), II, 500.

5. Michel Foucault, *Discipline and Punish: The Birth of the Prison*, trans. Alan Sheridan (London: Penguin, 1991), 49–50.

6. Thomas Wright, ed., *The Chronicle of Pierre de Langtoft: In French Verse, From the Earliest Period to the Death of King Edward I*, 2 vols., Rolls Series 47 (London: Longmans, 1866–8), II, 256, but with my translation.

7. Broughton, 'The Snowden Affair', 10.

8. 25 Edward III, c. 2: *Statutes of the Realm*, ed. John Raithby, 11 vols. (London: Dawsons, 1810–28), I: 319–20. See also J. Willard Hurst, *The Law of Treason in the United States: Collected Essays* (Westport, CT: Greenwood, 1971), 130–40.

9. James Wilson (1742–98), cited in Broughton, 'The Snowden Affair', 14, n. 45.

10. Broughton, 'The Snowden Affair', 24.

11. Bellamy, *The Law of Treason*, 100.

12. Bellamy, *The Law of Treason*, 63.

13. Bellamy, *The Law of Treason*, 101; Richard Firth Green, *A Crisis of Truth: Literature and Law in Ricardian England* (Philadelphia: University of Pennsylvania Press, 1999), 213.

14. *Statutes of the Realm*, I, 319.

15. Natalie Fryde, *The Tyranny and Fall of Edward II, 1321–26* (Cambridge: Cambridge University Press, 1979; repr. 2003), esp. 190, 195.

16. May McKisack, *The Fourteenth Century, 1307–1399* (Oxford: Oxford University Press, 1959; repr. 1991), 257.

17. Thomas Wright, ed., *Political Songs of England: From the Reign of John to That of Edward II* (London: Camden Society, 1839; repr. with intro by Peter Coss, Cambridge: Cambridge University Press, 1996), 268–72. Simon de Montfort's death is also associated with Becket's martyrdom in 'The Lament of Simon de Montfort', ed./transl. Susanna Fein, with David Raybin and Jan Ziolkowski in *The Complete Harley 2253 Manuscript*, 3 vols., TEAMS Middle English Text Series (Kalamazoo, MI: Medieval Institute, 2015), II, 88–97, ll. 40–5.

18. Pollock and Maitland, *The History of English Law*, II, 502.

19. Maurice Powicke, *The Thirteenth Century, 1216–1307*, 2nd edn (Oxford: Oxford University Press, 1962; repr. 1991), 137.

20. *Statutes of the Realm*, I, 13.

21. Pollock and Maitland, *The History of English Law*, II, 506.

22. Bellamy, *The Law of Treason*, 23; Green, *A Crisis of Truth*, 211.

23. Bellamy, *The Law of Treason*, 23.

24. Glyn Burgess, *Two Medieval Outlaws: Eustace the Monk and Fouke Fitz Waryn* (Cambridge: Brewer, 1997), 151.

25. Powicke, *The Thirteenth Century*, 191–2.

26. C. L. Kingsford, ed., *The Song of Lewes* (Oxford: Clarendon, 1990). On the MS, see Neil Cartlidge, 'Cultures in Confrontation in BL MS Harley 978', in *Language in Medieval Britain: Networks and Exchanges Proceedings of the 2013 Harlaxton Symposium*, ed. Mary Carruthers and Christian Steer (Donington: Shaun Tyas, 2015), 179–98.

27. Cf. Bracton, II, 33: 'Ipse autem rex non debet esse sub homine sed sub deo et sub lege, quia lex facit regem' ('The king must not be under man but under God and under the law, because law makes the king'). I cite the Woodbine/Thorne text/translation at http://bracton.law.harvard.edu.

28. Justinian, *Digest*, 1.4.1, trans. Alan Watson, *The Digest of Justinian*, 4 vols. (Philadelphia: University of Pennsylvania Press, 1998), I, 14; *Institutes*, I.2.6, trans. J. B. Moyle, *The Institutes of Justinian Translated into English*, 5th edn (Oxford: Clarendon, 1913; repr. 1949), 5.

29. John W. Conlee, ed., *Middle English Debate Poetry: A Critical Anthology* (East Lansing: Colleagues, 1991), 200–9, ll. 31, 36.

30. Kingsford, ed., *Song of Lewes*, ll. 537–41.

31. Kingsford, ed., *Song of Lewes*, ll. 542–3.

32. Kingsford, ed., *Song of Lewes*, l. 546. In the 'Song upon the Divisions among the Barons' (Wright, *Political Songs*, 121–4, ll. 28–31), he is urged to fight for the country ('Pugna nunc pro patria') and to defend the state ('Rem defende publicam').

33. Cf. 'Trailbaston', in Fein, ed., *The Complete Harley*, III, 144–9.

34. Bellamy, *The Law of Treason*, 24. Cf. Michael Prestwich, *Edward I* (New Haven: Yale University Press, 1997), 202: 'Clemency towards his enemies was not in Edward's character.'

35. Bellamy, *The Law of Treason*, 57.

36. Bellamy, *The Law of Treason*, 24: 'In the various trials for treason, Edward was involved at a personal level, for he considered each traitor as his own private enemy.'

37. Andrew Fisher, *William Wallace*, 2nd edn (Edinburgh: Donald, 2002; repr. 2005), 243–8; Prestwich, *Edward I*, 503, 508.

38. Fein, ed., *The Complete Harley*, II, 198–209. On these MSS and their scribe, see Carter Revard, 'Scribe and Provenance', in Susanna Fein, ed., *Studies in the Harley Manuscript: The Scribes, Contents, and Social Contexts of British Library MS Harley 2253* (Kalamazoo, MI: Medieval Institute, 2000), 21–109.

39. Both here and at lines 18–19, I suspect that 'anhonge, al quic biheueded' is better read as 'anhonge, al quic, bi þe heued', the point being that both Wallace and Fraser were still alive after they were hanged and while they were being disembowelled.

40. Wright, ed., *The Chronicle of Pierre de Langtoft*, 362–3. Cf. Anthony Musson, *Medieval Law in Context: The Growth of Legal Consciousness from Magna Carta to the Peasants' Revolt* (Manchester: Manchester University Press, 2001), 20: 'The significance of the decollation lay in [Wallace's] status as an outlaw and a traitor, while the burning of the entrails was in respect of their believed role in producing blasphemous thoughts.'

41. Fisher, *William Wallace*, 239–40.

42. Wright, ed., *The Chronicle of Pierre de Langtoft*, 180–3; Prestwich, *Edward I*, 202–3; Bellamy, *The Law of Treason*, 24–6.

43. Wright, ed., *The Chronicle of Pierre de Langtoft*, 188–9; Powicke, *The Thirteenth Century*, 440; Bellamy, *The Law of Treason*, 29–31.
44. In the 'Song on the Scottish Wars' (Wright, *Political Songs*, 160–79, l. 21), the Scots and the Welsh are accused of being 'faithless' because they 'molest' England by force of arms ('Prædicantur undique fraudes infidorum, / Qui molestant Angliam viribus armorum').
45. Pollock and Maitland, *The History of English Law*, II, 501, n. 1; Bellamy, *The Law of Treason*, 20–1.

Further Reading

Bellamy, J. G., *The Law of Treason in England in the Later Middle Ages*, Cambridge: Cambridge University Press, 1970.

Fein, Susanna, ed., *Studies in the Harley Manuscript: The Scribes, Contents, and Social Contexts of British Library MS Harley 2253*, Kalamazoo, MI: Medieval Institute, 2000.

Fein, Susanna, with David Raybin and Jan Ziolkowski, ed./trans., *The Complete Harley 2253 Manuscript*, 3 vols., TEAMS Middle English Text Series, Kalamazoo, MI: Medieval Institute, 2015

Green, Richard Firth, *A Crisis of Truth: Literature and Law in Ricardian England*, Philadelphia: University of Pennsylvania Press, 1999 (see esp. ch. 6, 'Truth and Treason').

Kingsford, C. L., ed., *The Song of Lewes*, Oxford: Clarendon, 1990.

Pollock, Frederick and Maitland, F. W., *The History of English Law before the Time of Edward I*, 2nd edn, 2 vols., Cambridge: Cambridge University Press, 1898. Repr. with intro. by S. F. C. Milson, Cambridge: Cambridge University Press, 1968.

Scattergood, John, 'Authority and Resistance: The Political Verse', in *Studies in the Harley Manuscript: The Scribes, Contents, and Social Contexts of British Library MS Harley 2253*, ed. Susanna Fein, Kalamazoo, MI: Medieval Institute, 2000, 163–201.

Wright, Thomas, ed., *Political Songs of England: From the Reign of John to That of Edward II*, London: Camden Society, 1839. Repr. with intro by Peter Coss, Cambridge: Cambridge University Press, 1996.

ed., *The Chronicle of Pierre de Langtoft: In French Verse, From the Earliest Period to the Death of King Edward I*, 2 vols., Rolls Series 47, London: Longmans, 1866–8.

8

WENDY SCASE

Complaint Literature

To the right sage and full wise Comunes of this present parlement
Besecheth mekely your right sage and wyse discrecions Isabell that was
the wife of Iohn Boteler of Beausey in the Shire of Lancaster Knight to
consider that where one william Pulle ... the seid Isabell beyng atte
Beausey ... with force and armes ... felonousely and most horribely
rauysshed ... her naked except hir kirtyll and hir smokke ledde with hym
into the wilde and desolate places of wales ... if he appier not ... that
than he stand atteint of high Tresoun ... consideryng that the seid
rauysshyng is done in more horrible wise and with more heynouse
violence than any hath be sene or knawen before this tyme.
    (Petition of Isabel Boteler to Parliament, 1437)[1]

Isabel Boteler's petition to parliament that her rapist, William Pulle, be
brought to justice, exemplifies the form of complaint used in the law courts
and other kinds of audience empowered to give judgements. A petition
customarily begins with a courteous and flattering formal address, in the
example, 'To the right sage and full wise Comunes.' The address is designed
not merely to make sure that it reaches the right recipients but also to indicate
humble respect for their authority. A petition identifies itself as such with
a suitable formal verb phrase in the third person: here 'beseketh mekely';
sheueth (show) is a regular alternative (*sheuen* being the English equivalent
of *moustre*, or *se pleyn* in French petitions, French being the more usual
language of complaint until the fifteenth century).[2] It identifies the complainant and their legal status (often more indications of humility are included
here, such as *ȝoure pore bedeman*, and *ȝoure pore prest*).[3] Here, the information that Isabel is a widow explains why she, and not her husband, is
presenting the petition. In the exposition section, a petition lists the sufferings
for which remedy is sought: as well as stating that she has been raped and
abducted, Isabel complains that Pulle broke into her house along with many
other 'misdoers' and has now gone into hiding. The main purpose of a legal
petition is to establish the legal basis for the request for remedy; formulaic

legal phrases and adverbs here serve – 'force and armes' 'felonousely' and 'horribely'.[4] As form dictated, the petition ends with a statement of the remedy sought (Isabel wants Pulle to be brought before a court or, if he refuses to appear, to be outlawed) and a conventional closing formula; here, 'And that for the love of god and in werk of charitee'.

Legal complaint is an important and often overlooked resource for complaint literature, serving medieval authors alongside complaint's more readily recognised biblical and classical models, such as texts from Jeremiah and the Psalms,[5] Ovid's *Heroides*,[6] and Boethius's *Consolation of Philosophy*.[7] Claudius's petition in Chaucer's *Physician's Tale* (*c.* 1386–90), the story of a conspiracy to rape Virginia, provides a good example of the creative engagement of medieval literary authors with legal complaint, its forms, language and processes. Recognising that the fair Virginia will never consent to his desires, Apius, a judge, by means of bribery and intimidation, has the 'cherl' (l. 140) Claudius accuse Virginius, Virginia's father, of having stolen her. The conspirator Claudius makes an accusation before Apius in the form of a written 'bille' (ll. 166, 170, 176, 190).[8] *Bill* was a term regularly used for a written petition or complaint. In the thirteenth-century *Le Roman de la Rose*, Chaucer's source for the story,[9] there is no mention of a written complaint and no use of legal form or vocabulary.[10] However, in Chaucer's version Claudius's bill is included:

> 'To yow, my lord, sire Apius so deere,
> Sheweth youre povre servant Claudius,
> How that a knyght, called Virginius,
> Agayns the lawe, agayn al equitee,
> Holdeth, expres agayn the wyl of me,
> My servant, which that is my thral by right,
> Which fro myn hous was stole upon a nyght,
> Whil that she was ful yong; this wol I preeve
> By witnesse, lord, so that it nat yow greeve.
> She nys his doghter nat, what so he seye.
> Wherfore to yow, my lord the juge, I preye,
> Yeld me my thral, if that it be youre wille.'
> Lo, this was al the sentence of his bille.   (ll. 178–90)

Following the form, Claudius's bill opens with a courteous address to its intended recipient ('To yow, my lord, sire Apius so deere'), identification of the complainant, and the petitionary verb 'sheweth' ('Sheweth youre povre servant Claudius'). It provides an exposition of the matter at issue. Virginia belongs to Claudius as his 'thral' (slave) 'by right'; she was stolen; Virginius holds her expressly against his wish and against law and equity; he has witnesses to prove his claim. Claudius's bill finishes with statement of the remedy requested: 'Yeld me my thral'. Two aspects of complaint process interest Chaucer here. First, Chaucer engages with a common theme in law and literature: complaint, although designed to achieve justice, may be used falsely and vexatiously. Second, Chaucer is interested in rendering the form and formulas of legal complaint in English. The result is a claim for the status of English (the earliest surviving petition to parliament written in English dates to 1344),[11] but also an uncomfortable analogy between legal falsehood and vernacular literary fiction.

Medieval legal complaint was associated with a vigorous culture of textual production in the later medieval period. Reforms in the reigns of Henry II and Edward I extended the range of grievances that could be heard in the royal courts. They also expanded the opportunities and means for getting a complaint heard. From the reign of Edward I, it became possible to initiate a suit by means of a written complaint (a bill). Bills could be submitted to itinerant royal justices. They could also be presented to special commissions of enquiry, and to parliament.[12] Reform in access to royal justice led to innovations in the forms and phrases of legal documents and, later, a move from Latin and French to English as their medium. There must have been, too, a considerable increase in the numbers of scribes and scriveners capable of producing bills and growing awareness among perhaps all social classes of the crucial role of writing in obtaining access to justice. From this period of reform and innovation survives a huge corpus of medieval petitions and related documents in the National Archives and other repositories. Many remain unpublished, but access to the originals is facilitated by online resources such as the digitised materials in The National Archives Special Collections: Ancient Petitions (SC 8).[13]

This chapter will seek to provide some approaches to analysing medieval literature in the light of the texts and processes of complaint in the law courts. It will examine authors' use of the forms and vocabulary associated with medieval bills and complaint procedure; their representations of, and critiques of, judicial process; their appropriations of the forms of the bill to mobilise opinion and to make political interventions; and their reflections on their role and their art in relation to the textual cultures of complaint. The range of source material, both literary and documentary, is vast (e.g., DIMEV categorises forty-two items as having complaint as their subject, and fifty-four as lovers' complaints, and this count omits texts that embed complaints and all prose materials). Therefore the present chapter will proceed by means of selected examples and case studies, drawing where possible on better-known texts and authors, although it will also discuss some lesser-known material in order to provide a fuller picture and to demonstrate how alertness to legal complaint can discover creativity in some very dull and dusty corners of the literary archive.[14]

Complaint and Social Justice

The forms and language of the complaint process are often used in literature that is concerned with good governance and the responsibilities of those in power to deliver social justice. The complaint process is discussed in literature as an institution designed to deliver justice, but it also becomes a metaphor for social processes and relationships more broadly. *Dede is worchyng*, one of the Digby Poems (*c.* 1413–14), instructs lords to uphold the truth; here the truth is figured as a plaintiff whom the lords should release from confinement so that his complaint may be heard:

> Þe lord þat wole haue good loos,
> Stonde fast in trouþe, waxe not faynt:
> Let trouþe goon out of cloos,
> Þat alle folk may here his playnt.   (ll. 57–60)[15]

The lord must allow Truth to appear, to come out of hiding ('goon out of cloos'); the metaphor is that of giving a hearing to complaint – everyone must have the opportunity to hear Truth's 'playnt' (legal complaint).

Similarly, *God kepe oure kyng and saue the croune*, also in the Digby MS, employs the metaphor of the complaint process in order to instruct those who judge cases:

> Eche a kyng haþ Goddis powere
> Of lyf and leme to saue and spille.
> He muste make God his partenere
> And do not his owen wille.
> For God reseyueþ pore mannys bille,
> And of here playnt God hereþ þe sowne,
> Sette ȝoure [domes] in euene skille   (ll. 105–11)[16]

God hears the prayers of the poor; metaphorically, he hears the 'playnt' of the poor and receives the poor man's 'bille'. Judges should make their judgements likewise.

While the Digby poet employs the language of the complaint process as a source of occasional metaphors and images to enrich his sententious moralising on social themes, Langland, in contrast, uses the process of complaint in an extended allegorical narrative about 'mede' (bribery and corruption). In *Piers Plowman* (quoted here from the B-text, *c.* 1377–79), Pees comes into 'parlement' and presents a complaint before the king, his son and Reason:

And thanne com Pees into parlement and putte up a bille –
How Wrong ayeins his wille hadde his wif taken,
And how he ravysshede Rose, Reignaldes loove,
And Margrete of hir maydenhede maugree hire chekes.
'Bothe my gees and my grys hise gadelynges feccheth;
I dar noght for fere of hem fighte ne chide.
He borwed of me bayard and broughte hym hom nevere
Ne no ferthyng therfore, for nought I koude plede.
He maynteneth hise men to murthere myne hewen,
Forstalleth my feires and fighteth in my chepyng,
And breketh up my berne dores and bereth awey my whete,
And taketh me but a taille for ten quarters otes.
And yet he beteth me therto and lyth by my mayde;
I am noght hardy for hym unnethe to loke!'   (B.4.47–60)[17]

Pees 'putte[th] up a bille' (l. 47), meaning, as we have seen, that he issues
a formal written document to the court. The usual opening and closing
sections are not included, but the exposition is detailed. Pees's wife and
other women have been raped, his horse taken, his wheat seized, his crop
sales disrupted (Pees uses the legal term 'forstalleth', l. 56) and his servants
murdered. Such is Wrong's power, Pees complains, that the process of complaint itself has been corrupted. Pees has not dared to 'fighte ne chide' (l. 52)
for fear of Wrong's 'gadelynges' ('fellows', l. 51); no amount of pleading (l. 54)
has been able to get compensation for his horse, and Wrong 'maynteneth'
('bribes', l. 55, another legal term) supporters to murder Pees's 'hewen' ('servants'; perhaps those members of his household to whom Pees would turn for
legal advice). The sequence develops with grim comedy. Wrong at first
attempts bribery to win the king's favour, recognising that he would then
have nothing to fear even if 'Pees and his power pleyned hym evere' (l. 66).
Next he attempts to silence Pees using intimidation ('Pees putte forth his heed
and his panne blody', l. 78); finally he pays Pees off, making him his advocate:

Pitously Pees thanne preyde to the Kynge
To have mercy on that man that mysdide hym so ofte   (ll. 98–9)

Although the passus ends with a rousing commitment to justice on the part of
the king, the process of complaint has been undermined (some of the detail
chiming with the corruption of the process we have seen illustrated in
Chaucer's Physician's Tale). The process yields a positive outcome for Pees,
but it is Lady Mede, not the king, who has given him redress: 'Mede hath
maad myne amendes – I may na moore axe' (l. 103). The suit against Wrong
remains unconcluded. Mede has undermined social justice and there is no
clear resolution.

Complaint and the Individual

In amatory literature the process of complaint gave an opportunity to explore human desire and the joys and pains of the human condition. The disappointed, betrayed or unrequited lover is regularly aligned with the plaintiff and the expression of his or her pain is sometimes imagined as a legal bill of complaint. The addressee may be the cruel love object herself (sometimes himself), or some presiding deity (Lady Fortune, Nature, Venus, etc.). Some manuscripts of Chaucer's *Fortune* (probably early 1390s) include subheadings that suggest a legal framework for the poem's dialogic balade series. The first balade is 'Le Pleintif countre Fortune'; the second balade is Fortune's 'respounse' to the 'Pleintif'; the third includes a further response and counter-response; in the envoy Fortune addresses '[p]rinces' (l. 73); should it please them to 'releve him [the plaintiff] of his peyne' (l. 77), Fortune petitions that the plaintiff's 'beste frend' (l. 78) might also be favoured. Lydgate's *Temple of Glas* (first quarter of the fifteenth century) imagines wronged lovers (Dido, Medea, Penelope, Thisbe, Griselda and others) as plaintiffs in the court of Venus. Some of the classical lovers depicted on the temple walls are kneeling 'with billis in hir honde' (l. 50), while within the temple thousands of lovers complain of many amatory and other grievances, including a mystery woman who 'held a litel bil' to 'shewe' the gods her 'quarel' (from French *querele* and Latin *querela*, another term for a legal complaint, 317–19).[18]

The narrative of the aborted, corrupted or unconcluded complaint process, which we have already encountered in *Piers Plowman*, was a favourite with amatory writers, giving opportunities to represent the frustrations of unfulfilled desire and the pain of the human condition. The anonymous *Assemblie of Ladies* (c. 1470–80) represents the complaints of women who have been betrayed by their lovers as bills presented and read out in the court of Lady Loyalty. The dreamer has her own complaint read out, and a further assembly is to take place where judgements and redress will be given, but she wakes up before the process can be completed.[19] Chaucer's *Complaint unto Pity* (mid- to late fourteenth century) offers a complex variation on this scenario. A preamble of eight stanzas explains that the speaker has been prevented from presenting his bill by fear of those who conspire for his death:

> Confedered alle by bond of Cruelte
> And ben assented when I shal be sleyn.
> And I have put up my complaynt ageyn,
> For to my foes my bille I dar not shewe   (ll. 52–5)

Withheld from the sight of his foes, the speaker's 'bille' is nonetheless included in the poem, where it is framed in relation to the terms and form of legal complaint. The poem includes a section headed 'The Bill of Complaint' in some manuscripts; following the form of legal bills, this section opens with an elaborate address, identification of the speaker, and the verb 'sheweth':

> Humbleste of herte, highest of reverence,
> Benygne flour, coroune of vertues alle,
> Sheweth unto youre rial excellence
> Youre servaunt, yf I durste me so calle,
> Hys mortal harm in which he is yfalle....   (ll. 57–61)

However the bill gradually unravels, showing that 'pity' is prevented from giving redress by her opponent Crueltee, and at the end reframing the cause of complaint; the speaker complains because Pity is dead: 'Sith ye be ded' (l. 117). Even as it appropriates the form of the legal request for remedy, it undoes the pragmatics of the form: this is a bill that complains of the impossibility of remedy.

George Ashby offers the *reading* of a complaint *poem* as a means of gaining remedy when the *legal* complaint process fails, adapting and modifying the structure of the legal complaint to align with this purpose. *Complaint of a Prisoner in the Fleet* (1463) (also known as *A Prisoner's Reflections*) begins with a list of grievances: the speaker has been imprisoned 'geynst ryght and reason' (l. 7); no one has been allowed to testify on oath for him (ll. 15–17); he has been falsely accused (l. 26); he has been stripped of his assets (ll. 20–1); imprisonment is bringing him into debt (l. 44).[20] Like a bill of complaint, too, the poem identifies the plaintiff in its opening lines: 'George Asshby ys my name' (l. 29). Unlike a legal complaint, however, Ashby's poem withholds the identification of the addressee. The speaker does not know any process for getting remedy – 'Knowyng no meane there to be releved' (l. 31)– nor to whom his complaint could be addressed and 'shown': 'What may I do? To whom shall I compleyn / Or shew my trouble or myne hevynes, / Beyng in pryson wrongfully, certeyn?' (ll. 50–2).

Ashby's poem is not alone in lamenting the lack of someone to whom to complain and the state of being without remedy. These are common tropes in amatory and courtly verse, taking for example this quatrain (reign of Henry VIII) in Oxford, Bodleian Library, MS Ashmole 176:

> Alas to whom should I complayne
> or shewe my wofull heavynes
> syth fortune hathe me in disdayne
> & am exyled remedylesse.[21]

This quatrain also appears in a poem (after 1521) in the voice of the exiled Edward Stafford, in which each of the twenty-two stanzas finishes with the word 'remedyless'.[22] Ashby differs from these examples, however, in his conclusion. As Ashby's poem unfolds, the speaker reveals that he has attained a new perspective on his suffering: troubles and tribulations are a means of learning patience and attaining God's grace. The addressees of the poem, when eventually revealed, are appropriate to this shift in perspective; rather than being those who might give justice, they are fellow sufferers:

> Goo forth, lytyll boke, mekely, without rous,
> To folk troubelyd and vexed grevously,
> Steryng theym by thy counseil vertuous
> To kepe pacience thereyn joyously,
> Redyng thys tretyse forth seryously,
> By the whyche they shall fynde grace as I suppose
> To comfortable entent and purpose.   (ll. 309–15)

Here Ashby offers the reading of the poem ('[r]edyng thys tretyse forth seryously') as an alternative process by which the afflicted may attain 'grace'. Ashby repurposes the complaint poem as an efficacious alternative to actual complaint in a legal process.

The Legal Status of Literary Complaint

In the examples of complaint literature discussed so far, there is a clear division between legal complaint and literary complaint. We will now turn to practices where the conceptual divisions between the literary and the legal break down and to literary writings which claim the status and agency of legal complaint. Central to this breaking down of boundaries was the legal concept of clamour. *Clamour* was a term used for many complaints on a subject. The existence of clamour could be enough to initiate a court case, even if it comprised informal complaint, in other words, complaint made outside of the formal legal channels. Clamour was a well-known concept in legal and literary sources. It is mentioned, for example, in relation to the rapist's trial in Chaucer's *Wife of Bath's Tale* (c. 1390–5)

> He saugh a mayde walkynge hym biforn,
> Of which mayde anon, maugree hir heed,
> By verray force, he rafte hire maydenhed;
> For which oppressioun was swich clamour
> And swich pursute unto the kyng Arthour
> That dampned was this knyght for to be deed,
> By cours of lawe, and sholde han lost his heed –   (ll. 886–92)

Here, there is great 'clamour' – much complaint – concerning the rape as well as suits made to the king for justice and as a result of both kinds of complaint the knight is condemned to be executed.[23]

Some literary texts claim legal agency by virtue of the concept of clamour. Falling into this category are verses against William de la Pole, Duke of Suffolk and unpopular minister of Henry VI. One brief stanza, said to have been posted up at St Paul's Church in London c. 1448, calls for the execution of Suffolk together with the bishop of Salisbury and Lord Saye:

> But Suthfolke, Salesbery and Say
> Be don to deathe by May
> England may synge well away.[24]

This stanza assumes that the reader (or hearer) will know the charges against these ministers. It calls for justice and predicts national clamour if justice is not delivered: England may sing 'well away', that is, express complaint.[25] Around the same time, complaints were issued against the Duke of York in the form of five quatrains.[26] These verses are written in the voices of dogs who complain that they have been unjustly slain when it is their master who is at fault:

> My mayster ys cruell and can no curtesye,
> ffor whos offence here am y pyghte.
> Hyt ys no reson þat y schulde dye
> ffor hys trespace, & he go quyte.   (ll. 1–4)

A chronicler records that the verses were displayed in the mouths of five dogs' heads.[27] Satirical complaints such as these claim the status of legal complaint through their assertion that they are part of clamour. The verse against Suffolk claims that all of England will complain if Suffolk and his fellows are not executed. Likewise, the verses against the Duke of York, constituting five complaints ostensibly by different dogs, invoke clamour. What is more, a final address to the readers suggests that more will join in. The dogs address 'maysterys' (l. 21) – perhaps those who might walk along Fleet Street where the gruesome display was said to have been installed opposite the Duke's lodging. The masters are instructed not to 'taketh for no grewe' the dogs' death ('do not accept willingly', l. 21),[28] implying, perhaps, that they should join in the clamour.

The claims of such literary complaints to legal status and agency through their self-identification as clamour were roundly contested by the authorities when it suited their purposes to do so.[29] Texts of this kind were often cited as evidence of treason or sedition. A satirical bill against Alexander Neville, one of the unpopular ministers of Richard II targeted in the Appellants crisis of 1388, appears among the records of parliament.[30] This text is very much a parody of a legal complaint. It addresses the Commons of England, calls God, the World and the Devil as witnesses, and alleges that Neville has abused his position in myriad ways. Supporters of Neville petitioned (complained to) parliament, objecting that such bills were slander: the most horrible and heinous slander ('desclaundre ... plus horribles et heynouse') aimed at any lord in parliament.[31] We can infer from this petition that the offending bills were originally attached to it as evidence, and it seems likely that this is how the satirical bill against Neville came to survive among the records. The bill against Neville demonstrates how a single text could be categorised on both sides of the boundary that distinguished legal complaint from illegal slander.

The Material Culture of Complaint

We have seen that literary and legal complaint were closely related in many ways, to the extent that there was ambiguity about the boundary between literary and legal complaint texts. How far did this go? Did literary complaints ever imitate the *material form* of legal complaints? And did the scribes of legal complaint have a hand in complaint literature?

Unfortunately, but unsurprisingly, few satirical bills survive in their original material form. Most texts appear in the context of chronicles or anthologies. However, there is the occasional piece of evidence for material similarities between legal and literary complaints. The Neville bill is a rare example. It has the form of a parchment bill, being 12.5 cm high x 32 cm wide and being written on one side only and across the wider dimension. Given that some satirical bills were displayed in public places, though, we can deduce that they too most likely were written on one side only. We can also infer that, because parchment was expensive, the same care for economy displayed in the choice of materials used for legal complaints would have influenced the size and shape of satirical complaints. Adopting the material form of the legal complaint would also have supported the claim of such materials to have legal status – they looked like clamorous texts. Ironically, their physical form, designed to facilitate their wide and public distribution, was also a basis for legal action against their authors and disseminators.

There is more evidence available to address the question of shared infrastructure. Some scribes copied both legal and literary complaints. Notaries and scriveners are associated with the mid-fifteenth-century rebellion and may have been responsible for the associated bill campaigns.[32] Some legal scribes were also *authors* of complaint literature; for example, Thomas Usk, George

Ashby and Thomas Hoccleve. Ashby was a clerk in the Royal Signet Office which received and answered petitions, referring to his service in *Complaint of a Prisoner/A Prisoner's Reflections* ('Havyng pen and inke evyr at my syde', l. 68) and complaining that despite his having served royalty loyally for forty years he has now been thrown into prison. Hoccleve's activities as clerk of the Privy Seal, where he copied legal documents, are regularly part of his reflections on his role as a poet. His failures to get payment for his scribal work form the pretext and subject for his begging poems, such as *La Male Regle* and the balade to Henry Somer (both early fifteenth century).[33] In the prologue to the *Regiment of Princes* (1410–11), 'Thomas' complains to the old man that his work in copying petitions is regularly not paid for by dishonest clients; he and his fellow scribes dare not complain for fear of false counter claims (ll. 1499–533).[34] The old man points out the irony that this long-standing Privy Seal scribe has not written his own complaint (ll. 1849–58). Thomas's petition to the Prince (ll. 2175 ff.) is, however, a request that he receive his translation of Giles of Rome's *De Regimine Principum*. He offers the literary work, rather than his scribal work, as a request for payment. In these complaint works Hoccleve imagines and reinvents literary production within the textual production and patronage frameworks of the professional legal scribe.

Conclusion

This chapter has sought to demonstrate that a knowledge of legal complaint can illuminate imaginative literature in the later medieval period. Literary complaint can be an evasive and coded textual practice that is hard to relate to the specificities of medieval society. A knowledge of the institutions, functions and textual corpus of legal complaint can help us see beyond the opaque surfaces of the literature. Badly in need of further editing and study, this vast corpus still has much to offer the literary scholar.

Notes

1. John H. Fisher, Malcolm Richardson, and Jane L. Fisher, eds., *An Anthology of Chancery English* (Knoxville, TN: University of Tennessee Press, 1984), 244–5. Lightly edited. All dates of texts in the present chapter are based on the information in the editions cited.
2. *MED* sheuen (v. (1)), sense 7 (b).
3. For example, Fisher et al., eds., *Anthology*, 198, 207.
4. See *MED* 'force' (n.), 3 (b) and examples of 'felonessement' and 'horriblement' in *AND*.

5. For example, Ps 137:1 and Jer. 9:1; see Wendy Scase, '"Heu! Quanta desolatio Angliae praestatur": A Wycliffite Libel and the Naming of Heretics, Oxford, 1382', in *Lollards and Their Influence in Late Medieval England*, ed. Fiona Somerset, Jill C. Havens and Derrick G. Pitard (Woodbridge, UK: Boydell, 2003), 19–36; Wendy Scase, *Literature and Complaint in England, 1272–1553* (Oxford: Oxford University Press, 2007), 97.

6. Nancy Dean, 'Chaucer's Complaint: A Genre Descended from the *Heroides*', *Comparative Literature* 19:1 (1967), 1–19.

7. Ian Cornelius, 'Boethius'*De consolatione philosophiae*', in *The Oxford History of Classical Reception in English Literature*, vol. 1: *800–1558*, ed. Rita Copeland (Oxford: Oxford University Press, 2016), 269–91.

8. All Chaucer references are to Larry D. Benson, gen. ed., *The Riverside Chaucer*, 3rd edn (Oxford: Oxford University Press, 1988).

9. *Le Roman de la Rose, par Guillaume de Lorris et Jean de Meung*, ed. Pierre Marteau (Paris: 1878), 100–7, ll. 5843–946.

10. *Roman*, ll. 5853–60.

11. R. W. Chambers and Marjorie Daunt, eds., *A Book of London English* (Oxford: Clarendon Press, 1931), 272–3.

12. See Scase, *Literature and Complaint*, 8–10 and references there.

13. http://discovery.nationalarchives.gov.uk/details/r/C13526.

14. The present chapter builds on and extends the analysis in Scase, *Literature and Complaint*, but focuses more centrally on the wide variety of uses to which literary authors could put complaint textuality and discusses, for the most part, a different set of examples.

15. Helen Barr, ed., *The Digby Poems: A New Edition of the Lyrics* (Exeter: Exeter University Press, 2009), 202–14. The poems survive in Oxford, Bodleian Library, MS Digby 102.

16. Barr, ed., *The Digby Poems*, 191–201.

17. A. V. C. Schmidt, ed., *William Langland, The Vision of Piers Plowman* (London: Dent, 1987).

18. *MED* 'querele' (n.), sense 2. The references are to J. Allen Mitchell, ed., *The Temple of Glass by John Lydgate* (Kalamazoo, MI: Medieval Institute Publications, 2007).

19. Derek Pearsall, ed., *The Floure and the Leafe, The Assemblie of Ladies, and The Isle of Ladies* (Kalamazoo, MI: Medieval Institute Publications, 1990).

20. Linne R. Mooney and Mary-Jo Arn, eds., *The Kingis Quair and Other Prison Poems* (Kalamazoo, MI: Medieval Institute Publications, 2005).

21. Bernard M. Wagner, 'New Songs of the Reign of Henry VIII', *Modern Language Notes* 50 (1935), 452–5, at 455. My lineation.

22. London, British Library, Harley MS 2252, fols. 2v–3. Quoted from *DIMEV* 301.

23. For *clamour of the people* as a kind of legal complaint, see Scase, *Literature and Complaint*, 56–7.

24. C. L. Kingsford, *English Historical Literature* (Oxford: Clarendon Press, 1913), 370.

25. *MED* 'weilawei' (interj.), sense 1; for occurrences in expressions of complaint, see 1 (b) and 1 (d).

26. R. H. Robbins, ed., *Historical Poems of the XIVth and XVth Centuries* (New York: Columbia, 1959), 189–90.

27. See further Scase, *Literature and Complaint*, 135.
28. *MED* 'taken' (v.), 9 b (c, d). I disagree with Robbins's gloss of 'no grewe' as 'not a whit' (355).
29. Scase, *Literature and Complaint*, 133–4.
30. TNA C 49/9/22.
31. TNA SC 8/262/13079.
32. Scase, *Literature and Complaint*, 115–18, 134.
33. Roger Ellis, ed., *Thomas Hoccleve, 'My Compleinte' and Other Poems* (Exeter: Exeter University Press, 2001), 64–78, 79–81.
34. Charles Blyth, ed., *Thomas Hoccleve, The Regiment of Princes* (Kalamazoo, MI: Medieval Institute Publications, 1999), 247.

Further Reading

Boffey, Julia, '"Forto Compleyne She Had Gret Desire": The Grievances Expressed in Two Fifteenth-Century Dream-Visions', in *Nation, Court and Culture: New Essays on Fifteenth-Century English Poetry*, ed. Helen Cooney, Dublin: Four Courts, 2001, 116–28.
Dodd, Gwilym, *Justice and Grace: Private Petitioning and the English Parliament in the Late Middle Ages*, Oxford: Oxford University Press, 2007.
Dodd, Gwilym and McHardy, Alison K., eds., *Petitions to the Crown from English Religious Houses, c. 1272–1485*, Woodbridge: Boydell, 2010.
Giancarlo, Matthew, *Parliament and Literature in Late Medieval England*, Cambridge: Cambridge University Press, 2007.
Oliver, Clementine, *Parliament and Political Pamphleteering in Fourteenth-Century England*, Woodbridge: York Medieval Press, 2010.
Ormrod, W. Mark, Dodd, Gwilym and Musson, Anthony, eds., *Medieval Petitions: Grace and Grievance*, Woodbridge: York Medieval Press, 2009.
Patterson, Lee, 'Writing Amorous Wrongs: Chaucer and the Order of Complaint', in *The Idea of Medieval Literature*, ed. J. M. Dean and C. K. Zacher, Newark, NJ: University of Delaware Press, 1992, 55–71.
Scase, Wendy, *Literature and Complaint in England, 1272–1553*, Oxford: Oxford University Press, 2007.

9

ANDREW GALLOWAY

Political Literature and Political Law

The proliferation of political complaints, satire and 'advice' in poetry and prose surviving from the twelfth century on suggests that medieval England's steeply hierarchical world was pervaded by political debate and satire, in both of which law, in its tangled conceptual and institutional forms, was a central focus. This is partly because law was crucial to the two most important centres of medieval authority, by which everyone's lives were in some measure guided: the king and the church. From the Conquest on, those were separate centres of increasingly massive written and unwritten bodies of law, courts and legions of legal professionals, whose numbers grew from the thirteenth century especially. Their proliferation, reliance on payment, and power over those seeking justice but lacking powerful connections or wealth provided fodder for much satire and complaint. Behind institutional systems, some of the fundamental ideas of political authority were paradoxical and continually subject to debate, chief among which was the kind of authority held by the king, clashing with that held by other potentates or wider political representatives, in parliament and elsewhere.

Such writing, whether in Latin, French or – increasingly in the fourteenth and fifteenth centuries – English, often claims to present the voices of 'common' subjects of the law, although how truly representative such writing was is ultimately unanswerable. The fiction of constructing politically representative voices in writing, however, has a history and political importance of its own. Thus as well as discussing how the law figures in political writing and political clashes, this chapter will also consider the changing nature of the idea of being a subject of the law, as displayed through the narrators and implied readers of political literature.

Church Law, King's Law: Satire and Partisanship in the Thirteenth and Early Fourteenth Centuries

Church law was more bookish, and less political, than secular law, but it merits attention as a major source of legal thought and bureaucracy, both of

108

which it had built up long before secular bureaucracies and law-codes. In the twelfth century, the church's internationally unifying 'canon law' was established through Gratian's compendium of nearly 4,000 excerpts or 'canons', expanded by further collections of decretals compiled by thirteenth- and fourteenth-century popes and canonists.[1] Late medieval English satires of the church courts, not surprisingly, are full of a sense of corrupt bureaucracy. A 'Satire on the Consistory Courts' preserved in British Library MS Harley 2253, dating from the early fourteenth century, satirises these church courts of appeal. This poem follows the tried-and-true *sirventé* (denunciation poem) format of bob-and-wheel, to lead us to a scene of the episcopal judge, 'an old cherl in a blake hure [*cap*]' who 'semeth best syre [*the highest lord*]' of all sitting there, but on closer inspection is 'an heme in a herygoud with honginde sleven' ('a yokel in a cloak with hanging sleeves'). The place is a trap for anyone with peccadillos that ecclesiastical judges can catch out:

Ant mo then fourti him byfore
  my bales to breven
In sunnes yef Y songe.
Heo pynkes with heore penne on
  heore parchemyn,
Ant sayen Y am breved ant
  ybroht yn
Of al my weole wlonke.
Alle heo bueth redy myn routhes
  to rede![2]
	more than forty before him to
	  record my penalty
	If I sink into sin.
	They stab with their pens on their
	  parchment
	And say I'm arraigned and
	  brought in
	For all my rich respectability.
	All are ready to declare my
	  punishments!

When a dishevelled woman arrives claiming that the narrator has promised marriage – a promise that, by canon law, is binding once sex has occurred – the narrator has no choice but to flee. The plot's basic elements are not uncommon in legal records, though the poem's presentation raises questions about the narrator's right to complain; the satire seems double-edged.[3]

King's law grew more gradually, into no less complex a system, evoking a larger range of political ideas, aspirations and satire. In twelfth-century England emerged a general or 'common law', a loosely combined body of written and unwritten law with a particularised approach to legal actions unlike elsewhere, featuring an array of kinds of 'writs' referring to specific kinds of suits requiring their own procedures. These were only rarely collected into general presentations, but notable are the early twelfth-century Latin collection of Anglo-Saxon laws, the *Laws of Henry the First*; the treatise attributed to Glanvill from the late twelfth century; and the mid-thirteenth-century compilation and rationalisation attributed to Henry

Bracton, *On the Laws and Customs of England* (now considered mostly to represent earlier compilations).[4]

The unification of royal courts was always a work in progress. The *Laws of Henry the First*, written *c.* 1115, before Henry II's great innovations in national law, states, 'the laws of the counties differ often from shire to shire, according as the rapacity and the evil and hateful practices of lawyers have introduced into the legal system more serious ways of inflicting injury'.[5] To address such variation, Henry II instituted various 'assizes' (sitting courts) to serve the entire nation. By the mid-thirteenth century, a professional legal culture was well established. Its workings, however, tended to provoke as much satire and complaint as its absence had by the writer of *The Laws of Henry the First*.

The king's court travelled where the king was, but in the thirteenth century royal justices also travelled 'in eyre', in circuits settling local cases held over for their arrival. This system became backlogged, however, and as an attempt to catch up, a new system, the Trailbaston courts, was established, with the idea that the 'eyres' would later resume (they never did). Here too was fodder for complaint. In the same manuscript as the English 'Satire on the Consistory Courts' is a French poem denouncing the Trailbaston courts, as rushed and brutal efforts to impose justice on local communities. As with the 'Satire on the Consistory Courts', however, the narrator is not an innocent victim of the courts' persecution. The narrator's lament is 'from a woods', where, he claims, he has been unfairly outlawed because he struck his servant to 'correct' him ('pur ly amender'); the servant has procured a 'bille' for the narrator's arrest.[6] This prototype or parallel of Robin Hood invites his readers to join him in a life of freedom, archery and forest life, denouncing in its totality 'la commune loy' (l. 56): a rare early instance of the term 'the common law' to refer to the king's law. The ideal community, the narrator claims, would be based on the shared celebration of unhindered rights. Best would be to stand wholly unreachable by the 'treachery' of evil laws created and enforced by outsiders: 'Pur ce me tendroi antre bois sur le jolyf umbray, / La n'y a fauceté ne nulle male lay' ('That's why I shall stay in the woods under lovely shade, / Where there's neither treachery nor any bad law', ll. 18–19). In one sense this turns Trailbaston into archetypal state oppression. But we cannot forget that the speaker has brutally beaten his servant. Is this an unreliable narrator, like the fornicator who fled in the 'Satire on the Consistory Courts'?

These two poems suggest that political satire, although sometimes seeming simpler than other kinds of poetry, does not provide a transparent addendum to history. All texts have formal and perspectival complexities, whether they are by a king's justice arguing for more centralisation or a satirist opening doubts about both the unfairness and corruption of the legal system and the human tendency to protest it. Some of the complexity in political writing on law, moreover, derives from the underlying paradoxes of the principles themselves found throughout the culture. A particularly paradoxical and crucial set of ideas clustered around the top of the political and (secular) legal pyramid. Was the king above the law?

The Prince and the Law in the Thirteenth and Fourteenth Centuries

This question is reflected in a wide variety of political writing in the later Middle Ages, and it was played out by continual conflicts between the king and his higher baronage. John's reign produced Magna Carta (1215), and subsequent reigns increasingly display such conflicts. The mid-thirteenth-century Latin poem *The Battle of Lewes*, describing the battle producing the brief triumph of the baronial revolt led by Simon de Montfort in 1258 against Henry III, begins by announcing its 'national' liberation – 'Now England breathes in the hope of liberty!' ('Jam respirat Anglia, sperans libertatem'), since it records the victory of the 'English' against the impositions of 'French' courtiers invited by Henry III. (The fact that Simon was French does not seem to have dampened the views of writers who considered this a return to true Englishness.) Amid the triumphant narrative of Henry's defeat, the author advances the curious idea that the king is himself 'liberated' if he keeps himself 'bound' by the law, as kingship, he claims, demands:

> Ad quid vult libera lex reges arctari?
> Ne possint adultera lege maculari.
> Et haec coarctatio non est servitutis,
> Sed est ampliatio regiae virtutis.

To what will a free law bind kings? – to prevent them from being stained by an adulterated law. And this constraint is not one of slavery, but rather an enlarging of the kingly faculty.[7]

The writer's witticism ties a knot in a long tradition of paradox. In the late twelfth century, Glanvill in his *The Treatise on the Laws and the Customs of the Realm of England* quoted a maxim from Roman ('civil') law, 'what pleases the prince has the force of law'.[8] By this position, first clearly influential in the twelfth century, the prince makes the law, thus is not subject to it. The Roman *lex regia*, however, from Justinian's *Institutes*, directly contradicts other sources becoming available, especially Aristotle. In the *Politics*, Aristotle focuses on the principles of rule and different kinds of government, observing that in every case, 'the rule of law ... is preferable to that of any individual ... he who bids the law rule may be deemed to bid God and Reason alone rule, but he who bids man rule adds an element of the beast; for desire is a wild beast, and passions pervert the minds of rulers, even when they are the best of men'.[9]

Aristotle's Greek *Politics* was not, however, available to Western Latin readers until the 1260s, though the influence of the *Politics* was thereafter rapid. Already by 1215, however, Magna Carta's clause 39 states, 'no free man shall be arrested or imprisoned, or disseised or outlawed or exiled or in any way victimised, neither will we attack him or send anyone to attack him, except by the lawful judgement of his peers or by the law of the land'. Regularly read and reaffirmed in later parliaments, Magna Carta was the first document asserting the king's subordination to law; it was often thereafter invoked to this end. The arrival of Aristotle's thought vastly bolstered this claim. By the 1270s, Thomas Aquinas, an exceedingly alert and up-to-date reader of the new Latin translations of Aristotle, insisted that Roman civil law's claim that 'the will of the prince has the force of law' had to be carefully interpreted. It could only mean that in order for the prince's actions to have the 'character' of law, those actions must themselves possess a lawful nature – a denial of any prince's automatic claims to authority.[10]

Aquinas was read mainly by other clerics, but his and Aristotle's ideas were further publicised by others. Giles of Rome's *De regimine principum* (*Regiment of Princes*), written 1277–88 for the French prince Philip the Fair (later Philip IV), builds on Thomistic ideas that 'reason' and 'virtue' should be the true 'rulers' of the self. As analogies to that, Giles's work granted that in the same way, the *pater familias* should govern the household, and the prince the state. But he is clear that ethical principles, not fallible individuals, should control the law. If English lawyers and judges had Glanvill and Roman law to insist on the king's transcendence of the law, they soon had Giles and Aquinas to argue that this was not so certain.

Giles's was the most widely influential political treatise of the next two centuries. *De regimine* was soon translated into French, and *Li Livres du Gouvernement des Rois* appears in book lists of English and French nobility and kings through the rest of the Middle Ages.[11] At the end of the fourteenth century, it was translated into English by John Trevisa for Thomas, lord of Berkeley, during Richard II's reign, a harrowing moment of royal claims discussed below.[12]

Mid-thirteenth-century English political poetry was rarely so sophisticated, but often no less pointed in claiming the need to constrain to some degree an individual king's authority. If the Latin *Battle of Lewes* offered a witty conundrum about the king's 'freedom' under the law, a roughly contemporaneous English *Chronicle* attributed to Robert of Gloucester espouses in different ways a similar perspective. When 'Robert' follows Henry III's battles down to Henry's grant of the Provisions of Oxford in 1258, by which Henry conceded to the barons the power to set up a council to monitor him and his government, the chronicler describes the Provisions as the recovery of ancient English freedoms, a return to the 'gode lawes' of Magna Carta. With the Provisions, Robert claims, Henry III agreed

To remue the frensse men to libbe bi yonde se	*To remove the French men to live overseas*
Bi hor londes her & ther & ne come nott age	*By their lands here and there, and not come back*
& to graunti gode lawes & the olde chartre al so	*And grant good laws and the old charter also*
That so ofte was igraunted er & so ofte vndo	*That so often was granted before, and so often undone.*[13]

To be sure, this completely misunderstands the Provisions of Oxford, but this English chronicler's nostalgic nationalism and atavistic idea of Magna Carta may grasp a different kind of truth, concerning what this event meant for some English pondering their nation's legal history. For Robert, 'good law' is what can be recovered as an ancient 'right', often granted and 'so ofte undo'. A similar view often attaches to later invocations of Magna Carta, and even some other statutes having a reputation for enshrining a principle of law above corrupt authorities and even whole legal systems.

Such a view is evident, for instance, in medieval England's most widespread popular revolt, in 1381, some of whose spokesmen demanded a return to the 'law of Winchester'. By this they apparently meant the 1285 statute emphasising the need to seize and hold felons in local courts. They might, therefore, have found congenial the 1285 statute's idea of communal self-policing, as they confronted new nationally imposed poll taxes and other legal and financial demands, disproportionately oppressing villagers, labourers and serfs in the period of the post-Black Death population crash and the financial demands produced by the war with France. In response, massed communities across the eastern and midland counties attacked archives, lawyers and other authorities they deemed the source of these novel impositions.[14]

The rebels seemed to view 'the king and the true commons' as the basis of pristine community, 'true' law and order. But their versified English 'letters' – cryptic but potent pieces of 'political poetry' – also exemplify a more existential sense that laws and courts can constitute in sum an imposition on fundamental moral or historical rights, of communities if not individuals. 'Knoweth your freend fro your foo. / Haveth ynow [*enough*], and seith "Hoo!" [*stop!*]'.[15] Though lacking in legal detail, their 'letters' suggest a shift in general legal perspective.

Cultivating the Voice of Complaint in the Fourteenth and Fifteenth Centuries

All political verse makes some claim to speak to and for a wide public, and the development of more 'popular' legal forms such as 'bills of complaint' conveyed by the Commons in parliament in the fourteenth century certainly spurred this 'voice' in political poetry.[16] Moreover, even before 1381, such writing sometimes implies that communities and individuals have 'rights' preceding any institutional or legal system.

We recall the poems from the early fourteenth-century manuscript (Harley 2253) with which this chapter opened. Both 'A Satire on the Consistory Courts' and 'A Satire on Trailbaston' end by affirming the speakers' right to flee or hide or establish a community somehow 'outside' the systems of law and politics against which he inveighs – although, as noted above, in both poems the authority of the narrators to claim those 'rights' is tricky. Yet both poems put the reader in the narrator's position, establishing a sense of participation opposing 'the system', whether that is the church or the royal courts. Thus from a wider perspective, we may ask (as Cary Nederman does) whether the fourteenth century saw the birth of what political historians usually attribute to the later age of John Locke: a sense of 'subjective' rights, imagined as pre-political, individual rights that serve as foundation for rather than dependent on any political system.[17]

Nederman takes as his example the Latin prose *Speculum Edwardi Tertii* (*Mirror of Edward III*) from the 1330s, by the learned parish priest William of Pagula, better known for his *Oculus sacerdotum*, widely used as priestly guidance in pastoral care. Like the *Oculus sacerdotum*, the *Speculum* relies on canon law, emphasising the premise of individual consent for any transaction to be legitimate. The idea of individual 'rights' emerges first and most emphatically in canon law.[18] However, unlike anything in canon law, the *Speculum* uses this premise to rail against the evils of the king's 'provisions': forced military requisitions of grain and other goods at sub-market prices. If the 'Satire on the Consistory Courts' displays church law courts as oppressive, the *Speculum Edwardi Tertii* nonetheless shows that canon law could support individual 'rights' in wholly economic domains, including those of the poor against the powerful who, when they take goods needed to sow fields, 'do great harm to the people'. In so doing, William's *Speculum* creates a posture of speaking for a 'common voice', well before any actual national community of readers.[19] From this perspective William's *Speculum* also takes up the question of the king's obligation to the law, concluding that although 'an emperor [*princeps*] is not subject to the laws, nevertheless it is fitting for him to live for his own part according to the laws'.[20] For, as he asks, 'are not you, King, required to obey the precepts of God as much as any peasant?'[21] If all individuals have rights pre-existing any legal system, how could one individual, the king, dictate and impose the law on everyone else?

This emphasis on subjective rights returns us to the puzzle of the *lex regia*, adding further force to its contradictions. Political tensions in that topic did not lessen as the Middle Ages came to an end. Outsized royal claims and personalities dominated, and fewer judges and legal commentators dared to openly refute claims that kings were above the law. At the same time, parliaments showed new confidence in their representative political authority. Clashes were inevitable, and seem to have inspired further ambitions in political literature focused on the law, amid which the idea of cultivating a 'common' reader's or listener's political understanding, articulateness, and even involvement assumes larger importance.

The contradictions of absolutism and parliamentarism are amply evident in the parliamentary trials dominating late fourteenth-century England, the historical and poetic narratives of which indicate a dense interweaving of positions, partisans and new legal procedures.[22] In the 'Good Parliament' of 1376, impeachment was first used, when the Commons, having first elected a Speaker, as a body indicted and ousted the associates of the senile Edward III for financial mismanagement.[23] Greater parliamentary battles and more extreme administrative tactics unfolded during Richard II's reign (1377–99). In the 'Wonderful Parliament' (1386), the chancellor, Michael de la Pole, was impeached for financial corruption, while the nineteen-year-old king was restrained, as Henry III had been, by a 'continuous commission' charged with examining royal expenditures.

This goaded Richard to a more extreme position. In 1387 he assembled the royal judges under Chief Justice Robert Tresilian, posing a list of provocative questions concerning the king's freedom from the law, and the legitimacy of anyone constraining that freedom. The judges – not surprisingly, given the menacing circumstances in which they were assembled – answered that the king was 'above the law' (*supra iura*), and those imposing constraints such as the 'commission' should be punished as traitors (*ut proditores*). The judges had read their Roman law, and ignored contrary precedents.

By most accounts, this was a turning point in Richard's reign. In the 'Merciless Parliament' the next year, a group of higher nobility tried and executed 'misleaders' of the king for treason, including Tresilian, citing 'the law of parliament', a new notion (it would return during Cromwell's revolution). Richard's response was more aggressive still. In the 'Revenge Parliament' of 1397, he packed parliament with followers, surrounding it with archers, while he and his supporters convicted and summarily executed many of those responsible for 1388. Richard's unflagging assertion of royal transcendence of law led to his adopting almost godlike new royal titles, such as 'Your Highness' and 'Royal Majesty'.[24] Two years later he was deposed, in a parliament managed by Henry of Lancaster's supporters, largely justified by arguments against the *lex regia*.

These outlines of a long and lethal controversy indicate why this period, and Richard himself, inspired so much politically implicated literature, and continued to do so. Some of the period's most complex political poetry was by John Gower, Geoffrey Chaucer and William Langland, 'Ricardian' poets offering important perspectives on law (thus treated in separate chapters elsewhere). Here we may end by considering a poem offering a retrospective view of Richard's fall: the alliterative poem *Richard the Redeless*, uniquely preserved in a quasi-academic but entirely English manuscript, written after Richard's deposition though narrated as if continuing *Piers Plowman* (also in the manuscript).

The year is 1399, at the brink of the deposition, 'whyle [Richard] werrid be west on the wilde Yrisshe, / Hennri has entrid on the est half', a setting lifted from historical narratives of Richard's deposition.[25] *Richard the Redeless* expands on that moment, drawing on notorious complaints, including those from the 'Record and Process', the formal account of Richard's deposition and Henry's coronation issued shortly after those events. The poem transforms this history into a surreal allegory, requiring careful decoding. Richard's notorious use of 'livery' and 'badges', emblems indicating the followers of lords or the king, serving as virtually private armies, is given elaborately metonymic treatment in the poem. 'Signes ... swarmed so thikke / Thoru-oute his lond in lengthe and in brede' that someone wandering – an Everyman – would encounter those. Richard's emblem of a 'hart' is just one of many thronging England:

Or hertis or hyndis on hassellis brestis,	*Either 'harts' or 'hinds' on retainers' breasts*
Or some lordis lyveré that the law stried,	*Or the livery of some lord who destroyed the law*
He shulde have ymette mo than ynowe.	*He would encounter more than enough.*
For they acombrede the contré and many curse servid,	*For they oppressed the land and 'handed up' many a curse*

And carped to the comounes with the kynges mouthe.	*And addressed the common people as the king's spokesmen.*

(2.21–29)

In this dizzying world, no ethical certainties or solid identities remain. The king, 'sette in your se as a sir aughte' ('sitting in your throne as a lord ought to' [1.86]), is addressed, wearing a crown whose meanings of law-giving we learn but he ignores. He presides over countless abuses and failures of 'loyalty' in which the narrator can only lament the loss of 'ledinge of [*carrying out*] lawe with love well ytemprid [*tempered*]' (1.19). The poem then shifts to a complex beast-allegory of parliaments, invoking the 'Revenge' parliament and the 'tyranny' of Richard's final years. But the allegory ruptures with word-play; 'nedy [*needy*] nestlingis', for example, are those hurt by the king who look to their Eagle – Henry of Lancaster – to save them; they 'bablid [*babbled*] with her billis, how they bete [*beaten*] were' (3.73, 78). Their 'bills' evokes 'beaks', but also parliamentary bills of complaint.

Amid such mingling allegory and word-play, the narrator pauses to scold 'Hick Heavy-head' for missing the point – 'hard is thi nolle [*head*]' (3.66). Obscure signs are part and parcel of the increasing political and literary complexity that English writers confronted and exploited. The poem is a stern test for readers' interpretive powers. It is unlikely that the poet thought that crowning Henry could in itself clarify such confusion. Indeed, anatomising Richard's evils allows *Richard the Redeless* to emphasise the personal sophistication necessary for the widening audience of English readers. Such readers are, for instance, challenged to understand a mathematical simile – parliamentarians silently accepting the king's execution of his enemies during the 'Revenge' parliament are 'empty' like zeroes, an Arabic mathematical concept still new to Western culture: 'Than satte summe as siphre [*cipher*] doth in awgrym [*Arabic numbers*], / That noted a place, and no thing availeth' (4.53–4). Not coincidentally, one of first guides to arithmetic in English is included in the poem's manuscript.[26]

Although political poetry can be direct and even simplistic, this is just one of the complicated political English poems from the fifteenth century.[27] Just as Henry IV distributed the 'Record and Process' in English – rather than Latin or French as usual for official legal documents[28] – so *Richard the Redeless*'s condemnation of Richard's abuses focuses on the depth of knowledge, thought, and rhetorical and poetic analysis that every free English reader needed, even Hick Heavy-head, for pondering politics, the law and the inherent right to understand them.

Notes

1. See James A. Brundage, *Medieval Canon Law* (New York: Longman, 1995).
2. *The Complete Harley 2253 Manuscript*, ed. and trans. Susanna Fein with David Raybin and Jan Ziolkowski (Kalamazoo, MI: Medieval Institute Publications, 2014–15), II, 188, ll. 19–26.
3. See the case before the York consistory court in *Women in England, c. 1275–1525*, ed. and trans. P. J. P. Goldberg (Manchester: Manchester University Press, 1995), 137–40.
4. See R. C. Van Caenegem, *The Birth of the English Common Law*, 2nd edn (Cambridge: Cambridge University Press, 1988). Useful too are A. Harding, *The Law Courts of Medieval England* (London: George Allen and Unwin, 1973); *Sources of English Constitutional History, vol. I: A Selection of Documents from A. D. 600 to the Interregnum*, ed. Carl Stephenson and Frederick George Marcham, rev. edn (New York: Harper and Row, 1972); Robert C. Palmer, *The Whilton Dispute, 1264–1380* (Princeton: Princeton University Press, 1984); and the searchable database for 'Bracton' at http://bracton.law.harvard.edu/.
5. *Leges Henrici Primi*, ed. and trans. J. L. Downer (Oxford: Clarendon Press, 1972), 98–9.
6. *Harley 2253*, III, 145, ll. 9–12.
7. *Political Songs of England: From the Reign of John to That of Edward II*, ed. Thomas Wright, with new forward by Peter Coss (1839; rept. Cambridge: Cambridge University Press, 1996), 72–121, ll. 667–74.
8. Van Caenegem, *Birth of English Common Law*, 3, n. b; see also Kenneth Pennington, *The Prince and the Law, 1200–1600: Sovereignty and Rights in the Western Legal Tradition* (Berkeley: University of California Press, 1993).
9. *Politics*, 1287a, in *The Complete Works of Aristotle*, ed. Jonathan Barnes (Princeton: Princeton University Press, 1984), II, 2042.
10. *Summa Theologiae*, 2a 2ae qu. 90; *St. Thomas Aquinas on Politics and Ethics*, trans. Paul E. Sigmund (New York: Norton, 1988), 44.
11. Charles F. Briggs, *Giles of Rome's De Regimine Principum: Reading and Writing Politics at Court and University, c. 1274–c. 1525* (Cambridge: Cambridge University Press, 1999).
12. *The Governance of Kings and Princes: John Trevisa's Middle English Translation of the De regimine Principum of Aegidius Romanus*, ed. David Fowler, Charles F. Briggs, and Paul G. Remley (New York: Garland, 1997).
13. *The Metrical Chronicle of Robert of Glocester*, ed. W. A. Wright, 2 vols. Rolls Series (London: HMSO, 1887), I, 734, ll. 11016–19.
14. See Alan Harding, 'The Revolt against the Justices', in *The English Rising of 1381*, ed. R. H. Hilton and T. H. Aston (Cambridge: Cambridge University Press, 1984), 165–93.
15. 'The Letter of John Ball', in *Medieval English Political Writings*, ed. James M. Dean, Teams Middle English Texts Series (Kalamazoo, MI: Medieval Institute Publications, 1996), 135, ll. 10–11. See also Steven Justice, *Writing and Rebellion: England in 1381* (Berkeley: University of California Press, 1994). Justice does not make the point proposed here.

16. See Wendy Scase, *Literature and Complaint in England, 1272–1553* (Oxford: Oxford University Press, 2000).
17. Cary J. Nederman, 'Property and Protest: Political Theory and Subjective Rights in Fourteenth-Century England', *The Review of Politics* 58 (1996), 323–44.
18. Brundage, *Medieval Canon Law*, 80–2.
19. *Political Thought in Early Fourteenth-Century England: Treatises by Walter of Milemete, William of Pagula, and William of Ockham*, ed. and trans. Cary J. Nederman (Tempe, AZ: Arizona Center for Medieval and Renaissance Studies, 2002), 82. See also David Matthews, *Writing to the King* (Cambridge: Cambridge University Press, 2010), 108–34.
20. *Political Thought*, 96.
21. Ibid., 93.
22. See Andrew Galloway, 'The Literature of 1388 and the Politics of Pity in Gower's *Confessio Amantis*', in *The Letter of the Law: Legal Practice and Literary Production in Medieval England*, ed. Emily Steiner and Candace Barrington (Ithaca, NY: Cornell University Press, 2002), 67–104.
23. Gabrielle Lambrick, 'The Impeachment of the Abbot of Abingdon in 1368', *EHR* 82 (1967), 250–76.
24. Nigel Saul, *Richard II* (New Haven: Yale University Press, 1997), 238–9.
25. *Richard the Redeless and Mum and the Sothsegger*, ed. James M. Dean (Kalamazoo, MI: Medieval Institute Publications, 2000), ll. 10–11; see *Annales Ricardi Secundi*, in *Chronicles of the Revolution*, trans. Given-Wilson, 115.
26. Andrew Galloway, '*Piers Plowman* and the Schools', *The Yearbook of Langland Studies* 6 (1992), 100–4.
27. See also, e.g., *The Digby Poems: A New Edition of the Lyrics*, ed. Helen Barr (Exeter: University of Exeter Press, 2009).
28. *The Deposition of Richard II: The 'Record and Process of the Renunciation and Deposition of Richard II'(1399) and Related Writings*, ed. David Carlson (Toronto: University of Toronto Press, 2007), 9, 58, 61, 63–5.

Further Reading

Agamben, Giorgio, *State of Exception*, trans. Kevin Attell, Chicago: University of Chicago Press, 2005.
Barr, Helen, *Signes and Sothe: Language in the Piers Plowman Tradition*, Woodbridge: Boydell, 1994.
Brundage, James A., *Medieval Canon Law*, London: Longman, 1995.
Burns, J. H., *The Cambridge History of Medieval Political Thought c.350–c.1450*, Cambridge: Cambridge University Press, 1991.
Galloway, Andrew, 'The Common Voice in Theory and Practice in Late Fourteenth Century England', in *Law, Governance, and Justice: New Views on Medieval Constitutionalism*, ed. Richard Kaeuper, Leiden: Brill, 2013, 243–86.
Giancarlo, Matthew, *Parliament and Literature in Late Medieval England*, Cambridge: Cambridge University Press, 2007.
Harding, A., *The Law Courts of Medieval England*, London: George Allen and Unwin, 1973.
Jussen, Bernard, 'The King's Two Bodies Today', *Representations* 106 (2009), 102–17.

Justice, Steven, *Writing and Rebellion: England in 1381*, Berkeley: University of California Press, 1994.

Oliver, Clementine, *Parliament and Political Pamphleteering in Fourteenth-Century England*, Woodbridge: York Medieval Press, 2010.

Sobecki, Sebastian, *Unwritten Verities: The Making of Vernacular Legal Culture, 1463–1549*, Notre Dame, IN: University of Notre Dame Press, 2015.

Taylor, Jamie K., *Fictions of Evidence: Witnessing, Literature, and Community in the Late Middle Ages*, Columbus: University of Ohio Press, 2013.

10

EMILY STEINER

William Langland

William Langland's *Piers Plowman*, one of the most influential poems of the English Middle Ages, is a poem steeped in law. The poet's profound engagement with legal concepts, with fourteenth-century legislation and with legal instruments, such as charters and seals, is key to his innovative poetics as well as to his larger project of making English verse a discourse of theology, ethics and reform. Throughout the poem, Langland explores the dynamics of justice and mercy; along the way he touches on such bread-and-butter legal topics as contract, crime, inheritance and bondage.[1] As the poem shows, legal language, whether derived from scripture, from canon, civil, or common law, or from contemporary practice can forge creative, even daring links between politics, religion and social life.

A Law unto Itself

Medieval law is not limited to set of codes or practices, nor is it simply an object, such as a charter, or a place, such as a courtroom, representable in literature or art. On the contrary, law bridges several areas of medieval thought and several discourses that have come to seem distinct: theology, political theory, ethics and aesthetics. In *Piers Plowman*, Langland views law as an all-encompassing idea and as a set of general rules governing behaviour and belief, whether those rules take the form of biblical precepts or of common-law maxims. Consequently, references to fourteenth-century English law in the poem can seem somewhat disparate and inchoate. However, the diverse strands of law woven throughout *Piers Plowman* help account for Langland's distinctive poetics, while showing how complex and sophisticated the relationship was between medieval English literature and law.

Perhaps the aspect of law most familiar to modern readers is its corruption and the always pressing need for legal reform. In Langland's Westminster, law is a 'labor of the tongue' (B.19.33)[2] easily corrupted by money, which greases the palms of a host of middlemen, including jurymen, summoners and executors. Conscience complains to the king that Meed (money, reward) controls the law and prevents poor people from obtaining justice: 'And doth men lese thorugh hire love that lawe myghte wynne – / The maze for a mene man, though he mote evere! / Law is so lordlich, and looth to maken ende: / Withouten presents or pens he pleseth ful fewe' (3.159–62). The ecclesiastical court of appeals of the archbishop of Canterbury (the Court of Arches) is also rife with lies and greed, fur mantels paving the way for divorce: 'And for a menever mantel he made lele matrymonye / Departen er deeth cam, and a devors shapte' (20.136ff.). These passages tend to cluster towards the beginning of the poem (Prologue, B.2–4), a series of satires about political life, where a marriage charter between Lady Meed (payment) and False, drawn up in Westminster, serves as an allegory of all legal fraud; and then again in passus 20 where Covetousness, in league with Antichrist, with 'glosynges and gabbynges', brings down 'the wit and the wisdom of Westmynstre Halle' (l. 133).

The need for legal reform is dire, but its impetus comes neither from the centre nor from the locales of medieval government. The poet downplays the role of parliament, which, at the time the B-text was likely written (mid-1370s), was beginning to assume its modern shape. In *Piers Plowman*, parliament's function is advisory or petitionary (as opposed to representative or legislative) and even in these capacities, severely limited.[3] Indeed, the poet depicts the role of collective bodies in creating law and maintaining justice only very abstractly, in contrast to other medieval allegories, such as John Gower's *Mirour de l'omme*, in which devils' parliaments and heavenly councils, for instance, play a bigger role. In *Piers Plowman* what would consolidate into the House of Commons is obscurely drawn as a generalised community of the realm. We learn, for example, that the King, along with the Commune and Kind Wit, 'shopen lawe and leaute – ech lif to knowe his owene' (l. 122). In the belling of the cat episode in the Prologue, two parliament-like groups of mice and rats conspire to bell a menacing cat, perhaps referring to the king's uncle, John of Gaunt, who dominated court politics, but they are too 'unhardy' to get the job done (Prol. 180). We are made vaguely aware of the existence of the King's council, but his royal advisors, Reason and Conscience, represent every man's ability to choose for the good rather than particular magnates or officers.

The well-meaning King decries corruption but is largely ineffectual. In this sense, law points to the irony at the heart of allegorical satire: personifications are, by their very nature, ill-equipped to reform society. If an allegorical King should permit his ward, Lady Meed, to marry False, or permit Wrong and Peace to settle out of court, 'to make pees with his pens, handy-dandy payed' (4.75), all of society would be irrevocably damaged. Unlike his contemporary John Gower, Langland offers no practical guide for English princes. For him there is no stable centre of worldly justice and no human embodiment of law. When Reason is called upon to advise the King, he conjures up a scene of total submission, in which monks adhere to their rules without deviation, wayward children and wives are beaten, in which the king's counsel is inseparable from the common profit, and law itself serves as 'a laborer and lede afeld donge' (5.47), always subordinate to the power of love. In *Piers Plowman*, examinations of worldly kingship are scattershot and under-theorised. Only the most marginal figures – a goliard, a lunatic and an angel on high – weigh in on whether the King is above the law, answerable only to God and divine law, or beholden to the law of the realm. The commons are left to shout (in Latin) their unqualified obedience: 'The king's precepts are for us the binding force of law!' (*Precepta regis sunt nobis vincula legis*) (l. 145).[4] The image of a truly law-giving and law-enforcing monarch appears only in B.19, which portrays the risen Christ as a conquering king, entitled to institute new laws, upend hierarchies and enslave those who resist him: 'To make lords of laddes, of lond that he synneth, / And fre men foule thralles, that folwen noght hise lawes' (ll. 33–4). True legal reform lies in the past and in an apocalyptic future in which nothing remains but total overhaul.

Personal Liability

Corruption in Westminster may be intractable, and Reason too lofty to combat it. Nonetheless, in *Piers Plowman*, the definition of a good person – someone who has what it takes to be saved – is intrinsically bound up in the law. Indeed, the poem shows that it is virtually impossible to imagine goodness and its reward without recourse to legal language and to a vivid legal imagination. Most obviously, for the poet, all of human society participates in a divine system of justice and mercy, in which sin is punished or pardoned and virtue rewarded in the afterlife. Within this system, one does well, in part, by obeying worldly laws or by using law to help, rather than hurt, other people. For example, in the Plowing of the Half-Acre (B.6), agricultural labourers flaunt the Statute of Labourers (1351, and subsequent statutes), which decreed that all able-bodied beggars be forced to work and that labourers not leave their estates or demand higher wages, thus making landlords compete for workers.[5] Piers the Plowman, unsure whether to compel 'wasters' to work by starving them, is assured by Hunger that God will punish them in the afterlife (l. 226). Piers' moral quandary is thus resolved by a collusion between theological precept (you will be rewarded or punished in the afterlife) and statute law (all able-bodied labourers to do well must work). To take a slightly more nuanced example, Truth's Pardon (B.7) condemns lawyers for accepting money to defend the innocent (from a moral standpoint, can advocacy be paid?), but then pardons them if they argue for the poor *pro bono*, and refrain from injurious speech. These lawyers, in their turn, will suffer no injury post-mortem from the notoriously litigious devil ('And [for Oure Lordes love lawe for hym sheweth] – / Shal no devel at his deeth day deren hym a myte', ll. 49–50).

These examples point to a complex interface between divine and human law: the poet, in the form of a divine pardon, imagines a reciprocal justice for principled lawyers (those who refrain from injuring others with legal language will not be injured themselves in a divine court of law). But they also suggest that law frames what it means to be good. To look at this idea from a different angle, *Piers Plowman* uses law to model goodness by asking its readers to imagine themselves as persons in law. That is, those seeking eternal salvation – those hoping to access divine grace, atone for their sins and join the community of the saved – must be able to express legal 'personality' (i.e., their advantages and disadvantages in law). They need to be able to picture themselves entering into contracts, suing or being sued, paying penalties for crime or debt, or, conversely, suffering disability in law by virtue of status, gender, age, or mental or physical incapacity.[6] Although the poet discourages social mobility, he asks his readers to become penitents by envisioning themselves in different legal situations as different kinds of persons in law.

We see the expression of legal personality through the various legal documents in the poem, which together attest to a contract drawn up between God and humanity, in which Christians may earn salvation rather than being automatically condemned to hell as a punishment for Original Sin. The recipient of these documents must shuffle a number of legal roles: debtor, heir, pardoned offender, or witness. In B.14, for instance, Patience assures Hawkyn the Active Man that sincere penance (i.e., a poor heart) operates like a quittance, a document proving payment for debt which the debtor can present to the devil in the heavenly court: 'Ac if the pouke wolde plede herayein, and punysshe us in conscience, / He sholde take the acquitaunce as quyk and to the queed shewen it, / *Pateat &c: Per passionem Domini*' (ll. 189–90a). Likewise Moses/Hope assures the dreamer that the benefits conferred by his letters patent (the Ten Commandments), once sealed by Christ hanging on the cross, will apply to anyone who loves God and his neighbour: 'And whoso wercheth after this writ, I wol undertaken / Shal nevere devel hm dere, ne deeth in soule greve' (B.17.16–17). Conversely, Meed's feoffment damns everyone who participates, the notaries, scribes, beneficiaries and witnesses, drawn from various social ranks: Simony and

Civil Law (clerics), 'unfoldeth the feffement', Mede and False, portrayed as highborn aristocrats, are enfeoffed with the earldom of Envy and the lordship of Lechery; and Piers the Pardoner, Reynald the Reeve, Munde the Miller and others serve as witnesses to the translation.[7]

Conceiving of oneself as a legal person is an enabling activity in several respects. First, it suggests that earthly law has an imaginative purchase on divine law that can be expressed in a variety of ways. Second, the notion that a Christian of any status, gender or age may be legally saved suggests that earthly law, too, might confer privileges and penalties more expansively. For example, at the core of legal personality is the ability to inherit, whether as an individual or as a collective. Like many medieval poets, Langland describes salvation as an inheritance that good Christians have the right to claim through their relationship with Christ. Thus inheritance raises questions not only about who has the right to claim but also about how kinship and belonging are defined. Such questions drive a number of debates towards the middle of the poem (B.11–12). Scripture insists, for instance, that only the poor can inherit their 'eritage in hevene – and by trewe right' (10.339), to which the dreamer protests that baptism is the main requirement for salvation, not poverty. Scripture agrees that baptism organises a class of redeemable people who can claim inheritance from Christ, a class that includes even Saracens, Jews and other 'heathens', but only if they convert at the eleventh hour and have been living all along in conformity to Christian beliefs. The Emperor Trajan breaks into protest that some pagans, such as himself, can be saved under exceptional circumstances. All the various people who can, under certain exceptions and conditions, inherit the kingdom of heaven, are described by the poet as blood brothers ('blody brethren'), sharing kinship ties: 'For alle are we Cristes creatures, and of his cofres riche, / And bretheren as of oo blood, as wel beggeres as erles' (11.198–9). Christian salvation changes the terms of inheritance by changing the definition of kinship; at the same time, however, inheritance offers an invitation to the legal imagination that enables people to think of themselves as one of the possibly saved. The crucial question is not simply who has the chance to be saved, but also under what conditions we can conceive of ourselves as legal persons, able to inherit.

A parallel to inheritance is the concept of mainprise. Mainprise refers to the medieval legal practice in which someone accused of a crime is temporarily released from custody before the trial. A mainpernour agrees to provide surety for the accused by putting up bail. In theory, the mainpernour promises his own body in exchange for that of the accused, agreeing to suffer the punishment should the accused not return ('corpus pro corpore' [a body in exchange for a body], probably deriving from hostageship), but, in practice,

EMILY STEINER

that promise has been commuted to a fine.[8] Those who benefit from main-prise have access to influential people willing to vouch for them. Not surpris-ingly, in the king's court at Westminster (B.2–4), mainprise is portrayed as a potential obstruction of justice. The King, learning of False's and Favel's intrigues, threatens to hang them, should they be captured, and refuses them the right to post bail: 'Shal nevere man of this molde maynprise the leeste. / But right as the lawe loketh, lat falle on hem alle' (2.198–9). Later, Wrong's friends plead for lenience: 'lat Maynprise hym have / And be borgh for his ble, and buggen hym boote' (4.87) and agree amongst themselves that 'Mede moste be maypernounr', that is, that money should provide surety for Wrong's release (l. 112). In these examples, mainprise, though a useful way of buying time in a system in which people languished in prison before trial, is portrayed as partial, a legal stopgap for those with deep pockets, and an impediment to justice should the accused escape.

One would assume that, in the next life, perfect justice would obviate the need for such remediations. As the poem called the 'Quatrefoil of Love' (c. 1400) affirms, at the Last Judgement, when the dead rise up, 'Thar may no gold ne no fee make owre maynpryse, / Ne kyn.'[9] Neither gold nor kin can buy a reprieve from prison, here conceived as penal rather than merely custodial. By contrast, in *Piers Plowman* the poet is determined to redeem mainprise, and indeed any legal practice that offers remedy or respite from the severity of the law. Not every accused person has the cash and kin to go free, but every faithful Christian does, insofar as Christ embodies both the payment and the connection. In a Christian era, God assumes the liability. As Abraham/Faith explains to the dreamer,

> Out of the poukes pondfold no maynprise may us fecche
> Til he come that I carpe of: Christ is his name
> That shal delivere us some day out of the develes power,
> And better wed for legge than we ben alle worthi
> That is, lif for lif –   (B.16.264)

In this passage, Abraham/Faith is talking about a one-time event, the Harrowing of Hell, when Christ freed the patriarchs and prophets from the devil's prison, laying down his life for theirs 'corpus pro corpore', a phrase that simultaneously evokes English legal practice and the sacrifice of the Holy Sacrament, the Corpus Christi. Christ's mainprise however, turns out to be a repeated rather than singular event: although the prisoners change, the mainprenour stays the same, forever granting and posting bail for those who deserve it. The idea is that, in a Christian era, mainprise, under certain conditions, is available to all: at the end of B.18, for example, Peace declares that God has granted that she and her sister Mercy mainprise 'al mankynde'

(l. 186). Mainprise is thus refurbished and repurposed to serve salvation theology, but the point is not that divine law transforms and redeems earthly law. It is rather that earthly law provides the apparatus through which one can imagine oneself as a legal person – able to inherit or be mainprised, to be pardoned or not – and thus able to participate in the scheme of salvation.

The Long Arm of the Law

Piers Plowman's encounter with law is eclectic and vast, drawing upon a repository of terms, practices and perspectives. As the poem abundantly shows, law is a language-making machine: it is nearly impossible to talk about one's relationship to other people (or to God) without recourse to law. Although the practice of law is often corrupt, and its application to other discourses often misunderstood, in *Piers Plowman* the virtue of law is that it is neither rigid nor restrictive. Law makes things happen 'for real', and Langland often invokes legal performativity in order to make a point about social or ecclesiastical reform; for example, just as a poorly written charter, with interlinear notes or bad Latin, will not hold up in court, so a priest who botches his prayers is doing no one any service (B.11.303–8).[10] At the same time, for the poet, working with the law also requires such qualities as flexibility of thought, the ability to think concretely and abstractly at once, and the will to inhabit a range of identities. Law is thus critical to a poetry that demands the same qualities from its readers.

In many passages in *Piers Plowman* the wonderful elasticity of law, and of the medieval legal imagination, is exemplified by metaphor. As suggested above, however, in medieval literature the application of earthly law to salvation is not exactly figurative. You might say that a legal metaphor such as 'heaven is my inheritance' is not metaphorical at all; it describes instead the disciplinary overlap between theology and law. In medieval literature, this overlap has surprisingly material dimensions. For example, the religious poet Guillaume de Deguileville (fl. 1330–50), whose well-known dream-vision poetry influenced *Piers Plowman*, portrays a heavenly court complete with judge, advocates, witnesses and written instruments.[11] Did Deguileville believe in a literal court? Quite possibly the image of a post-mortem courtroom was so conventional by the later Middle Ages that it had shed whatever metaphoricity it might have had in the first place. And certainly a legal metaphor such as 'the devil's prison' will cease to be metaphorical when theology is retrofitted to explain it (e.g., in the case of the doctrine of Purgatory). Perhaps a better way to think about medieval legal metaphor is the following: because law crossed various discourses it was always available as both a literal and a figurative concept.

This problem of legal metaphor can be approached in still a different way. If the metaphoricity of law describes the overlap between law and theology, it is also built into theological literature, and particularly into Paul's epistles. When Paul speaks of the circumcision of the heart (Romans 2:25–9) or the bond of debt nailed to the cross (Colossians 2:14), he is speaking metaphorically but not merely so; he also showing that legal language is indispensable to Christian hermeneutics and to Christian salvation. For Paul, the law, through its suitability for metaphor, bridges an Old Testament and New Testament worldview. Moreover, in the Pauline epistles, and elsewhere in biblical hermeneutics, a crucial part of grasping the rules of salvation is to experience the gap between spiritual and temporal law. That gap has emotional power, making readers feel anxious or relived about their future. Part of what legal metaphor does in *Piers Plowman* is to maintain that gap – or tension – between law and theology, and thereby sustain the emotion necessary for theology to function as law.

In many passages in *Piers Plowman* legal metaphors are deployed to heighten and deepen the emotional life of salvation and to shock the reader into gratitude or fear. In B.11.129–36, for example, the dreamer, desperate to ensure his salvation, perversely insists that baptism is a contract of unfreedom between a lord and a churl:

> Ac he may renne in arerage and rome fro home,
> And as a reneyed caytif recchelesly aboute.
> Ac Reson shal rekene with hym and rebuken hym at the laste,
> And Conscience acounte with hym and casten hym in arerage,
> And putten hym after in prison in purgatorie to brenne,
> For his arerages rewarden hym there right to the day of dome,
> But if Contricion wol come and crye by his lyve
> Mercy for hise mysdedes with mouthe or with herte.

In this extended metaphor, Paul's bondservant of Christ is reimagined as a churl, who is not allowed to draw up a charter, alienate property or leave the manor without his lord's permission. Although a churl may rack up debt and run away from his manor, the lord's henchmen (i.e., his own faculties, Reason and Conscience) will force him to confront his crime and throw him into the manor jail, until he confesses and begs pardon. There are two medieval English legal situations operating in this extended metaphor. One is the situation in which a bondsman leaves the manor, becoming officially a 'fugitive'. After a year, if the lord fails to file a claim, or to apprehend the fugitive, the bondsman earns his freedom and cannot legally be coerced. But if the lord files a claim initially, or catches up with the villein, he can force the villein to return to the manor.[12] Overlaid on top of this fugitive metaphor, in

Piers Plowman, is a related one regarding imprisonment for debt ('he may renne in arerage'). In the fourteenth century, a debtor could be held in close imprisonment until he paid his debt or his creditor allowed for his release. Here Reason and Conscience, playing the role of the lord's agents, catch up with the sinner/villein, confront him with the (spiritual) debts he owes, to his lord or someone else, and incarcerate him until the debt is paid, that is, the sinner is purged in Purgatory, unless he proves himself contrite.

In this playful if disquieting analogy, inclusion in the community of the saved is compared to unfreedom on the manor, thus yoking together one kind of anxiety ('will I be saved?') with another ('will I, or do I want, to be caught?'). To feel like a Christian, bound to Christ, one is supposed to feel like a villain, bound to the lord and to his law, and it is through the legal metaphor that such emotions are freshly felt and through which one can imagine oneself as someone who presumably many of Langland's readers were not, that is, unfree. From a theological perspective such metaphors may seem superfluous – and somewhat perplexing: is it not enough for Langland's dreamer to claim that baptism is a contract, in which God promises to redeem all Christians who do penance for sin, after a purgative stint in Purgatory? But the 'fugitive churl' critically re-figures the relationship between law and theology, if theology can be said to be law because of the tension that metaphor maintains between the two. The passage is emotional in part because it uses medieval English law to animate and narrativise spiritual law: a churl falls into debt and is imprisoned; he leaves the manor and is caught. But its emotional punch is derived from the gap that metaphor opens up between law and the Law: we are meant to feel like God's servant by feeling like a fugitive, reluctant, trapped, coerced – and safe.

Giving the Slip: Literature at the Limits of the Law

Legal metaphors in *Piers Plowman* point to the overlap between secular law and salvation theology, while maintaining a productive tension between the two, stressing the gap between the certainty and uncertainty of being saved. These metaphors aim to startle readers out of aesthetic or spiritual complacency: what would it feel like to be a renegade churl thrown into his lord's prison? Would one be relieved or aggrieved, happily or unhappily constrained? The poem's most powerful metaphors, however, turn on the legal exception, the unexpected or archaic remedy that saves you from certain death. Because pre-modern English law prescribed capital punishment for crimes that modern Western readers would consider minor, it also mediated the severity of the law by providing escape hatches that later jurists would consider unjust. Such remedies, loopholes and exceptions show what it means to write poetry 'in the shadow of the gallows', or in other words to create a high-stakes literature that saves.

In Passus B.18/C.20, for example, Christ, having triumphantly harrowed hell, gives a victory speech jam-packed with rationales for saving human-kind. In this speech, he is prepared to be generous. He affirms that, at Doomsday, it is possible that even those Christians consigned to hell will not be judged perpetually to death. As the divine judge Christ is authorised to pardon even condemned criminals. What follows are two legal analogies:

> It is noght used on erthe to hangen a feloun
> Ofter than ones, though he were a tretour.
> And if the kyng of that kyngdom come in that tyme
> There the feloun thole sholde deeth or oother juwise,
> Lawe wolde he yeve hym lif, and he loked on hym.
> And I that am kyng of kynges shal come swich a tyme
> Ther doom to the deeth dampneth alle wikked;
> And if lawe wole I loke on hem, it lith in my grace
> Wheither thei deye or deye noght for that thei diden ille.
> Be it any thyng abought, the boldenesse of hir synnes,
> I may do mercy thorugh rightwisnesse, and alle my wordes trewe.
>
> (B.18. 380–90)

In the first lines we are told that felons are not hung twice, which may refer to the rare event in medieval law that, if someone inadvertently 'gives the slip' at the gallows – if the rope breaks, or the condemned man is cut down before he gasps his last breath – that person is not re-hung, however disappointed the crowd.[13] The unlikelihood of the person's survival meant that his escape was seen as a miraculous event; kings would often give pardon to the hanged man out of the charity that such miracles demand. This passage in *Piers Plowman* may allude to the well-known case of one Walter Wynkeburn who was hung in 1363 at Leicester, revived in the cart, was rushed to the abbey to protect him from being hung a second time and pardoned by King Edward III, who happened to be at Leicester.[14] Even traitors are not hung twice, Langland adds with cold comfort, reminding us that, after the 1351 Statute on Treason, traitors might suffer multiple deaths: drawn, hung and disembowelled.[15]

The second legal analogy explains that, if the king should arrive at the gallows and give a sign ('and he loked on hym'), he may release a condemned man. This is an appeal to ancient tradition that a king could pardon anyone about to be executed if he happened to be passing by. For example, in 1397, one William Walshman was convicted of stealing a silver 'pendant' and sentenced to death. The king happened to pass by the site of execution and ordered William's release.[16] Likewise Christ can make an exception and grant mercy, even to those already in hell.[17] In this passage, the legal exception (the failed hanging) and the rarely used legal remedy (the royal look) heighten the emotional drama of salvation. Christ through his absolute power can give mercy even to the worse sinner, but that man has a noose about his neck, which may or may not break. The king may or may not ride by; he may turn and look. This passage is at once literature as legal compendium and poetry in the shadow of the gallows.

One final example of legal exception in *Piers Plowman* is the benefit of clergy, or what later medieval writers called 'neck-verse', a peculiarly English practice that tried to reconcile canon law and common law. In England, after the late thirteenth century, those accused of crimes in secular court (always excluding certain crimes such as treason) had the option of proving their clergy by reading aloud a verse from a Latin psalm, which eventually became identified with penitential psalm 50/51, 'Miserere mei', a psalm considered relatively easy to recite. If the accused passed the literacy test, he would be transferred to ecclesiastical court, where he might be retried, and where he was unlikely to receive the death penalty. By the end of the fourteenth century, the 'neck-verse' was becoming a legal fiction of clergy: the Gaol Delivery Rolls record many cases of laymen, who, lacking tonsure and habit, proved their 'clergy' by reciting the psalm.[18] In sum, by the late fourteenth century, psalmic literacy provided a remedy at the same time that it enabled social mobility in law.

In *Piers Plowman*, neck-verse shows how literature and law collude in shaping narratives about near-death escapes and, in the process, construct hair-raising theological poetics. With neck-verse, Langland places his own risky poetic project at the limits of the law. In B.12 (also in C), Imaginative is defending the special status of the clergy, by which he means both 'the clergy', that is, the men who preach and teach, and 'clergie' the learning that priests transmit to others to save them from eternal damnation:

> Wo was hym marked that wade moot with the lewed!
> Wel may the barn blesse that hym to book sette,
> That lyvynge after lettrure saved hym lif and soule.
> *Dominus pars hereditatis mee* is a merye verset
> That hath take fro Tybourne twenty strong theves,
> Ther lewed theves ben lolled up – loke how thei be saved!
>
> (12.185–190)

The passage begins by claiming that it is spiritually detrimental to be a layperson. Lucky are the ones who learn to read Latin psalms as children, because the psalms tell you what to believe and how to mourn your sins. In short, learning to read the psalms may save your soul. Yet the example of the benefit of clergy and its 'murye verset' links the idea that psalmic reading can save you to a more contested site of legal performance. According to the poet, in his day, thuggish thieves (twenty 'lewd' and 'strong') locked up in Tyburn prison can dodge the noose by reciting a verse from the psalm.

This outrageous comparison between psalmic reading and neck-verse feels like a travesty of spiritual literacy: surely the poet realises that the saving power of the psalms with respect to the soul is not on the same level as the literacy which any lowborn thief can use to save his neck! Presumably, the speaker, Imaginative, is contrasting criminality in the temporal mode with sin and forgiveness in the spiritual mode. That is to say, the psalms are so essential as expressions of contrition and faith that their application to the most instrumental of worldly causes highlights their value for all humanity. And yet, the poet, who loves a risky comparison, is also using the literacy test as a radical test case for clergie. Reading can save us in a pinch if are willing take that leap and imagine that mercy can be justice and that anyone, cleric or lay, knight or knave, saint or thief can claim the benefit.

Relief for a thief, temporal or spiritual, is never a sure thing. As Imaginative concedes, their status is ever precarious: 'for he that is ones a thef is everemoore in daunger / And as lawe liketh to lyve or to deye' (12.205). Yet medieval English law, with its battery of compromises and exceptions, makes spiritual benefit possible to imagine and to claim. Neck-verse may bridge the gap between earthly and heavenly salvation because English common law has the resources to remediate its own rules and to accommodate other legal systems. This is law – and literature – on the edge.

Notes

1. See James Simpson, *Piers Plowman: An Introduction to the B Text*, 2nd rev. edn (Exeter: University of Exeter Press) for a thorough explanation of the dynamics of justice and mercy in the poem.
2. Law plays an important role in the three major versions of the poem. I focus on examples from the B-text following A. V. C. Schmidt's edition (*The Vision of Piers Plowman: A Critical Edition of the B-Text based on Trinity College Cambridge MS B.15.17* (London: Dent, 1995)).
3. See Emily Steiner, 'Commonalty and Literary Form in the 1370s and 80s', *New Medieval Literatures* 6 (2003), 199–221; Matthew Giancarlo, *Parliament and Literature in Late Medieval England* (Cambridge: Cambridge University Press, 2007), 179–208.
4. See Fiona Somerset, '"Al þe comonys with on voys at onys": Multilingual Latin and Vernacular Voice in *Piers Plowman*', *The Yearbook of Langland Studies* 19 (2005), 107–36; and Larry Scanlon, 'King, Commons, and Kind Wit: Langland's National Vision and the Rising of 138', in *Imagining a Medieval English Nation*, ed. Kathy Lavazzo (Minneapolis, MN: Minnesota University Press, 2003), 191–233.

5. For *Piers Plowman* and labour legislation in the fourteenth century, see Anne Middleton, 'Acts of Vagrancy: The C Version "Autobiography" and the Statute of 1388', in *Written Work: Langland, Labor, and Authorship*, ed. Stephen Justice and Kathryn Kerby-Fulton (Philadelphia: University of Pennsylvania Press, 1997): 208–317.

6. On legal person and medieval allegory, see Elizabeth Fowler, 'Civil Death and the Maiden: Agency and the Conditions of Contract in *Piers Plowman*', *Speculum* 70:4 (1995), 760–92.

7. On Langland's documents, see Emily Steiner, *Documentary Culture and the Making of Medieval English Literature* (Cambridge: Cambridge University Press, 2003), 93–142.

8. See Kathleen Kennedy, *Maintenance, Meed, and Marriage in Medieval Literature* (New York: Palgrave, 2009), esp. 61–88; and Jonathan Rose, *Maintenance in Medieval England* (Cambridge: Cambridge University Press, 2017), esp. 150–80.

9. 'The Four Leaves of the Truelove', ed. Susanna Greer Fein, ll. 398–9. http://d .lib.rochester.edu/teams/text/fein-moral-love-songs-and-laments-four-leaves-of -the-truelove.

10. Bruce Holsinger, 'Langland's Musical Reader: Liturgy, Law, and the Constraints of Performance', *Studies in the Age of Chaucer* 21:1 (1991), 99–141.

11. See Andrew Galloway, *The Penn Commentary on Piers Plowman*, Vol. 1: *C Prologue-Passus 4; B Prologue-Passus 4; A Prologue-Passus 4* (Philadelphia: University of Pennsylvania Press, 2011), 5; Emily Steiner, *Reading* Piers Plowman (Cambridge: Cambridge University Press, 2013), 13.

12. See Henry de Bracton, *On the Laws and Customs of England*, ed. Samuel E. Thorne (Cambridge, MA: Belknap Press, 1977), II, 36. http://bracton .law.harvard.edu.

13. See Robert Bartlett, 'Death by Hanging', in *The Hanged Man: A Story of Miracle, Memory, and Colonialism in the Middle Ages* (Princeton, NJ: Princeton University Press, 2004), 42–52.

14. See Henry Knighton, *Knighton's Chronicle 1337–1396*, ed. G. H. Martin (Oxford: Clarendon Press, 1995), 188–9; Helen Lacey, *The Royal Pardon: Access to Mercy in Fourteenth-Century England* (York: York Medieval Press, 2009), 71.

15. See generally, J. G. Bellamy, *Law of Treason in England in the Later Middle Ages* (Cambridge: Cambridge University Press, 2004).

16. G. O. Sayles, *Select Cases in the Court of King's Bench*, Selden Society 88 (London: Quaritch, 1971), IV, 89.

17. Thomas McSweeney, 'The King's Courts and the King's Soul: Pardoning as Almsgiving in Medieval England', *Reading Medieval Studies* 40 (2014), 159–75; Lacey, *The Royal Pardon*, 70–7.

18. For histories of medieval benefit of clergy, see Richard H. Helmholz, 'Conflicts between Religious and Secular Law: Common Themes in the English Experience, 1250–1640', *Cardozo Law Review* 12 (1990), 707; Leona Christine Gabel, *Benefit of Clergy in England in the Later Middle Ages* (New York: Octagon, 1928); Katherine Zieman, *Singing the New Song: Literacy and Liturgy in Late Medieval England* (Philadelphia: University of Pennsylvania Press, 2013), ch. 22; John G. Bellamy,

The Criminal Trial in Later Medieval England: Felony before the Courts from Edward I to the Sixteenth Century (Toronto: Toronto University Press, 1998).

Further Reading

Boboc, Andreea D., *Theorizing Legal Personhood in Late Medieval England*, Leiden: Brill, 2015.

Cole, Andrew and Galloway, Andrew, eds., *The Cambridge Companion to Piers Plowman*, Cambridge: Cambridge University Press, 2014.

Fowler, Elizabeth, 'Civil Death and the Maiden: Agency and the Conditions of Contract in *Piers Plowman*', *Speculum* 70:4 (1995), 760–92.

Galloway, Andrew, *The Penn Commentary on* Piers Plowman, Vol. 1: *C Prologue-Passus 4; B Prologue-Passus 4; A Prologue-Passus 4*. Philadelphia: University of Pennsylvania Press, 2011.

'Piers Plowman and the Subject of the Law', *The Yearbook of Langland Studies* 15 (2001), 117–40.

Giancarlo, Matthew, *Parliament and Literature in Late Medieval England*, vol. 64, Cambridge: Cambridge University Press, 2007.

Holsinger, Bruce W., 'Langland's Musical Reader: Liturgy, Law, and the Constraints of Performance', *Studies in the Age of Chaucer* 21:1 (1991), 99–141.

Kennedy, Kathleen, *Maintenance, Meed, and Marriage in Medieval English Literature*, New York: Palgrave Macmillan, 2009.

Middleton, Anne, 'Acts of Vagrancy: The C Version "Autobiography" and the Statute of 1388', in *Written Work: Langland, Labor, and Authorship*, ed. Steven Justice and Kathryn Kerby-Fulton, Philadelphia: University of Pennsylvania Press, 1997, 208–317.

Scase, Wendy, *Literature and Complaint in England 1272–1553*, Oxford: Oxford University Press, 2007.

Sobecki, Sebastian, *Unwritten Verities: The Making of England's Vernacular Legal Culture, 1463–1549*, Notre Dame, IN: University of Notre Dame Press, 2015.

Steiner, Emily, *Reading* Piers Plowman, Cambridge: Cambridge University Press, 2013.

Documentary Culture and the Making of Medieval English Literature, vol. 50, Cambridge: Cambridge University Press, 2003.

Steiner, Emily and Barrington, Candace, eds., *The Letter of the Law: Legal Practice and Literary Production in Medieval England*, Ithaca, NY: Cornell University Press, 2002.

Taylor, Jamie K., *Fictions of Evidence: Witnessing, Literature, and Community in the Late Middle Ages*, Columbus, OH: Ohio State University Press, 2013.

Thomas, Arvind, 'The Subject of Canon Law: Confessing Covetise in *Piers Plowman* B and C and the *Memoriale presbiterorum*', *The Yearbook of Langland Studies* 24 (2010), 139–68.

Yeager, Stephen, *From Lawmen to Plowmen: Anglo-Saxon Legal Tradition and the School of Langland*, Toronto: University of Toronto Press, 2014.

11

CANDACE BARRINGTON

Geoffrey Chaucer

The extent of Chaucer's direct involvement with legal practice has been an open question since the fifteenth century. Although a practical knowledge of both the law and legal procedure was expected of London's citizens, details from Chaucer's life-records and his ease with legal terminology and protocol would seem to associate him closely with the courts, though in ways broader and less reliant on institutional credentialing than experienced by the many legal professionals he encountered in his dealings. Beyond Thomas Speght's observation in the biographical note prefacing his 1598 *Workes of Chaucer* that 'It seemeth that [Chaucer was] of the inner Temple' (a note based on an already-lost document noted by Speght's contemporary, William Buckley), we have no evidence substantiating Chaucer's connection to formal legal studies.[1] Instead, we can understand his legal knowledge through a mass of extant records, now assembled in the *Chaucer Life-Records*, consisting 'largely of legal documents: records of expenses, exchequer writs, payments of annuities, appointments to office, witness statements, pleas of debt, house leases'.[2] Rather than record his career, they witness his multiple and lifelong transactions within England's legal systems. In fact, because we have no record of Chaucer's life as a poet, these legal documents provide the primary window into his biography.

These documents reveal less a legist granted a systematic legal education at the London Inns of Court and more a gentryman able to navigate England's multiple legal institutions, sometimes as the accused, sometimes as the accuser and sometimes as the one who hears (though not judges) the accusations.[3] Many times, the documents identify and solemnise his role as a guardian, a witness, a spokesman, a controller of the customs, a clerk of the King's Works, a mainprenor (a guarantor analogous to a modern bail bondsperson), a member of Kent's commission of the peace and a single-term member of parliament. Repeatedly, he was drawn into the legal realm and required to grapple with its forms, its languages and its rituals. The documents and roles provide the broad outline of an individual negotiating England's complex legal system, using the advantages it offered and avoiding the threats it posed a man of his station, advantages limited by and threats enlarged by the somewhat modest station in which he found himself. In these negotiations, we find not specialised legal knowledge but rather knowledge that someone with his combined mercantile and court background would likely have known.[4] Unlike his Canterbury pilgrim or possibly his contemporary, the poet John Gower, Chaucer was not a Man-of-Law. He was instead a man-in-the-law, immersed in its structures and its presuppositions.[5]

Because these engagements with the legal system placed Chaucer in multiple positions – as the accuser, the accused and the mediator – they seem to have granted him a strong sense of the impossible demands made on a system that depends on the goodness and selflessness of those charged with providing justice. In England, the law evolved to prosecute and punish those charged with abusing the law and, simultaneously, to protect the privileges of those who designed and enforced it. Problems occurred when those roles interfered with one another, when the law-enforcers were also the law-breakers. Chaucer's contemporaries bewailed the legal system's inability to restrain authority figures who, charged with upholding the law and protecting the weak, used their positions to degrade the laws and menace the weak. Unlike these contemporaneous condemnations, Chaucer's verse takes a more rhetorically nuanced approach. His verse questions the fourteenth-century English legal system by mimicking its protocols, adopting its language, assuming its forms, and mouthing its legal principles – and then enacting their inherent inability to deliver justice, suggesting a sense that England's intricate judicial system, tilting as it did to favour one small group, could not uniformly reward the obedient, punish law-breakers or protect the weak.

Throughout his *oeuvre*, Chaucer exhibits a distrust of legal forms and formulas for their failure to provide consistent or predictable results. When the frustrated lover in 'The Complaint unto Pity' combines the amorous complaint with the format of a legal bill (the document used to initiate a formal complaint in court), the legal formulas are met with silence. Embedded in the poem's amorous narrative, the Bill begins with an Address to Pity (ll. 57–63), moves to a briefly stated Statement of Grievance (ll. 64–70), expounds on the resulting hardship (ll. 71–91) and ends with a Prayer for remedy (ll. 92–8), all to no avail. The lover's complaint is not heeded. Similarly, in *The House of Fame* (a dream vision infused with the quotidian discourse of legal terms and protocols), Fama's petitioners are unable to decipher the codes for having their requests addressed, a confusion exemplified by the willy-nilly behaviours at Fama's court.[6] The petitioners' formalised supplications include various kneeling rituals, none of which correspond with either the validity of the petition or Fama's judgement. Despite what seems to be self-evident distinctions to the narrator – to him, some are clearly deserving to have their petitions answered positively, while others are not – the verdicts are uneven. Chaucer's Fama represents a defendant's worst fears, an imprudent and arbitrary judge. With no assurance that the court is following established procedures, the petitioners remain adrift, not knowing what to do next.[7] These two poems mimic how legal formulas cannot ensure the petitioner's desired outcome because they are either ineffective (in 'The Complaint unto Pity') or chaotic (in *The House of Fame*). A similar distrust is betrayed in the frameworks established to contain and control individual narratives of *The Legend of Good Women* and *The Canterbury Tales*. Both reveal Chaucer's ambivalence about the ability of any rigid framework, legal or literary, to sustain a civil society. Such prescriptive frameworks can be ignored, infiltrated, abused, desecrated, amended and appended. Unlike other fourteenth-century observers, Chaucer does not bemoan the frailty of the structures. Indeed, the structure of Harry Bailey's tale-telling contest seems designed to allow for permutations and ruptures, accommodating the evolving plans of the pilgrims, the intrusions of the Canon and his Yeoman and the postmortem additions in the fifteenth and subsequent centuries.[8] As these examples suggest, Chaucer seems aware of how undependable prescriptive frameworks and formulas can be, both open to abuse and failing to provide justice. Rather than argue for their reform, however, he seems to distrust any framework or formula so rigid that it cannot be circumvented in order to accommodate the unexpected and protect the weak.

In his exploration of legal and literary frameworks that can simultaneously resist abuse and allow resistance, Chaucer repeatedly relies on one particular trope: women under assault and with limited legal options and only a handful of extra-legal strategies for defending themselves, such as silence, delay, mercy, death and divine intervention. If Chaucer was particularly attuned to the ways the law constricts and binds a woman's access to justice, it might be because he had witnessed it first-hand. Among the trove of documents composing Chaucer's biography, one stands out for its tawdry implications by recording in Latin the formulaic close rolls entry of Cecily Chaumpaigne's 1380 agreement to release 'Galfrido Chaucer from all charges related to "*de raptu meo*"'.[9] The nineteenth-century discovery of this out-of-court settlement has provoked much consternation among scholars. Initially, the focus was to determine what crime '*de raptu meo*' referred to, whether to abduction or to rape. After nearly a century of denying that Chaucer could be accused of perpetrating such a heinous crime as rape, scholars had by the end of the twentieth century turned to careful semantic analysis of the term '*raptus* in contemporaneous legal documents and determined that, depending on the context, *de raptu meo* could indeed refer to either an abduction or to forced coitus.[10] If, as Sebastian Sobecki has recently suggested, the release is tied to Chaucer's wardship of Edmund Staplegate, then 'de raptu meo' could refer to Chaumpaigne's abduction in the context of arranging for a marriage.[11] Outside this or similar context, however, 'de raptu meo' refers to 'a charge of sexual violation'.[12] While acknowledging that the documentation provides no proof of Chaucer's guilt or innocence, the possibility that 'de raptu meo' could mean 'rape' has led to significant studies examining rape as a recurrent trope and lending important insight into Chaucer's verse.[13]

A more recent source of study has been on be an equally important aspect of the document: Cecily Chaumpaigne's release of all claims against Chaucer (her alleged assailant) and her apparent receipt of £10 in compensation.[14] This release's importance lies less in its possible exoneration of Chaucer of *raptus* and more in how it highlights the legal circumstances that might have compelled her to drop her charges, what those circumstances tell us about a woman's vulnerability to violent coercion, and how they illustrate a woman's limited legal options in late medieval England.[15] Among these legal circumstances would have been Cecily Chaumpaigne's legal status. In most cases, a woman's legal status, *feme covert*, placed her under the control of a legal guardian, who could be her father, brother, husband or other appointed warden. All legal actions conducted in her name were actually overseen by her guardian, who was also liable for her misdeeds. Thus when a woman charged *raptus*, the proceedings would involve not only her and the accused perpetrator but also a third figure, her male guardian. Under four-teenth-century England common law, *raptus* (whether abduction or rape) involving a *feme covert* was defined not as a crime perpetrated against a woman but as a crime that devalued the property of the man who held legal dominion over her. It seems, however, that these constricted legal circumstances would not have applied to Cecily Chaumpaigne, because evidence points to her being a twenty-year-old, unmarried daughter of a baker who had died when she was an infant, giving her legal status of *feme sole*, which allowed her to act without a male guardian. For her, *raptus* would have been a crime perpetrated against her alone.

A second legal circumstance involved the role of consent. At one point, thirteenth-century statutes had linked *raptus* to the question of the woman's consent. If a *feme covert* had not consented to the abduction or sex act, then a crime had been perpetrated against her husband or guardian. If she had consented, the legal situation became murkier because she technically had no legal agency and could not infringe upon her male guardian's finan-cial interests in his control of her sexual purity.[16] Granting her the ability to withdraw from his custody or to consent to sex outside of marriage granted her a legal subjectivity otherwise denied her. A century later, the Statute of Rapes (1382) went a step further, requiring the courts to determine whether or not she given her consent in order to determine her culpability.[17] Thus, when a woman cried 'raptus', she not only had to prove the assault had occurred but also had to convince the court of her absolute lack of consent to the act. If she could not prove that she had *not* consented, then she (along with the accused) could be convicted of a crime against her male guardian. For the *feme sole*, the legal circumstances and her options shift, and the crime would have been against her alone. Despite her status as a *feme sole*, Cecily Chaumpaigne would still have to demonstrate the *raptus* had been perpetrated without her consent.

With these two basic legal circumstances (the woman's legal state and the role of consent) in mind, we can reach two understandings about the 1380 documents releasing Chaucer of all charges. First, if Chaucer either abducted or raped Cecily Chaumpaigne, he would have been aware that her case was unusual in not including an aggrieved third party, her male guardian. Second, if Chaucer were charged and convicted of *raptus*, she could be charged with collusion if it were determined she gave her consent, a barrier notoriously easy to hurdle. Consequently, Cecily Chaumpaigne's withdrawal of the charges suggests neither Chaucer's innocence nor her consent but rather her vulnerability. Whatever she released Chaucer from, her decision could have been based primarily on what she saw as most benefitting her within a range of limited options.

To understand Chaucer's response to this experience, we can examine that combination of legal setting, male aggression and ownership, plus female obedience and vulnerability in four places in *The Canterbury Tales: The Physician's Tale, The Second Nun's Tale, The Man of Law's Tale* and *The Tale of Melibee*. All four feature female litigants with names establishing their purity and innocence: Virginia, Cecilia, Constance and Prudence. All four show the legal system limiting the women's options as they attempt to resolve the legal predicament they have been forced into by male violence. Ultimately, because no options within the legal system seem available, the four tales each propose extra-legal options for resolving or avoiding violent assaults against the women, with the limited utility of each option foregrounded.

The Physician's Tale relates the very limited legal options – first delay and then death at the hands of her father – of a girl (Virginia) on the verge of being abducted from her father (Virginius) through a rigged legal process. The setting, a Roman judge's chambers, very much resembles a fourteenth-century English court. The proceedings are initiated when Apius – unnamed for thirty lines yet labelled a 'justice' or 'juge' who 'jugged' (VI.228) or 'yaf his juggement' (VI.198) six times in that space and another nine times across the remaining 131 lines – allows himself to be bewitched by the beauty of fourteen-year-old Virginia.[18] In order to possess 'this mayde' (VI.129), the judge devises a sham legal hearing, a scheme abetted by both a greedy churl ready to act at the judge's behest and the judge's unchecked power in his court. Their conspiracy requires the churl, Claudius, to bring to Apius's court a formal complaint against Virginius. This counterfeit bill states that Virginia is not Virginius's daughter but a slave stolen from Claudius, who demands she be returned to him. In keeping with the court's deceptive procedures, Claudius's bill follows the standard format of a bill (as Scase details in Chapter 9, this volume). In further keeping with fourteenth-century English procedure, Claudius's complaint alone is not sufficient; Viriginius must be brought forward to answer the claim. After the bill is read to Virginius, he expects (as should be expected in an upright court) the opportunity to respond, to tell 'his tale' and to prove his case, via either trial by battle or bringing forth witnesses. Before Virginius can do either, Apius declares 'his juggement' (VI.193 and 198):

> I deeme anon this cherl his servant have;
> Thou shalt no lenger in thyn hous hir save.
> Go bryng hire forth, and put hire in our warde.
> The cherl shal have his thral, this I awarde.   (VI.199–202)

Virginius sees through this declaration studded with legal terms – 'deeme', 'warde' and 'awarde' – and realises that Apius's false sentence would force him 'his deere doghter [to yive] / Unto the juge in lecherie to liven' (VI.205–6). Rather than submit them both to the false judgement, Virginius beheads Virginia and returns *that* maidenhead to the court. For this transgression (against the judge himself, not the daughter), Apius orders the father hanged, an iniquity which finally rouses the people enough to cast Apius in prison (where he kills himself) and to condemn Claudius to be hanged (before allowing him to be exiled at Virginius's request).

In this tale, the Physician documents the legal system's limited ability to protect the weak against the powerful. While the laws prescribe specific protocols for ensuring justice in Apius's courtroom, the story witnesses the ease with which those protocols succumb to the judge's corrupting desires. In this tale, no courtroom protocol can thwart the wicked, lecherous plans of the 'false juge' (VI.154, 158, 161) who turns his courtroom hearings into staged performances with pre-determined outcomes. Such a system provides no justice. Virginia's sole tactic is delay, and it provides her no long-term relief from either Apius's false judgement or her murder by her father (VI.231–250). Ultimately, though, Apius's reach is limited by the outrage of righteous men who resort to extra-legal manoeuvres. Virginia is kept from Apius's clutch, but the price she pays is her life. Her desires – as well as her life – are made secondary to her father's determination that the only way to preserve her chastity is to kill her. The hue and cry required of rape victims is here transmuted into the clamour of 'a thousand peple' (VI.260) who demand Virginius be saved from the hangman's noose, and the mercy Virginius denied his daughter is extended to Claudius, saving him from execution. This tale, which closes with a series of extra-legal efforts to right wrongs, punish perversion and extend pity, limits those benefits to the men in the story. For the girl, though, there is 'no grace' and 'no remedye' (VI.236). *The Physician's Tale* closes with a moral that focuses on the danger of letting sin infect one's conscience, not on the flaws inherent in a juridical system whose ability to deliver justice depends upon the invulnerability of judges to temptation (VI. 277–86). The tale can illustrate the legal system's short-coming, but its extra-legal solutions are ad hoc, not systemic, and unable to assure justice.

The *Tales'* second Roman courtroom drama, *The Second Nun's Tale*, reconfigures the legal parameters enough to allow its virtuous woman, St. Cecilia, more legal autonomy. This hagiographic story of an early Christian martyr relates her virginal marriage, her subsequent widowhood, her trial before the Roman judge Almachius, and finally her execution. Her widowhood means she is not under any man's control, and she thus handles her trial defence in ways that preserve her interests rather than those of a male guardian. Although she, too, has been beheaded by the tale's end, she (and not a male guardian) has dictated the terms. She achieves this legal autonomy by rejecting the authority of earthly law courts and by relying instead on heavenly justice. Cecilia's recourse to extra-legal principles is anticipated in the Second Nun's prologue, where her '*Invocacio ad Mariam*' – with its references to 'advocate' (VIII.68), 'prison' (VIII.71), and a general plea for compassionate justice – establishes a vivid contrast to the rigged courtrooms of men shown in the tale itself. In heaven, the judgements are singular and certain, unlike on earth, where even simple interpretative enterprises, such as the etymology of Cecilia's name, multiply into uncertainty (VIII.85–119). This heavenly courtroom overseen by a 'rightful Juge' (VIII.389) is a ready contrast to the courtroom of Almachius and its enforcement of an unrighteous and unjust law requiring Christians to choose between sacrificing to 'the ymage of Juppiter' or losing their heads (VIII.364–66). The contrasting heavenly courtroom so closely hovers over the scene of the tale's first trial (of Cecilia's husband and brother-in-law) that one onlooker, Maximus, claims '[t]hat he hir soules saugh to hevene glyde / With aungels ful of cleernesse and of light' (VIII.402–3). When Cecilia is then brought to Almachius's court, she is subjected to a trial that she turns into a confession of faith, a tactic resembling one used in later Lollard trials in which the accused heretic answers by questioning the legitimacy of the question and the principles on which the court operates.[19] When Almachius has finally been overcome by Cecilia's intractable faith and relentless argumentation, he falls into a wrathful fit and orders her slain. The executioner's three strokes, however, fail to cleave her head from her neck. The law forbids a fourth stroke (so we are told), and she is left half dead (VIII.529–33). When the executioner stands by the letter of the law and refuses to go beyond it, he and the law he enforces unwittingly become agents of a divine justice that allows her to control her defence and the final settlement of her worldly goods.[20] This courtroom scene concurs with the story of Virginia and shows that earthly justice is unavailable to women, no matter their virtues. It does suggest, however, that a woman, who is not limited by the constraints of her male guardian's desires, can seek out her own extra-legal measures and thereby access a divine justice that overshadows earthly injustice.

The Man of Law, the pilgrim tale-teller who might be most expected to set a tale inside an English common-law courtroom, instead places his heroine's treacherous encounters at royal courts from Syria to Northumberland, all at a time before either ecclesiastical or common laws had a firm hold in England. Because the multiple episodes each involve a king, God's earthly agent for delivering justice, each tribulation becomes a figurative trial testing Constance's constancy, or rather her identity as 'constant'. One if these scenes resembles a courtroom trial (II.610–89). Here, she faces charges of murdering her companion, Hermengyld. Her accuser, a knight of standing in king Alla's court, proffers both his spoken testimony and a bloody knife as evidence. Constance, mute and pale, has only her moral purity and good repute ('the peple ... seyn they kan not gesse' how she could do such a thing [II.621–23]), neither one sufficient to counter the false evidence. The tale's audience knows that the knight is the murderer and that the murder and set-up were provoked by Constance's rejection of the knight's sexual advances. This audience might know her innocence, but it can also recognise that the evidence is stacked against her. In an impromptu courtroom scene, Alla the king must deal with two sets of contradictory evidence. First there is the evidence against Constance. The knight provides sworn testimony, a form of evidence (along with written documents such as deeds, letters, contracts, writs, and grants) that provided the primary mode of legal evidence in medieval England. His sworn testimony is supplemented by the mute material object, the bloody knife, which the knight claims can stand in for events and motives otherwise unknown. Not limited to symbolic or metaphoric meanings, it asserts a specific relationship between itself, an event, and others involved in the event.[21] That is, the knife is no longer a symbol of treachery or a metaphor for deceit; instead, it is the visible evidence of a crime as well as a witness to who committed the crime. Until it is not. The 'bloody knyf', like the knight's sworn testimony, has been manipulated and cannot help discern the truth.[22] Suspicious of the knight's story and bloody knife, the king turns to an ancient form of evidence, the oath. He orders the knight to swear on a Bible that Constance is guilty. At the instant of his oath, he is smitten by the hand of God, in 'sighte of every body in that place' (II.672). Of all the forms of evidence, only the oath, an ancient method 'designed to harness the word of God as testimony of legal truth', delivers an accurate testimony and supports Constance's uncontesting silence.[23] Although all forms of terrestrial evidence are found wanting, vulnerable to manipulation and fraud, Constance's innocence is determined by divine intervention, and she is saved from execution.

The fourth courtroom tale, *The Tale of Melibee*, again adjudicates the constraints limiting women's autonomy by placing an assaulted woman, Prudence, in a juridical space and allowing her to speak, momentarily, in terms that favour her judicial wishes over those of her husband. One of the two tales told in the voice of pilgrim-Chaucer as his own contribution to the tale-telling contest, the tale opens with a crime against Prudence and her daughter: Melibee's three 'olde foes' ... 'betten his wyf and wounded his doghter with fyve mortal woundes in fyve sondry places' (VII.970–971). From the beginning, the crime against the two women is reconfigured as a crime against Melibee, the husband and father of the victims. His first impulse – and that of his male advisors – is to seek vengeance. Prudence, assuming the role of prudent wisdom frequently allocated to women in medieval allegory, advocates a different course. She begins, like Cecilia, to look to divine justice by reminding Melibee that 'God which that is ful of justice and of rightwisnesse' (VII.1407) has let this happen. The righteous can turn to earthly judges, who have 'the jurisdiccion' to take 'vengeance' and 'punysse hem as the lawe axeth and requireth' (VII.1441–42). Or the righteous can wait for the divine Judge who 'vengeth all vileynyes and wronges' (VII.1455–58). Unable to take personal vengeance and forced to wait for either juridical or divine retribution, she continues, the affronted should make peace with their enemies through a mediator, a role she volunteers to provide (VII.1719–20).

Though momentarily accepted by Melibee, Prudence's solution is quickly transformed so that her husband's roles as prosecutor and judge are affirmed. Prudence's mediation convinces Melibee's enemies to come 'to the court', and Melibee assumes the role of attorney and judge, laying out their misdeeds and their deserved punishment, 'deeth' (VII.1807 & 1810). Then, directly contravening Prudence's advice, he gives them the option of putting 'the punyssement and the chastisynge and the vengeance of this outrage in the wyl of me and of my wyf Prudence' (VII.1811–14). After they admit their guilt and give themselves over to his judgement, Melibee adjourns the court, a hiatus that allows Prudence to ask what he proposes to do. His plan – 'I thynke and purpose me fully / to desherite hem of al that evere they han and for to utte hem in exil for evere' (VII.1834–35) – is somewhat more benign than death, but, as Prudence asserts, it cannot assure Melibee and his people a long-standing peace. Eventually, she convinces Melibee to forgive his enemies as God has forgiven humankind (VII.1878–83). Melibee accepts and follows (in a modified form) Prudence's counsel in a way that allows him to reassert his legal authority by making himself the judge who offers mercy, an extra-legal prerogative that Chaucer and his contemporaries had seen King Richard II wield erratically in pursuit of political advantage rather than disinterested justice.[24] The tale ends with Melibee's dispensing mercy, without letting us know if his adversaries accept his mercy, if they remain in Melibee's good graces, or if Melibee is able truly to forgive and forget. Because Melibee repeatedly transforms Prudence's advice into justifications that reassert the old ways, her legal destiny remains limited to his husband's desire for retribution against his enemies.

   With these four tales of virtuous women undone or ignored by the established legal systems, *The Canterbury Tales* presents bleak prospects for a woman's ability to turn to the land's law courts for justice as long as she remains under the control of a male guardian. A rebuke to this bleak prospect comes from an unsurprising voice, the Wife of Bath. Neither quiet nor virtuous and flaunting a name – Alisoun – that points to no noble virtue, the Wife of Bath exploits the bind that being legal property places women in. In her prologue, the Wife of Bath uses legal concepts of property (those dealing with objects both inanimate and animate, including wives) to make 'her husbands liable for her own misdeeds', a maneuver that the Wife can make because her husbands (and the law) deem her incapable of holding legal responsibility.[25] The Wife exploits the paradoxical fact that at the same time a wife was legally the same person as her husband and had no legal personhood apart from her husband, she was also capable of acting outside her husband's wishes, thereby forcing him to decide whether or not to take responsibility for her actions.[26] Like the biting dogs and working oxen she compares herself to, she can act against the best interests of her 'owner'. The Wife of Bath's dramatic monologue becomes in this context an extended legal plaint establishing her strategy for subverting the very laws that would bind her (III.235–378). Rather than look to extra-legal means for reducing her vulnerability, she embraces the legal principles that reduce her to the status of property and thereby absolves herself of any blame for her infractions against her husband. As the Wife demonstrates, women's 'metaphorical status as "bodies" subject to husbands as rational "heads" gives them, ironically, the power to revoke certain kinds of contracts'.[27] In the Wife's performance, Chaucer seems to show how a woman can circumvent a legal system designed to limit her.[28] By embracing the paradoxical aspects of consent, a woman can transform a principle that condemns a woman to the status of property so that it liberates her. Like the Wife, she might 'han the governance of hous and lond' (III.814) turned over to her by her husband. Or she might, as Cecily Chaumpaigne seems to have done, collect her aggressor's £10 fine, an amount comparable to the price of a London house.[29]

When Chaucer places good, virtuous women in situations where the legal system fails to deliver justice, where only extra-legal interference provides a suitable resolution to their troubles, he seems to be pointing to the corruptions endemic to any system that grants a husband, father, or guardian the legal right to circulate or use the women under their dominion without regard for the women's wishes. His experiences in and out of the common-law courts of fourteenth-century England had taught him to be on the watch for the disobedient woman who chooses to give or withhold consent as she pleases.

Notes

1. Martin M. Crow and Clair C. Olson, eds., *Chaucer Life-Records* (Austin, TX: University of Texas Press, 1966), 12, n. 5.
2. Ruth Evans, 'Chaucer's Life', in *Chaucer: An Oxford Guide*, ed. Steve Ellis (Oxford: Oxford University Press, 2005), 9.
3. Crow and Olson, *Chaucer Life-Records*, 356.
4. Derek Pearsall, *Chaucer* (Oxford and New York: Blackwell, 1992), 30.
5. Joseph Allen Hornsby, *Chaucer and the Law* (Norman, OK: Pilgrim Books, 1988); Joseph Allen Hornsby, '"A Sergeant of the Lawe, War and Wyse"', in *Chaucer's Pilgrims: An Historical Guide to the Pilgrims in* The Canterbury Tales, ed. Laura C. Lambdin and Robert T. Lambdin (Westport, CT: Greenwood Press, 1996), 116–34.
6. Mary Flowers Braswell, *Chaucer's 'Legal Fiction': Reading the Records* (Cranbury, NJ: Fairleigh Dickinson University Press, 2001), 49–66.
7. Jennifer Hough, '"On Kneys I Knelyt and Mercy Culd Implore": An Examination of Kneeling in Relation to Emotions Experienced at Law', New Chaucer Society Congress, 14 July 2016.
8. Robert J. Meyer-Lee, 'Abandon the Fragments', *Studies in the Age of Chaucer* 35 (2013), 47–83.
9. Crow and Olson, *Chaucer Life-Records*, 343.
10. Christopher Cannon, '*Raptus* in the Chaumpaigne Release and a Newly Discovered Document Concerning the Life of Geoffrey Chaucer', *Speculum* 68: 1 (1993), 74–94; Christopher Cannon, 'Chaucer and Rape: Uncertainty's Certainties', in *Representing Rape in Medieval and Early Modern Literature*, ed. Elizabeth Robertson and Christine M. Rose (New York: Palgrave Macmillan,

2001), 255–79; Henry Ansgar Kelly, 'Meanings and Uses of *Raptus* in Chaucer's Time', *Studies in the Age of Chaucer* 20 (1998), 101–65.

11. Sebastian Sobecki, 'Wards and Widows: *Troilus and Criseyde* and New Documents on Chaucer's Life', *ELH*, forthcoming.

12. Kelly, 'Meanings and Uses of *Raptus* in Chaucer's Time', 101.

13. Christine M. Rose, 'Reading Chaucer Reading Rape', in *Representing Rape in Medieval and Early Modern Literature*, ed. Elizabeth Robertson and Christine M. Rose (New York: Palgrave Macmillan, 2001), 23–60.

14. Kelly, 'Meanings and Uses of *Raptus* in Chaucer's Time'.

15. Christopher Cannon, 'The Lives of Geoffrey Chaucer', in *The Yale Companion to Chaucer*, ed. Seth Lerer (New Haven, CT: Yale University Press, 2006), 41.

16. Cannon, 'Chaucer and Rape: Uncertainty's Certainties', 260.

17. Cannon, 'Chaucer and Rape: Uncertainty's Certainties', 261.

18. All Chaucerian references are taken from Larry Benson, ed. *Riverside Chaucer*, 3rd edn (Boston: Houghton Mifflin, 1987).

19. Andrew Cole, *Literature and Heresy in the Age of Chaucer* (Cambridge: Cambridge University Press, 2008), 3–22; Jamie Taylor, *Fictions of Evidence: Witnessing, Literature, and Community in the Late Middle Ages* (Columbus, OH: The Ohio State University Press, 2013), ch. 5.

20. Nicola Masciandaro, 'Half Dead: Parsing Cecelia', in *Dark Chaucer: An Assortment*, ed. Myra J. Seaman, Eileen Joy and Nicola Masciandaro (Brooklyn, NY: Punctum Books, 2012), 71ff.

21. Bill Brown, 'Thing Theory', *Critical Inquiry* 28:1 (2001), 4.

22. Taylor, *Fictions of Evidence*, 25–6 and 28.

23. Taylor, *Fictions of Evidence*, 44.

24. Andrew Galloway, 'The Literature of 1388 and the Politics of Pity in Gower's *Confessio Amantis*', in *The Letter of the Law: Legal Practice and Literary Production in Medieval England*, ed. Emily Steiner and Candace Barrington (Ithaca, NY: Cornell University Press, 2002), 67–104.

25. Jeanne Provost, 'Vital Property in *The Wife of Bath's Prologue and Tale*', *Studies in the Age of Chaucer* 38 (2016), 72.

26. Kathleen E. Kennedy, *Maintenance, Meed, and Marriage in Medieval English Literature* (New York: Palgrave Macmillan, 2009), 32.

27. Provost, 'Vital Property in *The Wife of Bath's Prologue and Tale*', 62.

28. For forms of 'rape justice' in the Wife's tale, see Carissa Harris, 'Rape and Justice in *The Wife of Bath's Tale*', in *The Open Access Companion to* The Canterbury Tales, ed. Candace Barrington, Brantley Bryant, Richard Godden, Daniel T. Kline, and Myra Seaman (2017), https://opencanterburytales.dsl.lsu.edu/wobt1/.

29. Cannon, 'The Lives of Geoffrey Chaucer', 41.

Further Reading

Cannon, Christopher, 'Chaucer and Rape: Uncertainty's Certainties', in *Representing Rape in Medieval and Early Modern Literature*, ed. Elizabeth Robertson and Christine M. Rose, New York: Palgrave Macmillan, 2001, 255–79.

'The Lives of Geoffrey Chaucer', in *The Yale Companion to Chaucer*, ed. Seth Lerer, New Haven, CT: Yale University Press, 2006, 31–54.

'*Raptus* in the Chaumpaigne Release and a Newly Discovered Document Concerning the Life of Geoffrey Chaucer', *Speculum* 68:1 (1993), 74–94.

Hornsby, Joseph Allen, *Chaucer and the Law*, Norman, OK: Pilgrim Books, 1988.

Kelly, Henry Ansgar, 'Meanings and Uses of *Raptus* in Chaucer's Time', *Studies in the Age of Chaucer* 20 (1998), 101–65.

Kennedy, Kathleen E., *Maintenance, Meed, and Marriage in Medieval English Literature*, New York: Palgrave Macmillan, 2009.

Provost, Jeanne, 'Vital Property in *The Wife of Bath's Prologue and Tale*', *Studies in the Age of Chaucer* 38 (2016), 39–74.

Rose, Christine M., 'Reading Chaucer Reading Rape', in *Representing Rape in Medieval and Early Modern Literature*, ed. Elizabeth Robertson and Christine M. Rose, New York: Palgrave Macmillan, 2001, 23–60.

Sobecki, Sebastian, 'Wards and Widows: Troilus and Criseyde and New Documents on Chaucer's Life', *ELH*, forthcoming.

Taylor, Jamie, *Fictions of Evidence: Witnessing, Literature, and Community in the Late Middle Ages*, Columbus, OH: Ohio State University Press, 2013.

12

R. F. YEAGER

John Gower

Conventional wisdom holds 1330 to be the year the English poet John Gower was born, following a line of speculation that he was older than his friend and fellow poet Geoffrey Chaucer, whose birth traditionally has been assigned to 1340. No contemporary records are known to exist to confirm either date, for either man, however – and as is not the case with Chaucer, no accounts at all have surfaced to shed light on Gower's early life. Lacking firm evidence to the contrary, and for a variety of circumstantial reasons, his birthdate is perhaps better set a bit later, between 1335 and 1340. Most likely John Gower hailed from armigerous gentry, with lands in Kent. His father – or more plausibly, the poet's uncle – may have been one Sir Robert Gower (d. 1349), buried in Brabourne, south-east Kent – a township where John Gower also owned property, at least in his later years.[1] Armorial blazons on a manuscript of Gower's Latin poems *Vox Clamantis* and *Cronica Tripertita* match both one on the poet's tomb, preserved in Southwark Cathedral, and those of Sir Robert Gower; another indication of the poet's Kentish origins are the many Kentish dialectal elements present in the language of his English poetry.[2] If Sir Robert Gower was indeed John Gower's father, the family also possessed properties in Suffolk and East Anglia along with Kent, and probably had landed relations in Yorkshire as well.[3]

In any case, John Gower's educational achievements alone imply a background of sufficient, if untitled, means. Whether that education included formal legal training cannot be answered firmly. Early editors and biographers seized upon a first-person reference to dressing in striped sleeves in Gower's Anglo-French poem the *Mirour de l'Omme* (MO) to extrapolate a career in the law courts, rayed sleeves being a common uniform of lawmen.[4] How seriously the lines can be taken as autobiographical evidence of Gower's legal career remains an open question, however. Commonly quoted in excerpt, they nonetheless are part of a single sentence that extends for twelve lines – a full stanza – and are best considered in their larger context:

Mais s'aucun m'en soit au travers,
Et la sentence de mes vers
Voldra blamer de malvuillance,
Pour ce que je ne suy pas clers,
Vestu de sanguine ne de pers,
Ainz ai vestu la raye mance,
Poi sai latin, poy sai romance,
Mais l commune tesmoignance
Du poeple m'ad fait tout apers
A dire, que du fole errance
Les clercs don vous ai fait parlance
Encore son tils plus divers.   (MO 21,769–80)[5]

In addition to the standard difficulty of equating any medieval authorial 'I' with a 'real-life' author, the passage complicates such a reading in other ways, as well.[6] In the *Mirour*, the stanza in which it appears (above) concludes a segment critical of friars, which is itself the final subsection of more than 3,000 lines devoted not to the courts but to 'l'estat de ceux qui se nomont gens du sainte eglise' ('the estate of those called the people of Holy Church').[7] The context thus suggests an ecclesiastical allusion, not a legal one. In addition, the line 'Vestu de sanguine ne de pers' is best translated 'clothed [neither] in red nor in blue-black/purple', that is, not *one* bicolored garment but *two*, one red and one blue-purple.[8] At this point in the *Mirour*, one surmises that Gower's reference is more likely to ecclesiastical garments – a cardinal's red robe, possibly to blue and/or plum chasubles sometimes worn by celebrants of high mass.[9] Given Gower's overall criticism of avaricious churchmen of all types in this section, the intent of his comparison here would seem to be to contrast the peccant sumptuousness of Caesarian clergy with the humbler civilian garment – possibly a livery – worn by the narrator.[10]

Circumstantial evidence does suggest, however, that Gower had, in whatever fashion, acquainted himself with at least some aspects of the law, in particular those legal areas pertaining to real and moveable property. Such evidence is of three kinds: 1) documentation of significant purchase and sale of manor lands from 1365 (in fact, the earliest extant record of Gower's life known) through the early 1380s;[11] 2) Chaucer's conveyance of power of attorney to Gower and to one Richard Forester, a known attorney, when Chaucer travelled to Italy in 1378, implying his trust in his friend's legal capabilities;[12] 3) Gower's carefully prepared will, detailing distribution of his monies, chattels and lands primarily to his wife, but also to a few other named individuals, and to charity.[13]

In the first case, one land purchase is particularly noteworthy for the light it casts – or the shadow – on Gower's legal capabilities. The manor of Aldington Septvauns, in north Kent, acquired from an under-age heir by Gower and certain partners, possibly through manipulation of the young man, brought investigation by the Crown (and rather self-righteous condemnation from one or two late nineteenth-century readers).[14] Sharp dealing or no, from a purely legal point of view Gower's participation in the so-called 'Septvauns affair' suggests that his understanding of property laws in the Court of Chancery was considerable. Such knowledge seemingly stood him in good stead: Gower alone of the initial purchasing group of Aldington Septvauns was ultimately vindicated, and allowed to keep his portion of the property.[15] Subsequently he obtained the rest of the property once belonging to Septvauns, before passing title in 1373 to another consortium, headed by John, Lord Cobham.[16]

The case of Chaucer's power of attorney is similarly suggestive, since certainly Chaucer had ample choice of legal experts among his acquaintance to choose from other than Gower in 1378, as by then Chaucer's career as a royal courtier and civil servant had blossomed. Certainly the other named representative, Richard Forester, was a seasoned practitioner, quite able, from all accounts, of handling any legal issues likely to arise in the administration of the absent Chaucer's affairs.[17] Forester's capability has thus led some to assume that Gower's expected role was extra-legal, something like a literary executor. However, the intriguing suggestion has recently been offered that, since very little of Chaucer's currently extant poetry is thought to have been circulating in 1378, he and Gower were unlikely to have shared a poetic acquaintance so early – and that therefore their relationship at that time was likely 'professional in nature'.[18]

And in the third case, of his will: in 1408, when Gower died, written wills were relatively unusual, even among royalty, and among propertied Londoners were only starting to become the norm.[19] Common law usage, applied in the Court of Hustings, where wills were processed and recorded, divided the deceased's property into thirds: one to the widow, one to the children (not applicable in Gower's case), and the third, known as the 'dead man's part', was to be used for charitable purposes. Distribution was in the hands of an 'ordinary', in most cases a bishop.[20] Separate conditions developed for real property and for chattels, and varied by location. Household goods and other movables, such as jewellery, generally could be awarded to the widow. Frequently, rather than deeding actual lands, widows would be left sums of money, supplemented by the income from real estate owned by the husband. It was customary for precise provision for the widow – known as the dower, counterpart to the bride's dowry – to be made at the time of marriage, as the husband's part of the contract. Terms of the dowry and dower would have been set down in pre-nuptial documents, their legitimacy attested to by seal. Their details, however, would often surface in the will.[21]

Viewed in historical and social context, Gower's will has little to tell us about either his legal sophistication or activities. Although a generation earlier a man like Gower would likely not have made one, by 1400 the practice of leaving a will by propertied individuals was becoming more common among wealthy London bourgeoisie. His contemporaries William Walworth, John Northampton – both former mayors – Nicholas Exton and John Philippot, all made wills.[22] Moreover, 'although there were no necessary forma clauses' required of wills by the Hustings Court, something akin to a template was emerging, and Gower's will follows this closely.[23] That his will was proved at Lambeth Palace, by the archbishop of Canterbury (and not William of Wykeham, whose bishopric included Southwark), was, as Macaulay noted, standard procedure, 'because the testator had property in more than one diocese of the province of Canterbury'.[24] One item of potential interest, if only incidentally informative about Gower's legal acumen, is the confirmation of his bequest to his wife, Agnes, of the rents from two properties, 'as he has more fully determined in certain other writings given under his seal': there was, apparently, a dower pre-determined and officially documented at the time of his marriage.[25]

Beyond these facts and speculations, as many have noticed, there is nevertheless a demonstrable interest in the law and its practitioners, and an obvious easiness in the use of legal terminology apparent in Gower's work. This in itself is less unusual for the period than it has seemed in more recent times. Legal language offered speakers of English and Anglo-French like Gower and his contemporaries a kind of 'parallel discourse'.[26] Gower is, however, notably unique among all writers of his period – indeed, of any period, including the present – in that he wrote major poetry, about 30,000 lines each, in Anglo-French, Latin and English, the three salient languages of his place and time. That he did so purposefully, with an eye towards posthumous fame, is apparent from the tomb, likely of his own design, in Southwark Cathedral where the head of his effigy rests upon the trilingual volumes of his three greatest works, the *Mirour de l'Omme* in French, the *Vox Clamantis* in Latin and the *Confessio Amantis* in Middle English, the language of its title notwithstanding.[27] Gower also left lesser, but altogether important, poetry: the *Cronica Tripertita* in Latin, 'To King Henry IV In Praise of Peace' in English, a body of shorter Latin pieces and two groups of balades in Anglo-French, the *Traitié pour essampler les amantz marietz* and the *Cinkante Balades*. There is also, in addition to these works unquestionably by Gower, a Latin poem, 'Eneidos bucolis', present in five manuscripts of Gower's verse, in the production of two of which he may have had a hand.[28] The poem favourably compares Gower's trilingual *oeuvre* with Virgil's Latin, and while addressing him in the third person, very likely is by Gower himself.[29] Along with his self-representation on his tomb, and the unusually uniform care with which many of his manuscripts were prepared, 'Eneidos bucolis' attests to Gower's powerful identification with, and understanding of, his role – and hoped-for perpetual stature as – a poet comparable to classical *auctores*. Their greatness, Gower clearly believed, was intimately connected to their conscious particularity with language.

Such staking of a claim to be a modern *auctor* heavily underscores the importance of acknowledging terms and concepts in Gower's poetry borrowed from the law. The prominence in his writing in all three languages of legal vocabulary, and a not-infrequent quasi-legal presentation of narrative material, have seemed strong proof to many of Gower's careful study of the law, at least, if not evidence in fact of his direct practice of it.[30] Yet the problem first raised by Macaulay, that 'the statement of Leland that he practised as a lawyer seems rather improbable, in view of the way in which he ... speaks of lawyers and their profession', remains a vexing one, resiliently resisting easy reconciliation.[31]

Nowhere in his *oeuvre* is Gower's criticism of legal institutions stronger than in the *Mirour de l'Omme*, often considered Gower's initial poetic venture.[32] Certainly it was begun soonest of his known work, parts seemingly written perhaps as early as 1365 (tellingly, perhaps, amid the Septvauns litigation), although some argue for a date of composition a decade later. Gower was an inveterate reviser, however, and it is likely he returned to the *Mirour* several times before drawing it to a close not long after Richard II ascended the throne in 1377.[33] Such habits render precise chronology very difficult. Gower devotes over four hundred lines (24,181–625) to a scathing description of how greedy lawyers bend – or even break – the law to win cases for rich clients while turning a deaf ear to those who cannot pay high fees, choosing to prey upon the poor instead of defending them in their helplessness. A shorter, but equally damning exposure of the judiciary follows (24,625–816), and then of corrupt sheriffs, bailiffs and jurors who accept bribes (24,817–25,176). Gower's anger, however, is not at the law itself, which he describes (24,601–2) as 'juste et pure / Et liberal de sa nature' ('just and pure, and liberal by nature'), but invariably (24,603–5) 'cils qui sont la loy gardant / La pervertont et font obscure, / Si la vendont a demesure' ('those who maintain the law pervert it and obscure it, even sell it at an outrageous price').

These same sentiments – that the law is blameless, but not the corrupt practitioners – crop up again in Book VI of Gower's major Latin poem, the

Vox Clamantis (ll. 237–8); for example, 'Est bona lex in se fateor, tamen eius inique / Rectores video flectere iura modo' ('I acknowledge that the law itself is good, but I see its wicked masters now bending justice'). Indeed, the first 469 lines of the *Vox* Book VI are devoted to the same savaging of lawyers, judges and court officials found in the *Mirour*, and for identical reasons.[34] Because this Book of the *Vox* probably was composed for the most part prior to 1381, and at least a decade after his earlier critique of lawyers and legal institutions in the *Mirour*, it would thus seem to indicate a sustained opinion of Gower's, rather than merely a temporarily jaundiced response to an awkward period in the courts.[35]

On balance, then, the sum of evidence would suggest that Gower acquired his knowledge of the law as 'a litigant, but never [as] a lawyer'.[36] Indeed, his comparative success in the Septvauns case required careful navigating through the Chancery Court, a rather unorthodox approach; but while clearly the wisest course, nothing in the record confirms that the thinking behind it belonged exclusively to Gower *solo*. With the means to buy property, he also could afford good counsel if, as likely, the purchase had presented itself to him as a 'sticky wicket'.[37] Similarly, Chaucer's delegation of power of attorney to Gower and to Forester, a lawyer of some reputation, does not in itself reveal what lay behind Chaucer's interest in Gower's participation. It may, as has been speculated, have been requested one poet to another, to care for whatever writings Chaucer may have had at the time, but as Sobecki has noted, the date seems premature for either Gower or Chaucer to have known of each other's poetry. A more likely motive would therefore appear to be Gower's recognised skill as a successful buyer and seller of real property, something that by 1378 Gower might easily have learned through multiple transactions, not unlike the way an experienced real-estate agent today understands the legal ins and outs of property purchases and sales. In this regard the vindicating outcome of the Septvauns case, widely known in London due to its deliberation in parliament, would have burnished, rather than marred, his reputation among contemporaries such as Chaucer, the way it has in more recent times.[38] (Parenthetically it is perhaps noteworthy that Chaucer acted himself as one of several attorneys appointed by one Gregory Ballard to take seisin of lands on his behalf, in 1396.[39])

Ultimately, then, more interesting than the existence of any professional legal career are Gower's attitudes to the law itself. This is an entirely different question, and an important one. The examples from the *Mirour* and the *Vox Clamantis*, noted above, demonstrate that Gower's ire was focused on lawyers who abused the law for their own gain, and not with the conceptual framework of law *simpliciter*. The point seems immediately obvious, but nonetheless requires some clarification. Gower applied 'lawe' to a range of circumstances, which can be illustrated with reference to the *Confessio Amantis* (*CA*). Some usages currently retain the same linguistic force, others do not, having traversed over time from what, for Gower, abutted on the actual, to what today is primarily metaphoric, regulation. Universally applied, but unwritten, 'laws' such as the 'lawe of kinde' (*CA* II. 3275) or the 'lawe of charite' (*CA* Pro. 257) are cases in point: Gower, who understood these as established by God, defers to them directly, as binding in human affairs, even as their codification defies possibility.[40] The 'lawe of Moïses' (*CA* V. 6967), 'Cristes lawe' (*CA* II. 769), both contained in 'the Bible, in which the lawe is closed' (*CA* IV. 2655), he of course employs in the same way – as emanations of the infallible omnipotence of God. A second category of universals exists as well. The fact that 'tholde lawe' – that is, the Old Testament – (*CA* V. 7007) is term-limited and subject to supersession by 'the newe lawe' (*CA* II. 3432) – that is, Christ's law – nevertheless marks out their mutual difference from the universal and unchanging laws, such as of 'kinde' or of 'charite', both of which apply continuously from the Creation. These and similar universals, which for Gower were as 'lawful' as we today hold gravity, provide a valuable working parallel – *mutatis mutandis* – to a third, non-universal but related category: the impermanent and variable laws created by man in the processes of government.

These that man makes can be either 'goode lawe' (*CA* VII. 3006) or 'false lawes' (*CA* V. 1466), the latter of two distinct types. Laws at first 'goode' can become 'false' when conditions change that necessitated their establishment. Most of Gower's specific discussions of derivations of Mosaic law – for example, degrees of consanguinity permitting marriage – are of this sort, their original validity having been superseded by wider spousal availability and/or vacated with the advent of Christ. Their proper purview being canon law, however, and Gower's legalistic interests lying primarily elsewhere, he is generally content merely to acknowledge these changes and move on. There are a few exceptions, notably generated by the Schism. As a category they are germane. Because their motivation is human rapacity for wealth and/or power, edicts issued by a schismatic church brightly illuminate for Gower the nature of 'false lawe' at its worst. The 'lawes' of Avignon are thus potentially more damaging than heresy – even than lollardy – to the degree that they command obedience, on false threat of damnation.[41] The second sort of 'false lawe', then, is knowingly enacted with intent to do wrong. It is coercive and, most often, extractive; and in the political sphere represents both a sign and a result of tyranny.

'Justice' is a profounder creature altogether for Gower, at once simpler, and yet more complex. His understanding of it follows two eventually convergent tracks. One is that justice is synonymous with equity. The importance of this idea for the Middle Ages cannot be overstressed; it appears near-ubiquitously in multiple sources Gower knew, and he repeats it many times in every major work – for example, in the *Confessio Amantis* (VII. 2816): 'do justice and equite'.[42] 'To do justice', understood in this simpler sense, is humanly possible, and in most quotidian circumstances it should be equivalent to 'doing the law', if and when those caretakers of the law, from the king to the lowest bailiff, act rightly.

But justice in Gower's thought is also ultimately a deeper, even a mysterious, concept, outstripping ordinary human reach. We see this clearly in other verbal pairings Gower makes with it: 'such grace and such justice' (*CA* I. 3318); 'for love and for justice' (*CA* VII. 3014). 'Grace' and 'love' – like 'equite' itself – are attributes of God, and/or of 'God-in-man', which is to say, of Christ. It is a semantic connection that Gower regularly affirms directly: 'The hihe god of his justice' (*CA* I. 2778; III. 2251); 'And telle hou god of his justice' (*CA* V. 4918). The most telling – and common – pairings with 'justice' in Gower's parlance, however, are 'mercy' and 'Pite', the latter in the sense of 'compassion', rather than 'piety', with which meaning it alternates in all three of Gower's languages. 'Thi merci medle with justice' (*CA* I. 3014); 'To speke of justice and Pite' (*CA* VII. 3809) are examples. Further, if assessed transitively (in the mathematical sense; that is to say: 'a=b, b=c, thus a=c'), such examples as these are extendable: 'Do mercy forth with rihtwisnesse' (*CA* I. 2936); 'Of rihtwisnesse and of pite' (*CA* V. 1738); 'Of Pite forth with rihtwisnesse' (*CA* VII. 4206). 'Justice' and 'rihtwisnesse' in Gower's parlance were interchangeable synonyms – a recognition that identifies the broader nexus concatenating Gower's legal thought. It follows that 'truth' is a connected concept as well: 'Fulfild of trouthe and rihtwisnesse' (*CA* VII. 3917); 'Thurgh the verray trowthe of rihtwisnesse' (*CA* VII. 1959); and also 'And pes, which rihtwisnesse keste' (*CA* Pro. 109).

'Grace', 'love', 'equite', 'mercy', 'pite', 'trouthe', 'pes': evidently in Gower's mind an invocation of 'justice' and 'rihtwisnesse' opens out into the realm of theology.[43] Examples such as 'The hihe god of his justice' (*CA* I. 2778; III. 2251), set against 'To thing which god in lawe of kinde' (*CA* I. 31) and 'Which god hath sette be lawe of kinde' (*CA* I. 2231) suggest Gower's distinction between 'justice' as an attribute of God – hence immutable and timeless – and 'lawe' as created entity, whether directly by God or secondarily, by human beings. Even at its highest level, 'lawe' is applicable to the physical – but not the spiritual – world. In this Gower is a good Augustinian. The evident trajectory of 'justice' in Gower's parlance parallels Augustine's elevation of divine justice as the governing medium in the City of

God over the legal system, contrived by human reason, laid out by Cicero, in both *De Legibus* and *De Re Publica*, the latter of which *De Civitate Dei* was largely written to dismantle and replace.[44] The Augustinian consistency of Gower's thought thus suggests, on one level at least, that his concept of 'justice' may have been most nurtured, not in the Inns, but rather grown out of a deep study of the writings of Augustine that characterises Gower's worldview generally.[45]

Reading the poetry through an Augustinian lens helps make visible how Gower separates 'lawe' from 'justice'. For this purpose, the *Cronica Tripertita* (*CT*), with its focus on the fall of one king and the rise of another, is an especially rich source. It opens with King Richard busily creating 'law':

> Leges conduxit, pro parte suaque reduxit.
> Munere corrupti suadente timoreque rupti
> Legis in errorem regi tribuere favorem;
> Hii tunc legiste, quicquid rex dixerat iste,
> Federa component, que sigilla sub ordine ponunt.
>
> (*CT* I. 28–32)[46]

Striking here is the raw statement of how easily the outward appearance of legal procedures can be counterfeited: in accord with the king's will, laws can be manufactured, judges can be hired or intimidated, seals on documents – affixed as official confirmation of the legitimacy of their contents – can be forged. That a tyrant can shape the law to suit himself reveals, not merely the tyrant's nature, but also the fundamental problem Gower perceived as inherent in the law itself: it can be followed to an unjust conclusion. The first two parts of the *Cronica* are centred on Richard, portraying his villainies largely in legal terms – as perverse manipulations of English law. Indeed, because he has corrupted it so thoroughly and made it his creature, Richard the man's blatant dishonesties link him inseparably with the *idea* of law, the law as he has vitiated it: his and the law's failings, as a product corruptible by corrupt men, become synonymous.

Bolingbroke's return from exile in part three, however, brings an abrupt shift from the law to justice. In the *Cronica* the most common adjectives describing Henry and each of his initial acts as new monarch are 'iustus' and 'pius', the latter in this context oscillating between its dual meanings of 'pious' and 'merciful'.[47] The *Cronica* is of course primarily a triumph of bespoke Lancastrian propaganda, in which the brute fact of Henry's usurpation is glossed over as ordained by God: 'Predesintauit deus illum quem titulauit / Vt rex regnaret sua regnaque iustificaret' ('He whom God now proclaimed by Him was preordained / To rule his realm in justice and as king to reign' (*CT* III. 318–19)). What should not be overlooked, despite its propagandistic intensity, is that Gower's mechanism for structuring his poem is the radical division between, on the one hand, Richard and the law (and subsequently Satan), and God, Henry and justice, on the other. For the kingdom to function this division between the merely legal and the truly just must be re-conjoined in the person of the king, no less than the sundered population must be harmoniously reunited. In the *Cronica*'s closing verses, Gower explicitly shows Henry achieving both:

> Rex sedet, et cuncti proceres resident sibi iuncti,
> Stant et presentes communes plus sapientes.
> Tempus erat tale; communeque iudiciale
> Quod bene prouisum nichi est a iure recisum
> Est quia protectus, letatur sic homo rectus,
> Et metuunt reliqui sua dampna dolenter iniqui.
>
> (*CT* III. 344–9)[48]

This closing vision invokes three very powerful images. Two are biblical and messianic: the 'peaceable kingdom' of Isaiah 11:6, and Christ the judge of the world, of Matt. 25:31–46. In this way, in the *Cronica*, Gower is able to leverage his essentially Augustinian understanding of the difference between mere law and true justice, the latter the purview of God and of just kings as his rightful vicars, into support for Henry's rule.

The third image in the passage above, of the king amid his nobles and commons, determining *ensemble* the future course of the nation, is political in a different, primarily secular sense. Any attempt to understand Gower's legal views leads – by necessity – to an assessment (albeit necessarily brief) of his political ones, as well. To address these comprehensively is well beyond the scope of these pages. Assessments of what Gower's politics might have been are numerous, and – no surprise, given such a broad field – highly divergent: he has been labelled a 'middle-class, conservative' (even a 'rock ribbed conservative'), a 'moderate old-fashioned royalist with a strong distrust for the King's advisors', or 'motivated by conciliarism', his 'politics ... consensual and constitutionalist'. 'Effectively non-aligned', albeit a devoted Ricardian – until he became a Lancastrian 'apologist' and 'sycophant', he disdained peasants, although (in another view) he 'had great sympathy' for them; for still others, Gower held no political beliefs per se, but rather translated social questions into problems of personal ethics.[49]

Fortunately, a strict focus on how Gower understood the interrelationship of 'law', justice, and equity helps to circumvent some of the more tentacular issues here. It is clear that, in Gower's view, justice and equity ideally were equivalent: their perfect synonymy was embodied in the infallible judgement of God, whose laws as well were immutable, equitable and just. This ideal model Gower transposed onto the affairs of king and commons, with the former mirroring God's role rendering justice according to laws designed to ensure equity for all.[50] Thus along with his description of Justice in Book VII of the *Confessio Amantis*, Gower notes 'Hic tractat de tercia Principium regis Policia, que Iusticia nominate est, cuius condicio legibus incorrupta unicuique quod suum est equo pondere distribuit' ('Here he discourses about the third Policy of the Governance of rulers, which is called Justice, whose nature, uncorrupted by laws, distributes to each human being with an equal weight what is properly his').[51] The notion that Justice is the equitable distribution of what is due each person, without regard for rank or privilege, is borrowed from Roman legal theory (though the phrase 'condicio legibus incorrupta' is wholly Gower's insertion and recognises his persistent belief that human laws fall short of the ideal).[52] This is the royal role in Gower's legal structure: to ensure that the laws render justice, that is, equitable provision in all cases, for all. Although Gower accepted, following most contemporary English legal thought, that in order to accomplish this the king has unique power to act, unaccountable to any but God, his regal authority nonetheless is also a creation of the laws founded on common rights. Consequently, the king is also bound by them:

> [Each] schal be served of his riht.
> And so ferforth it is befalle
> That lawe is come among ous alle:
> God lieve it mote wel ben holde,
> And every king therto is holde:
> For thing which is of kinges set,
> With kinges oghte it noght be let.
> What king of lawe takth no kepe,
> Be lawe he mai no regne kepe.
> Do lawe awey, what is a king? (*CA* VII. 3066–75)

Appropriately used, royal power allows the king to order laws, and to bring justice by overriding unjust laws and inequitable decisions of lesser judges through the power to pardon – but he may act only to reassert equity, never to benefit himself or his favourites.[53] When Richard II fell into the latter practice, as the *Cronica Tripertita* shows him doing, Gower supports his deposition.[54]

Thus, Gower is not an absolutist, nor even, strictly speaking, a monarchist. Although the king occupies the centre of Gower's political thought, the royal purpose is ultimately to serve the common good. The king's justice is to benefit the many – and hence in Gower's view royal judgements should be rendered after consideration of advice from those his decisions will affect. The need of kings to hear – and to accept – counsel is a major theme of Gower's, and throughout his works he provides examples of counsel both good and bad.[55] At times these illustrations of the king engaged with counsel take the form of a 'parlement'. In the *Confessio* (VII. 2949) Lycurgus, for Gower an originary of just laws, calls one, to gain agreement for those laws to stand and continue; Apollonius of Tyre does the same (VIII. 1915), for essentially the same purpose. But such examples, and others like them, are not evidence of Gower's 'parliamentarianism', or even 'constitutionalism'. He accepts the idea that the 'comun vois' should be listened to, particularly when it cries out to royal authority for justice and redress.[56] In the end, however, it is the king's alone to legitimate the law by ensuring its equitable application.

Notes

1. As Sir Robert Gower's known heirs were two daughters, John Gower seems likely to have been a nephew; see Nicholas Harris Nicholas, 'John Gower, the Poet', *Retrospective Review* 2 (1828), 103–17, esp. 107 and 112.
2. On Gower's English, see G. C. Macaulay, ed. *The Complete Works of John Gower*, 4 vols. (Oxford: Clarendon Press, 1899–1902), III, xcii–cxx, esp. cxx; also reprinted as *The English Works of John Gower*, EETS, e.s 81and 82, I, same pagination. Hereafter references to Gower's works will be to Macaulay's edition. Also see further Michael L. Samuels and Jeremy J. Smith, 'The Language of Gower', *Neuphilologische Mitteilungen* 82 (1981), 295–304.
3. Almost nothing concrete is known of Gower's family or immediate background. The most extensive research, and plausible speculation, has been that of Nicholas, cited above, and of John H. Fisher; see *John Gower: Moral Philosopher and Friend of Chaucer* (New York: New York University Press, 1964), 37–69.
4. Notably, Macaulay dismissed any likelihood that these lines gave proof of Gower's legal career – a notion original to Leland on scant evidence, and subsequently parroted by Bale and Speght, though denied outright by Thynne. See *Complete Works*, IV, ix–x, and xxvi. The most thorough discussion of the passage is again by Fisher (*John Gower*, 54–6), who notes, rather cagily, both that 'striped garments connoted civil livery of some sort' and that 'rayed sleeves suggest a professional involvement with the law'. See also, more recently, Candace Barrington, 'John Gower's Legal Advocacy and 'In Praise of Peace'', in *John Gower, Trilingual Poet: Language, Translation, and Tradition*, ed. Elisabeth Dutton, with John Hines and R. F. Yeager (Cambridge: D. S. Brewer, 2010), 112–25, at 122; and Sebastian Sobecki, 'A Southwark Tale: Gower, the 1381 Poll Tax, and Chaucer's *The Canterbury Tales*', *Speculum* 92 (2017), 630–60, esp. 632–5.
5. 'But if someone should have an opinion on the subject opposite to mine and should want to blame the charges of my verses on ill-will (because I am not a cleric clothed in scarlet and blue but I have worn only striped sleeves – I know little Latin and

little French), it is the consensus of people that has determined me to say quite openly (as I have told you) that there is still greater diversity of foolish error among the clerics'. Trans. William Burton Wilson, *John Gower: Mirour de l'Omme (The Mirror of Mankind)*, rev. Nancy Van Baak (East Lansing, MI: Colleagues Press, 1992), 291.

6. The classic discussion of the autobiographical problem is Erich Auerbach's; see 'Figura', in *Scenes from the Drama of European Literature: Six Essays* (New York: Meridian, 1959), 11–76; and further E. Talbot Donaldson, 'Chaucer the Pilgrim', *PMLA* 69 (1954), reprinted in *Speaking of Chaucer* (New York: Norton, 1970), 1–12.

7. Prose heading following *MO* 21,780.

8. 'Pers' is among the more difficult of medieval colours to define, as its usages seem to encompass a range between light bluish-gray/livid and deep purple/plum; see, for example, *Old French-English Dictionary*, ed. Alan Hindley, Frederick W. Langley and Brian J. Levy (Cambridge: Cambridge University Press, 2000), s.v. 'pers'[2] and *MED* https://quod.lib.umich.edu/cgi/m/mec/medidx?type=id&id=MED33071&egs=all&egdisplay=open. Contemporary English limners, in their colour recipes, mix a 'purple-blue-grey color'; see *The Crafte of Lymmyng and the Maner of Steyning: Middle English Recipes for Painters, Stainers, Scribes, and Illuminators*, ed. Mark Clarke, EETS, o.s. 347 (Oxford: Oxford University Press, 2016), 432–3, s.v. 'perce' (perce) 'plunket/plongket' and 297/22. Gower himself uses 'pers' only in French, and then just once more, at *MO* 6979, 'Pent au Gibet et pale et pers' ('Hangs from the gibbet pale and livid [?]' – a difficult reference as well, since faces post-hanging are either blue or pale, depending on whether the carotid artery is broken or blocked).

9. For examples, see Oxford, Bodleian Library, Bodley MS 270 and London, British Library, Yates Thompson MS 13.

10. Chaucer's Physician should also be kept in mind, as a caveat to all: 'In sangwyn and in pers he clad was al, / Lyned with taffeta and with sandal', *Canterbury Tales*, I, 439–40. Riverside Chaucer, 3rd edn, gen. ed. Larry D. Benson (Boston: Houghton Mifflin, 1987). And see also the Reeve (*CT*, I, 617): 'A long surcote of pers upon he had', which to illustrate the Ellesmere limner presents over bright red stockings.

11. Macaulay, *Complete Works*, IV, xi–xvii, sets out most of what is known of Gower's land transactions, beginning with the purchase of the manor of Aldington Septvauns in 1364. Nicholas, 'John Gower, the Poet', contributes important documentary evidence, some of which (not always acknowledged) is incorporated by Fisher, *John Gower*, 51–8, gives greater detail, including, in translation, the record of the inquisition into the matter of under-age heir (Appendix C. 313–18). (But see also Andrew Galloway, 'The Common Voice in Theory and Practice in Late Fourteenth-Century England', in *Law, Governance, and Justice: New Views on Medieval Constitutionalism*, ed. Richard Kaeuper (Leiden: Brill, 2013), for an alternate translation of significant passages.) Recently this list has been supplemented by discoveries made by Martha Carlin (see 'Gower's Southwark', in *The Routledge Companion to John Gower*, ed. Ana Sáez-Hidalgo, Brian Gastle and R. F. Yeager (Abingdon and New York, 2017), 132–49; and Sobecki, 'A Southwark Tale').

12. For the 'King's Letter of General Attorney' granting to John Gower and Richard Forester legal power to represent Chaucer while overseas, see Martin M. Crow and Clair C. Olson, eds., *Chaucer Life-Records* (Oxford: Clarendon Press, 1966), 54. A version also appears in Fisher, *John Gower*, 337–78, n. 79.

13. Macaulay, *Complete Works*, IV, xvii–xviii, includes a copy of the will, in English translation.

14. Macaulay, indeed, was driven to defend Gower by doubting that the poet was the same individual involved in the case: 'It is impossible without further proof to assume that the villainous misleader of youth who is described in the report ... as encouraging a young man to defraud the Crown by means of perjury, in order that he may purchase his lands from him at a nominal price, can be identical with the grave moralist of the *Speculum Hominis* and the *Vox Clamantis*.' *Complete Works*, IV, xv. Even recently, the affair has been deemed 'Gower's Black Eye'; see Conrad van Dijk, *John Gower and the Limits of the Law* (Cambridge: D. S. Brewer, 2013), 1.

15. For a narrative account of the 'Septvauns affair', see Fisher, *John Gower*, 51–4. Gower's claim to Aldington was officially determined fully legal in 1368: Fisher, *John Gower*, 334, n. 55. The most complete account of the legal process followed by Gower is that of Matthew Giancarlo, 'The Septvauns Affair: Purchase and Parliament in John Gower's *Mirour de l'Omme*', *Viator* 36 (2005), 435–64.

16. Fisher took this transaction to be a straightforward sale, in the modern sense (*John Gower*, 53, 58–9). Michael Bennett, citing Nicholas, 'John Gower, the Poet', 106–7, in unpublished communication, argues instead that Gower's transfer was an 'enfeoffment to use', not a sale, and would have been carried out in chancery court. The procedure was a relatively common preemptive to entail in the latter half of the fourteenth century, when moneyed gentry acquired lands formerly owned by titled individuals. If the case, the transaction would demonstrate a level of legal sophistication on someone's part, either Gower's or his advisor(s).

17. Fisher, *John Gower*, 338, n. 79, notes that 'Forester appears at least 11 times as an attorney between 1378 and 1405 in the Calendars of Rolls of Assizes, Fresh Force, etc., London, Guildhall'.

18. Sobecki, 'A Southwark Tale', 639.

19. On royal wills, see *A Collection of All the Wills, Now Known to Be Extant, of the Kings and Queens of England, Princes and Princesses of Wales, and Every Branch of the Blood Royal, from the Reign of William the Conqueror, to That of Henry the Seventh Exclusive* (Union, NJ: Lawbook Exchange, 1999).

20. See Theodore T. F. Plucknett, *A Concise History of the Common Law*, 5th edn (Boston, 1956; Clark, NJ: Lawbook Exchange, 2010), 732–44.

21. On dower, see Plucknett, *Concise History*, 566–8; and also Barbara A. Hanawalt, *The Wealth of Wives: Women, Law, and Economy in Late Medieval London* (Oxford: Oxford University Press, 2007), 61–5.

22. See Reginald R. Sharpe, ed. *Calendar of Wills Proved and Enrolled in the Court of Husting, London* Parts I (1258–1358) and II (1358–1688) (London: HMSO, 1890), 321–36, for wills 20–1 Richard II.

23. 'Most wills', Plucknett points out, 'run on the same lines – the testator bequeaths his soul to God and the saints, his body to a particular church; there follow details of the funeral arrangements (often very elaborate) ... there was often express

direction for the payment of debts, sometimes with provisions as to how this was
to be done; long lists of chattels bestowed on friends and relatives ... gifts of the
residue of the estate only became frequent in the fifteenth century, when they are
commonly made to the executors with vague directions for their charitable
disposal.' *Concise History*, 739–40.

24. Macaulay, *Complete Works*, IV, xviii–xix. Plucknett observes that 'after a long
struggle the archbishop of Canterbury established his 'prerogative' to grant
probate when there were 'notable goods' in more than one diocese; the wills of
the well-to-do are therefore to be sought in the registers of the prerogative court
of Canterbury'. *Concise History*, 741.

25. Gower's will, quoted in translation by Macaulay, *Complete Works*, IV, xviii; for
the text in Latin, see Nicholas, 'Gower, the Poet', 103–5, n. 1.

26. The description is by Richard Firth Green; see 'Medieval Literature and Law', in
The Cambridge History of Medieval Literature, ed. David Wallace (Cambridge:
Cambridge University Press, 1999), 407.

27. On the tomb, in fact, the *Mirour* appears in Latin translation as *Speculum
Meditantis* – presumably for the sake of uniformity – the idea for consistent Latin
titles possibly having occurred to Gower after the *Mirour* had been completed.

28. Many have speculated on Gower's possible oversight of preparation of his
manuscripts; but see especially A. I. Doyle and M. B. Parkes, 'The Production
of Copies of the *Canterbury Tales* and the *Confessio Amantis* in the Early
Fifteenth Century', in *Medieval Scribes, Manuscripts and Libraries: Essays
Presented to N. R. Ker*, ed. M. B. Parkes and Andrew G. Watson (London:
Scolar Press, 1978), 163–210; and M. B. Parkes, 'Patterns of Scribal Activity
and Revisions of the Text in Early Copies of Works by John Gower', in *New
Science Out of Old Books: Studies in Manuscripts and Early Printed Books in
Honour of A.I. Doyle*, ed. Richard Beadle and A. J. Piper (London: Scolar Press,
1995), 81–121.

29. For text, English translation, and commentary, see *John Gower: The Minor
Latin Poems*, ed. and trans. R. F. Yeager (Kalamazoo, MI: Medieval Institute
Press, 2005), 83–85.

30. Candace Barrington has applied this assumption of a legal career most promi-
nently, making it the basis for detailed analyses of 'In Praise of Peace' and also of
the poems in London, British Library Additional MS 59495 (*olim* Trentham); see
her ' The Spectral Advocate in John Gower's Trentham Manuscript', in
Theorizing Legal Personhood: Medieval Law and Its Practice, ed.
Andreea Boboc (Leiden: Brill, 2015), 94–118. See also Matthew W. Irvin,
*The Poetic Voices of John Gower: Politics and Personae in the Confessio
Amantis* (Cambridge: D. S. Brewer, 2014), esp. 17ff.; Emma Lipton,
'Exemplary Cases: Marriage as Legal Principle in Gower's *Traitié pour essampler
les amantz marietz*', *Chaucer Review* 48 (2014), 480–501; Sobecki,
'A Southwark Tale', esp. 630–40.

31. Macaulay continues, 'Of all the secular estates that of the law seems to him to be
the worst, and he condemns both advocates and judges in a more unqualified
manner than the members of any other calling. Especially the suggestion of
a special tax to be levied on lawyers' gains (*MO* 24337ff.) is one that could
hardly have come from one who was himself a lawyer'. *Complete Works*, IV,
xxvi.

32. For a suitable, general-use overview of current opinion on the dating of Gower's works, see Russell A. Peck, ed. *John Gower: Confessio Amantis*, 2nd edn, 3 vols. (Kalamazoo, MI: Medieval Institute Press, 2006), I, 38–40.

33. On the staged completion of the *Mirour*, see R. F. Yeager, 'Gower's French Audience: The *Mirour de l'Omme*', *Chaucer Review* 41 (2006), 111–37.

34. Gower's attacks on legal practitioners in *Vox Clamantis* Book VI have been studied extensively by Robert J. Meindl; see his 'Nuisance and Trespass in the *Vox Clamantis*: Sheriffs, Jurors, and Bailiffs', *Interdisciplinary Journal for Germanic and Semiotic Analysis* 20 (2015), 181–213; and further 'Gower's *Speculum Iudicis*: Judicial Corruption in Book VI of the *Vox Clamantis*', in *John Gower: Others and the Self*, ed. Russell A. Peck and R. F. Yeager (Cambridge: D. S. Brewer, 2017), 260–82.

35. It is generally thought, based on manuscripts lacking what is now Book I (often referred to as the '*Visio anglie*'), that addresses the Peasants' Revolt (i.e., Oxford, Bodleian Library, MS Laud (Misc.) 719, Lincoln, Cathedral Library, MS A.72 (235)) that Gower initially envisioned, and completed, the *Vox* as a poem in six books; moved by the Revolt, he added the *Visio*. See *John Gower: Poems on Contemporary Events*, ed. David R. Carlson, verse trans. A. G. Rigg (Toronto: Pontifical Institute of Medieval Studies Press, 2011), 4.

36. The phrase is by van Dijk, see *Gower and the Limits of the Law*, 3.

37. The phrase is by Fisher, see *John Gower*, 51.

38. On parliament's involvement with the case, see Giancarlo, 'Septvauns Affair', 438–40.

39. See Crow and Olson, *Chaucer Life-Records*, 506–12; and further the discussion of Mary Flowers Braswell, *Chaucer's 'Legal Fiction': Reading the Records* (Madison, NJ: Fairleigh Dickinson University Press, 2001), 123.

40. See Kurt Olsson, 'Natural Law and John Gower's *Confessio Amantis*', *Medievalia et Humanistica* 11 (1982), 231–61; and generally, Hugh White, *Nature, Sex, and Goodness in a Medieval Literary Tradition* (Oxford: Oxford University Press, 2000).

41. Gower held very strongly against lollardy, in no small part because in his view such heretics were breaking the laws of the Church. See his *Carmen super multiplici viciorum pestilencia*, esp. ll. 1–93.

42. Or, in *Mirour* 15195–204: 'Justice est ferm constant / Du volenté que ja ne fine, / Q'au riche et povre en jouste line / Son droit a chascun vait donnant: / A nully triche et nul trichant / La puet tricher, car tout avant / Tient Equité de sa covine, / Q'ove sa balance droit pesant / Vait la droiture ensi gardant, / Q'al un n'al autre pat s'acline.' ('Justice is a firm and perpetual will that gives to each his due, rich or poor, in just order. She cheats no one, and no one can cheat her, for in her company she always has Equity, who, with her accurate scales, maintains uprightness without inclining to one side or the other.') Gower's image of Justice graces many courthouses today with her blindfold, scales, and sword. For a learned, summary of the development of this idea from Cicero forward, see Conrad van Dijk, "Giving each his Due": Gower, Langland, and the Question of Equity', *JEGP* 108 (2009), 310–35; a more concise version appears in his *Gower and the Limits of the Law*, 111–22.

43. Indeed, in the last example noted above – 'And pes, which rihtwisnesse keste' – Gower borrows straightforwardly from Psalm 84:11, verses unmistakable for his readers as a reference to the coming of Christ.

44. The relevant locus here is *De Civitate Dei* XIX.

45. Gower of course knew Cicero only fragmentarily: via Macrobius, incorrectly, via the mis-attributed *Rhetorica ad Herennium* – and through the window of Augustine. Ann Astell, *Political Allegory in Late Medieval England* (Ithaca, NY: Cornell University Press, 1999), 11–22, summarises the major points very clearly. For an excellent, succinct application of Ciceronian/Augustinian rhetorics to English jurisprudence in a slightly later era, see Sebastian Sobecki, *Unwritten Verities: The Making of England's Vernacular Legal Culture, 1463–1549* (Notre Dame, IN: Notre Dame University Press, 2015), esp. 155–7.

46. 'He hired the laws and brought the judges on his side. / By suasive gifts seduced, and broken down by fright, /They gave the king their aid, perverting what is right. / These lawyers did their best to follow royal writ: / They manufactured pacts and forged the seals to fit.' Latin text and translations from Carlson and Rigg, *Poems on Contemporary Events*, 252 and 253.

47. As well as other, apparently contradictory responses, for example, evidence of royal power, 'legal vengeance', 'judicial punishment': the case for a multiplicitous reading of 'pius/pité' is made by Andrew Galloway, 'The Literature of 1388 and the Politics of Pity in Gower's *Confessio Amantis*', in *The Letter of the Law: Legal Practice and Literary Production in Medieval England*, ed. Emily Steiner and Candace Barrington (Ithaca, NY: Cornell University Press, 2002), 67–104.

48. 'The king sits down and all the Nobles by his side; / The commons stand there too, the wise and dignified. / Such was the time: the common and judicial law, / If it was just, he promised he would not withdraw. / Since they were safe and sound, all upright men were glad; / The others grieved and feared a loss, if they were bad.' Translation from Carlson and Rigg, *Poems on Contemporary Events*, 318–19.

49. In order, these opinions are traceable to the following: George R. Coffman, 'John Gower, Mentor or Royalty', *PMLA* 69 (1954), 953–64 (and see also Coffman, 'John Gower in His Most Significant Role', in *Elizabethan Studies and Other Essays in Honor of George F. Reynolds*, ed. E. J. West, University of Colorado Studies, Series B, 2 (4) (Boulder, CO: University of Colorado, 1945), 52–61); Eric W. Stockton, ed. and trans., *The Major Latin Works of John Gower* (Seattle: University of Washington Press, 1962), 23; Gervase Mathew, *The Court of Richard II* (London: John Murray, 1968), 81; Sobecki, *Unwritten Verities*, 84; James Simpson, *Sciences and the Self in Medieval Poetry: Alan of Lille's Anticlaudianus and John Gower's Confessio Amantis* (Cambridge: Cambridge University Press, 1995), 283; Paul Strohm, *Social Chaucer* (Cambridge, MA: Harvard University Press, 1989), 31; Fisher, *John Gower*, 178, 133; Stockton, *Major Latin Works*, 19; George Boas, *Vox Populi: Essays in the History of an Idea* (Baltimore, MD: Johns Hopkins University Press, 1969), 24; Russell A. Peck, *Kingship and Common Profit in John Gower's Confessio Amantis* (Carbondale, IL, and Edwardsville, IL: Southern Illinois University Press, 1978), xxi; Elizabeth Porter, 'Gower's Ethical Microcosm and Political Macrocosm', in *Gower's Confessio Amantis: Responses and Reassessments*, ed. A. J. Minnis (Cambridge: D. S. Brewer, 1983), 135. And see further

Matthew Giancarlo, *Parliament and Literature in Late Medieval England*
(Cambridge: Cambridge University Press, 2007), for whom Gower is
a 'parliamentary' poet' (91).

50. The distinction is important here to recognise that, whereas for Gower God *is* the
law, ultimately the king is its administrator – 'merely', one might say.

51. Translation is by Andrew Galloway, in *John Gower: Confessio Amantis*, ed.
Russell A. Peck, 3 vols. (Kalamazoo, MI: Medieval Institute Press, 2004), III,
464; Gower's Latin at *CA* VII. 2699.

52. Gower's source would have been Justinian's *Institutes*: 'Iustitia est constans et
perpetua voluntas ius suum unicuique tribuens' ('Justice is the constant and
perpetual will to give to each his own'); see especially van Dijk's discussion,
Limits of the Law, 99–100.

53. The operative principle is, again, found in Justinian: 'Quod principi placuit, legis
habet vigorem' ('What pleases the prince has the force of law') but as van Dijk points
out, quoting Bracton, 'the English political context' refined that principle with 'facit
enim lex quod ipse sit rex' ('for the law makes that he himself is king'); see *Limits of
the Law*, 98–9; and further Russell A. Peck, 'The Politics and Psychology of
Governance in Gower: Ideas of Kingship and Real Kings', in *A Companion to
Gower*, ed. Siân Echard (Cambridge: D. S. Brewer, 2004), 215–38.

54. Gower's treatment of Richard in the *Cronica* – showing him separate from, and
manipulating, the law for the benefit of himself and his faction in violation of
rightful kingship – devolves from the primarily canonistic concept of the king's
'body natural (or mortal)' and 'body politic'; see Ernst Kantorowicz, *The King's
Two Bodies: A Study in Medieval Political Theology* (Princeton, NJ: Princeton
University Press, 1957). In his condemnation here of Richard, Gower shows his
adherence to general medieval legal theory, that the force of the law was properly
separate from the king; Richard's figure in the *Cronica* seems to act in accord
with the Roman principle, 'Quod principi placuit, legis habet vigorum' (roughly,
'What pleases the prince has the power of law'), variously supported in civil law:
see Justinian, *Digest* 1.4.1; and further 1.3.1.

55. For the good, see for example the tale of 'King, Wine, Woman, and Truth',
Gower, *Confessio* VII. 1782–1984; for the bad, see *Vox* VI. 550–80 (*540–*80).
Cf. also his many attacks on flatterers in these poems, and also in the *Mirour*.
On Gower and counsel, see especially Judith Ferster, *Fictions of Advice:
The Literature and Politics of Counsel in Late Medieval England* (Philadelphia:
University of Pennsylvania Press, 1996), 108–36.

56. Failure to do so lay at the root of the Revolt in 1381, in Gower's view. See, for
example, *Vox Clamantis*, VI. 545–46; *Mirour de l'Omme*, 26, 485–97.

Further Reading

Barrington, Candace, 'John Gower's Legal Advocacy and "In Praise of Peace"', in
John Gower, Trilingual Poet: Language, Translation, and Tradition, ed.
Elisabeth Dutton, with John Hines and R. F. Yeager, Cambridge: D. S. Brewer,
2010, 112–25
   'The Spectral Advocate in John Gower's Trentham Manuscript', in *Theorizing
Legal Personhood: Medieval Law and Its Practice*, ed. Andreea Boboc, Leiden:
Brill, 2015, 94–118.

Bellamy, J. G., *Bastard Feudalism and the Law*, Portland, OR: Areopagitica Press, 1989.

Brundage, James A., *The Medieval Origins of the Legal Profession: Canonists, Civilians, and Courts*, Chicago: University of Chicago Press, 2008.

Fisher, John H., *John Gower: Moral Philosopher and Friend of Chaucer*, New York: New York University Press, 1964.

Giancarlo, Matthew, 'The Septvauns Affair: Purchase and Parliament in John Gower's *Mirour de l'Omme*', *Viator* 36 (2005), 435–64.

Green, Richard Firth, 'Medieval Literature and Law', in *The Cambridge History of Medieval Literature*, ed. David Wallace, Cambridge: Cambridge University Press, 1999, 25–36.

Hanawalt, Barbara A. *The Wealth of Wives: Women, Law, and Economy in Late Medieval London*, Oxford: Oxford University Press, 2007.

Meindl, Robert J. 'Gower's *Speculum Iudicis*: Judicial Corruption in Book VI of the *Vox Clamantis*', in *John Gower: Others and the Self*, ed. Russell A. Peck and R. F. Yeager, Cambridge: D. S. Brewer, 2017, 260–82.

'Nuisance and Trespass in the *Vox Clamantis*: Sheriffs, Jurors, and Bailiffs', *Interdisciplinary Journal for Germanic and Semiotic Analysis* 20 (2015), 181–213.

Musson, Anthony and Ormrod, W. M., *The Evolution of English Justice: Law, Politics and Society in the Fourteenth Century*, New York: St Martin's Press, 1999.

Plucknett, Theodore T. F., *A Concise History of the Common Law*, 5th edn, Boston, 1956; Clark, NJ: Lawbook Exchange, 2010.

Sobecki, Sebastian, 'A Southwark Tale: Gower, the 1381 Poll Tax, and Chaucer's *The Canterbury Tales*', *Speculum* 92 (2017), 630–60.

van Dijk, Conrad, *John Gower and the Limits of the Law*, Cambridge: D. S. Brewer, 2013.

Yeager, R. F. 'John Gower's Poetry and the "Lawyerly Habit of Mind"', in *Theorizing Legal Personhood: Medieval Law and Its Practice*, ed. Andreea Boboc, Leiden: Brill, 2015, 71–93.

13

FIONA SOMERSET

Lollards and Religious Writings

The Middle English *Rosarium* (*c.* 1375–1415) an alphabetic compendium of religious knowledge compiled by sympathisers with John Wyclif (*c.* 1330–64), begins its discussion of 'Lex' in this way:

> 'Law' is spoken of in two ways, that is to say, true and pretended. True law is a truthful directive, or rectifying, of a created thing, in order to have it as it ought to be, as at its beginning. And this law is divided into God's law and man's law.[1]

Man-made laws, as much as God's law, can be true. That truth is evident in their capacity to bring about reform by restoring created things to how they were in the beginning. This understanding of law's place in the life of a Christian would surprise scholars who expect lollard writers to adopt a *scriptura sola* position, where only the Bible is a reliable source of moral rectitude. However, Wyclif and his followers ('lollard' or 'Wycliffite' are used interchangeably to describe these persons and their mostly anonymous writings) resembled reform-minded religious writers more generally not only in their tendency to seek models in the past, but also in their willingness to cite both church and secular law in order to advance their claims. The *Rosarium* says no more at this point about pretended law; but other lollard writings dismiss man-made laws only when they regard them as manifestly incompatible with scripture and reason. What is more, they commonly insist on leaving room for human doubt: only God is always sure of the truth. Rather than assuming that lollards simply rejected human law while orthodox writers accepted it unquestioningly, this chapter will take a fresh look at how lollard and other religious writings engaged critically with law and its practice, communicating legal knowledge as they sought to explain the best way to live in this world.

This brief survey will focus on defamation and heresy. Both topics have been well studied: both were central to how people thought of their roles within communities, their interactions and their moral worth. The audience for the writings we will discuss would have known about these offences, for the process of their investigation stipulated pastoral instruction upon them and involved ordinary lay people as plaintiffs, witnesses or defendants. These were legal processes where church law played a leading role in adjudicating cases, though in collaboration with secular law. Each is a focus for complaint and satire in some religious writings, and for various kinds of advice in a wide range of others.

England's law on defamation may be traced from ecclesiastical court formularies and the fifteenth-century English canon law commentator Bishop William Lyndwood's *Provinciale* to a provincial constitution of the Council of Oxford in 1222, called by Archbishop Stephen Langton to issue the decrees of the Fourth Lateran Council (1215), an ecumenical council convened by Pope Innocent III to affirm broad-ranging ecclesiastical reforms. The 1222 Council of Oxford issued the seventy decrees of the Fourth Lateran Councils supplemented with local rules, this constitution on defamation among them, as constitutions for the province of Canterbury. This constitution excommunicated anyone who maliciously imputed a crime to any person of good fame in such a way that that person was harmed.[2] Read publicly in parishes from the early thirteenth century, it was familiar to lay persons and clergy alike, and all were subject to it; it was a means of restoring reputation and community.[3]

Salient features of England's law on heresy, too, can be traced to the Fourth Lateran Council, which provided a new understanding of how not only false beliefs, but also the social networks that sustained them, should be investigated in seeking to root out heresy.[4] While canon law had required secular cooperation in the pursuit of heresy since the twelfth century, in England it was in the late fourteenth and fifteenth centuries that the Crown collaborated closely with the Church in the sustained pursuit of lollardy, identified as a new heresy and traced to Wyclif. Ian Forrest has shown that while many aspects of this pursuit were not new (e.g., the restriction on lay preaching and the investigation of heresy by bishops in the normal round of their duties), the concerted pursuit of heresy required and occasioned wider instruction on what constituted heresy and how it might be sought through communities.[5] The law on heresy became widely known through regular inquiries as part of many bishops' visitations in the late fourteenth and fifteenth centuries. Since lay persons, as often or more often than clerics, were subject to investigation for heresy, the process taught them, as well as those administering it, to recognise the faultlines between proper religious practice and dissident religion.

Subject to the Law: Defamation and Heresy

Defamation

The whole community is called upon to adjudicate defamatory speech, within and beyond legal processes. In pastoral writings defamation is often referred to as 'backbiting', and approached in moral rather than in explicitly legal terms: counselling against backbiting is a means of setting guidelines for everyday conduct, rather than providing legal recourse when those guidelines are not followed. As a positive alternative, pastoral writers advocate fraternal correction, a form of mutual criticism for moral improvement that should take place in private or before a few persons in authority, and should avoid making public even truthful claims about the recipient.[6] Anyone who listens to backbiting without reproving the speaker joins the speaker in his sin, pastoral writers advise. In a defamation case, witnesses were similarly called to speak on the plaintiff's behalf, testifying not only to what defamatory words were said, but also to the previous good reputation those words had damaged.[7]

Thus, readers of works that discuss defamation are often drawn into adjudicating the boundaries of legitimate criticism: where does correction end, and defamation begin? Lollard writings often seek to renegotiate how and to whom correction might properly be delivered, even as contemporary legislation sought to limit public condemnation of the sins of the clergy before the laity.[8] Drawing a wider audience into witnessing correction of the clergy was not a new phenomenon; Gratian cites multiple authorities to suggest that lay people should shun the masses of sinful priests in D.32 c.6.[9] Richard Fitzralph's polemical sermon the *Defensio Curatorum* (1357), widely copied across Europe and made accessible to readers of English through Trevisa's late fourteenth-century translation, explicitly invited lay parishioners to assess for themselves whether their spiritual ministers were living virtuously and providing proper services.[10] Similarly, lollard writings critical of incontinent clergy or of friars place judgement in lay hands, aiming to create in their readers the discernment to judge corruption against a consistent external standard. 'Of Dominion' (*c.* 1377–1410) suggests that laymen can judge the behaviour of their priests by means of their consciences just as well as they can judge by the means of their senses whether their food is good or spoiled.[11] Likewise, *Piers the Plowman's Creed* (*c.* 1390–1415) places its lay narrator on a journey in pursuit of pastoral instruction in which he observes the greed and corruption among all four orders of friars, and their mutual sniping, before being properly taught by a poor plowman who explains charitable correction to him. And the lay seeker in *Mum and the Sothsegger* (*c.* 1410) tours every social order and institution in England searching for someone who will dare speak the truth, observing myriad forms of legal corruption and eventually finding limited solace in a dream where a beehive's friar-like drones are culled by its beekeeper.

Some writers, however, attempted to expand the bounds of legitimate correction into the territory of defamatory speech, advocating a new, harsher type of public correction of religious groups or even named individuals that some of them called 'sharp speech'.[12] The 'Dialogue between Jon and Richerd' (c. 1375–1415) stages such a redefinition. Against Richard's complaint that his criticism of friars is 'too sharp . . . and not of the gospel',[13] Jon retorts that Christ himself spoke sharply against the pharisees, and Christian men should never speak of these sects (meaning the friars) except to speak sharply to reprove their vices.[14] Similarly, Margery Kempe's *Book* recounts her own sharp speech while visiting Archbishop Thomas Arundel at Lambeth Palace: she publicly rebuked members of the archbishop's retinue for their sins, so much that they wished she might be burned as a heretic. She then reproved the archbishop as well, for his failure to correct them. The archbishop responded meekly that he would do better.[15] This mild response implicitly justifies Margery's critique and invalidates the previous hostile reaction from his retinue.

Margery Kempe was not the only writer to report that sharp speech might incur accusations of heresy. A number of late fourteenth- and fifteenth-century writers complain that any public critique of morals might itself incur defamation, by bringing others to label one a 'lollare' or 'lollard'. Chaucer's Host in the *Canterbury Tales* smells a 'Loller in the wind' when the Parson protests at his swearing, and insists that the Parson should preach, but is diverted by the Shipman, who is concerned that the Parson's preaching might raise difficulties.[16] Chaucer's light touch in dramatising this conflict is unusual: most writers seem far more worried by the potential consequences of this sort of name-calling. John Audelay, for example, in his alliterative poem 'Marcolf and Solomon' is concerned that any poor parish priest who performs his service devoutly, like Chaucer's Parson, is at risk of being called lollard, but more worryingly yet, that priests and laymen who see covetous clerics will not speak out for fear of unlawful condemnation.[17] A prose treatise of spiritual advice centred on the five senses, *The Fyve Wyttes*, is similarly worried that fear of false slander will prevent people from reproving sin as they should; but also appeals to onlookers to make a correct judgement in favour of the reprovers, rather than their defamers: 'though they be called heretics or lollards ... beware, do not consent to call them so, nor easily believe the common slander ... if they truly preach Christ and his gospel'.[18] Thus, lollard writers and their reform-minded contemporaries seek to renegotiate the boundaries of legitimate correction by appealing to wider or alternative adjudication, even as they fear that doing so may bring accusations not merely of defamation, but of heresy.

Heresy

Accusations of heresy were not merely of concern because fear of them might prevent the public criticism of sinful behaviour, of course. The pursuit of the lollard movement as a heresy profoundly shaped how writers and readers interested in reform and in lay learning thought about their religious affiliation and practice, whether or not they saw themselves as followers of Wyclif. Any heresy case was a serious matter, even if most ended with the accused abjuring (publicly forswearing their erroneous beliefs and undergoing some sort of penance) or undergoing compurgation (dismissal of the case after a number of witnesses testified to the accused's innocence). Only those who had relapsed after a previous conviction, or those who refused to accept correction of their beliefs, were in danger of execution. Yet the process of accusation, arrest and imprisonment, trial, and punishment would disrupt lives and whole communities by drawing them into the detection and witnessing of religious error and its correction.[19]

Many lollard writings turn the threat of legal persecution on its head, encouraging readers to embrace the possibility of martyrdom as vindication of their true faith. The *Lanterne of Light* (c. 1409) invites its readers to imagine themselves as members of the true church, God's little flock who need not fear, the congregation of persons in whom there is knowing and true confession of faith and truth.[20] The *Wordes of Poule* (c. 1377–1410) exhorts its readers to imitate Christ's suffering: 'since Christ glorified the thief that suffered with him ... much more shall he glorify those that willingly suffer persecution for his law, not only for a little while but forever after'.[21] Some writings use the format of an examination for heresy, whether imagined or recounted as a dialogue, as an occasion for some sort of profession of faith.

Of lollard writings that address the movement's persecution as a heresy, perhaps the most direct instruction on self-defence under examination for heresy is found in the 'Sixteen Points' (c. 1382–99), whose rubric pointedly specifies that these are points that bishops' deputies 'put ... upon ... men which they call lollards'.[22] None of the articles can simply be affirmed because each is partly false, but a detailed explanation of what 'we believe' or 'we grant' in each article shows that when properly qualified, part of its content can be defended.[23] While the agenda and contents of this document are set by the hostile rendering of lollard belief it aims to counter, the explanations presented amount to a kind of a creed, even if a legalistic one couched in academic language.

William Thorpe, an Oxford-trained Wycliffite cleric known mainly from his own account of his examination for heresy in 1407, more overtly seizes the occasion of this examination in order to assert what he truly believes.[24] According to his own retelling of events in the *Testimony of William Thorpe* (*c.* 1407–15), Archbishop Arundel asked him to swear to forsake all the opinions held by the 'sect of Lollers', reading to him a deposition that listed five beliefs that he had recently preached in Shrewsbury. However, Thorpe presents the whole of his narrative in the form of a different legal document entirely, a charter, beginning with the standard opening 'Let it be known to all men that read or hear this writing', to suggest that he making a public declaration of his own accord, rather than being forced to submit.[25] (Charters begin with the tag line '*Sciant presentes et futuri*', 'let all men know whether present or in future'.) And in what is surely a creative reconstruction of events, he recounts that Arundel allowed him to take control of his own testimony. By his own account, Thorpe professed his belief and affirmed the value of what named followers of Wyclif had taught him before addressing the points on which he had been accused. And when he finally responded to the accusations, he redefined each one on his own terms before affirming them according to his own understanding.

Thorpe's *Testimony* is probably modelled on the less well-known *Letter of Richard Wyche*, which describes events in 1402–3.[26] Like the *Testimony*, Wyche's letter to his followers describes an examination for heresy from the point of view of the defendant. Wyche similarly attempts to manipulate legal forms to his advantage during his trial, in that he attempts to swear an oath with a mental reservation about his interpretation of its content. He is willing to swear an oath to obey the law of the Catholic Church as it pertains to him because his understanding is that that law is, or should be, equivalent to the law of God. But he is then required to swear obedience to the contents of the canonical books of canon law, which he thinks only partly conform to the law of God. Wyche's failed attempt at redefinition resembles the strategies shown in Thorpe's *Testimony* and the 'Sixteen Points'. His, however, is not a story of triumph, but of how to persevere through shame and despair.

The Subject of Law: God's Law and Man's

Lollard writers often had a broad and sometimes deeply informed interest in law. As Wyche's *Letter* shows us, they sought not only to redefine specific legal forms or provisions, but also to return law to the ground from which it was derived. There was no basic disagreement in late medieval thought about where that ground lay. Gratian had begun the first distinction of the *Decretum* (*c.* 1140), the basis from which all subsequent canon law developed, by explaining that the natural law that regulates the human race consists of what is contained in the Law and the Gospel (the Old and New Testaments).[27] And it was commonplace for later canonists to assert that any law contradicting scripture is not true law.[28] What was distinctive about the writings of Wyclif and his followers was the frequency with which they asserted that human laws or customs were invalid because such laws or customs were in conflict with God's law – though this did not prevent them from engaging in close detail with church and secular law, citing the laws approvingly in support of their positions, or imitating the form of legal documents and procedures.

All these strategies can be found in the *Thirty-Seven Conclusions* (c. 1384–1420). Like Thorpe's *Testimony*, it presents a defiant manifesto in support of Wyclif, advocating for critics of the church to be allowed to preach regardless of their licensing by bishops and disputing the heretical positions imputed to lollards on controversial topics such as the Eucharist, confession, swearing, images and pilgrimages. But most of the articles are instaurational, that is, aimed at restoring a proper order of church and realm that has perhaps never yet been attained in this world, but could be if the law were properly followed. These conclusions bristle with quotations drawn from scripture, authorities from the patristic to the thirteenth century, and canon and secular law. Canon law is frequently the substrate: scripture and other writings will be cited from their use in the *Decretum, Liber extra, Liber sextus*, or *Clementines* as well as their original source. One reason may be that for a writer well versed in it, canon law is a convenient topical finding aid; but it seems too that he wishes to demonstrate that except where corrupted, these sources of law should be compatible.

Where corruption of human law has set in, the writer is clear on what authorises its reform, and through what channels. Conclusions 26 and 27, which come at the end of a sequence of twelve conclusions on papal power, explain that Christians are not required to believe that each determination of the church is true (73). For the church of Rome often determines against holy scripture, and one council against another, and one pope contradicts another's sentence as it pleases him without needful reason (76). Holy scripture and the works of Christ are a ground that may not fail, while determinations of the Church of Rome should be relied on only insofar as they are grounded expressly in holy scripture or open reason (76–7).

Secular power is the proper recourse when the pope's determinations are corrupt, as conclusion 27 goes on to explain. If the pope imposes an interdict, it should be resisted by everyone, for the English king, lords, clerks and commons in parliament are strongly bound to maintain local prerogatives by their own statute of *Praemunire*, which forbids the pope to assert his jurisdiction within England (86–7). Similarly the *Thirty-Seven Conclusions*, conclusion 12 places the king's regal privilege above papal power, indirectly echoing the Statute of Treasons (28–9, 31). The *Grete Sentence of Curs*, a work disputing the pope's capacity to excommunicate anyone, places Magna Carta at the top of a hierarchy of human laws (326–7).[29] Plainly these lollard writers place statute law above canon or even civil law in their appeals to secular power to reform the church; however, we should note that their citations do not rely on detailed knowledge, but gesture at especially famous examples.

That canon law is unreliable because its statements contradict one another, as conclusion 26 of the *Thirty-Seven Conclusions* asserts, seems an odd claim. After all, describing and resolving discord between canons is of course the purpose of Gratian's *Decretum*, as well as much subsequent commentary upon canon law. But we would be wrong to take it as evidence for a general lollard preference for dogmatic certainty based solely on scripture. Conclusion 35 puts this claim in context, arguing in favour of uncertainty as it shows how to resolve contradictory canons. The glorious martyr St Cyprian was wrong in thinking that evil priests cannot make the sacraments, it points out (129–31). But rather than providing grounds for rejecting human law altogether, this example of human fallibility shows that anyone can be wrong – even the pope. And thus, when we are uncertain we should neither take a papal determination as belief, nor despise it as false, but remain in doubt (131).

The *Dialogue between Reson and Gabbyng*, too, uses uncertainty to make room for dissent. In response to the challenge that any speech against the court of Rome is speech against Christ and his law, Reason gives a lengthy explanation of the four possible replies to any statement: granting, denying, doubting and supposing.[30] In the *Thirty-Seven Conclusions*, however, the point is not merely to justify critique, but to defend Wyclif and oppose his posthumous condemnation. Wyclif, like Cyprian, should not be condemned for speaking according to his conscience, particularly when those condemning him cannot even understand his books (133–4). Lollard writers reject excommunication more generally on the same grounds: there can be no certainty in human judgement of any person's membership in God's church. Rather than being dogmatic about the relationship between God's law and human law and its practice, then, we find that lollard writings about law make careful distinctions, weigh decisions carefully, and open up spaces for uncertainty.

Notes

1. Cambridge, Gonville and Caius College MS 354/581. All translations are my own unless otherwise noted.

2. R. H. Helmholz, ed., *Select Cases on Defamation to 1600 Selden Society* 101 (London, 1985), xiv; *Councils and Synods with Other Documents relating to the English Church II: 1205–1313*, ed. F. M. Powicke and C. R. Cheney, 2 vols. (Oxford: Clarendon Press, 1964), I, 107.

3. Helmholz, *Select Cases*, xv.

4. John Arnold, 'Lollard Trials and Inquisitorial Discourse', in *Fourteenth Century England*, ed., Christopher Given-Wilson (Woodbridge: Boydell, 2002), II, 81–94.

5. Ian Forrest, *The Detection of Heresy in Late Medieval England* (Oxford: Oxford University Press, 2005).

6. Edwin D. Craun, *Ethics and Power in Medieval English Reformist Writing* (Cambridge: Cambridge University Press, 2010).

7. On backbiting, see, for example, Thomas Aquinas, *Summa Theologica*, II, 73.4, http://dhspriory.org/thomas/summa/SS/SS073.html#SSQ73OUTP1; on defamation proceedings, see Helmholz, *Select Cases*, xxvi–xli.

8. Archbishop Thomas Arundel's *Constitutions* (drafted Oxford 1407, issued 1409), article 3, in *Concilia Magnae Britanniae et Hiberniae*, ed. David Wilkins, 4 vols. (London, 1737), III, 314–19, at 316.

9. Gratian, *Decretum* part I, distinction 32, chapter 5. http://geschichte.digitale -sammlungen.de/decretum-gratiani/online/angebot.

10. John Trevisa, *Dialogus Inter Militem et Clericum, Richard Fitz-Ralph's Sermon: 'Defensio Curatorum' and Methodius: 'The Beginning of the World and the End of Worldes'*, ed. A. J. Perry EETS 167 (Oxford: Oxford University Press, 1925).

11. 'Of Dominion', in *The English Works of Wyclif Hitherto Unprinted*, 2nd edn, ed. F. D. Matthew, EETS o.s. 74 (London: Trübner, 1880), 282–93, at 291.

12. Edwin D. Craun, 'Discarding Traditional Pastoral Ethics: Wycliffism and Slander', in *Wycliffite Controversies*, ed. Mishtooni C.A. Bose and J. Patrick Hornbeck II (Turnhout: Brepols, 2012), 227–42.

13. *Four Wycliffite Dialogues*, ed. Fiona Somerset, EETS o.s. 333 (Oxford: Oxford University Press, 2009), 5, ll. 68–9.

14. Ibid., ll. 70–5.

15. Chapter 16 in *The Book of Margery Kempe*, ed. Lynn Staley (Kalamazoo, MI: Medieval Institute Publications, 1996). Lines 818–46 in the unpaginated online edition: http://d.lib.rochester.edu/teams/publication/staley-the-book-of-mar gery-kempe.

16. Geoffrey Chaucer, *The Canterbury Tales*, ed. Jill Mann (New York: Penguin, 2005), fragment II, ll. 1170–83.

17. John Audelay, 'Marcolf and Solomon', in *Poems and Carols*, ed. Susanna Greer Fein (Kalamazoo, MI: Medieval Institute Publications, 2009), online edition http://d.lib.rochester.edu/teams/publication/fein-audelay-poems-and-car ols-oxford-bodleian-library-ms-douce-302, lines 131–43, 664–76.

18. *The Fyve Wyttes*, ed. Rolf H. Bremmer, Jr (Amsterdam: Rodopi, 1987), 19, ll. 10–13.

19. J. Patrick Hornbeck II, 'Records of Heresy Trials', in *Wycliffite Spirituality*, ed. and trans. J. Patrick Hornbeck II, Stephen E. Lahey and Fiona Somerset (New York: Paulist, 2013), 45–52.
20. *The Lanterne of Light*, ed. L. M. Swinburn, EETS o.s. 151 (London: K. Paul, 1917), 22–5.
21. Fiona Somerset, 'A Mirror to See God in: An Edition of "Þe Wordes of Poule"', *Yearbook of Langland Studies* 31 (2017), 257–86.
22. 'Sixteen Points on which the Bishops Accuse Lollards', in *Selections from English Wycliffite Writings*, 2nd edn, ed. Anne Hudson (Toronto: University of Toronto Press, 1997), 19–24, at 19, ll. 1–2.
23. Ibid., 20, ll. 44–55.
24. On Thorpe's arrest, see Maureen Jurkowski, 'The Arrest of William Thorpe in Shrewsbury and the Anti–Lollard Statute of 1406', *Historical Research* 75:189 (2002), 273–95.
25. *The Testimony of William Thorpe*, in *Two Wycliffite Texts*, ed. Anne Hudson EETS o.s. 301 (Oxford: Oxford University Press 1993), 24–93, at 29. See also Emily Steiner, 'Inventing Legality: Documentary Culture and Lollard Preaching', in *The Letter of the Law: Legal Practice and Literary Production in Medieval England*, ed. Emily Steiner and Candace Barrington (Ithaca: Cornell University Press, 2002), 185–201.
26. Richard Wyche, 'The Letter of Richard Wyche: An Interrogation Narrative', ed. and trans. Christopher G. Bradley, PMLA 127 (2012), 626–42.
27. Gratian, *Decretum*, D.1 c.1.
28. See, for example, Panormitatus, 'the pope cannot arrange anything contrary to the Gospel'. Quoted in R. H. Helmholz, 'The Bible in the Service of the Canon Law', *Chicago-Kent Law Review* 70 (1995), 1557–81, at 1564 n. 29.
29. *Select English Works of John Wyclif*, ed. Thomas Arnold (Oxford, 1871), III, 267–337, at 326–7. See also Anne Hudson, 'The King and Erring Clergy: A Wycliffite Contribution', in *The Church and Sovereignty c. 590–1918: Essays in Honour of Michael Wilks Studies in Church History*, ed. Diana Wood, Subsidia 9 (Oxford: Blackwell, 1991), 269–78.
30. 'Dialogue between Reson and Gabbyng', in *Four Wycliffite Dialogues*, ed. Somerset, 52–3, ll. 349–75.

Further Reading

Arnold, John, 'Lollard Trials and Inquisitorial Discourse', in *Fourteenth Century England*, ed. Christopher Given-Wilson, Woodbridge: Boydell, 2002, II, 81–94.
Councils and Synods with Other Documents relating to the English Church II: 1205–1313, ed. F. M. Powicke and C. R. Cheney, 2 vols., Oxford: Clarendon Press, 1964.
Craun, Edwin D., 'Discarding Traditional Pastoral Ethics: Wycliffism and Slander', in *Wycliffite Controversies*, ed. Mishtooni C. A. Bose and J. Patrick Hornbeck II, Turnhout: Brepols, 2012, 227–42.
Ethics and Power in Medieval English Reformist Writing, Cambridge: Cambridge University Press, 2010.
The English Works of Wyclif Hitherto Unprinted, 2nd edn, ed. F. D. Matthew, EETS o.s. 74, London: Trübner, 1880.

Farr, William, *John Wyclif as Legal Reformer*, Leiden: Brill, 1974.

Forrest, Ian, *The Detection of Heresy in Late Medieval England*, Oxford: Oxford University Press, 2005.

'William Swinderby and the Wycliffite Attitude to Excommunication', *Journal of Ecclesiastical History* 60 (2009), 246–69.

Four Wycliffite Dialogues, ed. Fiona Somerset EETS o.s. 333, Oxford: Oxford University Press, 2009.

The Fyve Wyttes, ed. Rolf H. Bremmer, Jr, Amsterdam: Rodopi, 1987.

Heresy Trials in the Diocese of Norwich, 1428–31, ed. Norman P. Tanner, S. J. Camden Society, fourth series, vol. 20, London: Royal Historical Society, 1977.

Hornbeck II, J. Patrick, 'Records of Heresy Trials', in *Wycliffite Spirituality*, ed. and trans. J. Patrick Hornbeck II, Stephen E. Lahey and Fiona Somerset, New York: Paulist, 2013.

Hudson, Anne, *The Premature Reformation: Wycliffite Texts and Lollard History*, Oxford: Oxford University Press, 1988.

Jurkowski, Maureen, 'The Arrest of William Thorpe in Shrewsbury and the Anti-Lollard statute of 1406', *Historical Research* 75:189 (2002), 273–95.

'Lollardy and Social Status in East Anglia', *Speculum* 82 (2007), 120–52.

The Lanterne of Light, ed. L. M. Swinburn, EETS o.s. 151, London: K. Paul, 1917.

Lollards of Coventry 1486–1522, ed. Shannon McSheffrey and Norman Tanner, Royal Historical Society, Camden Society, fifth series, vol. 23., Cambridge: Cambridge University Press, 2003.

McNamara, Lawrence, *Reputation and Defamation*, Oxford: Oxford University Press, 2007.

Select Cases on Defamation to 1600, ed. R. H. Helmholz, Selden Society 101, London, 1985.

Select English Works of John Wyclif, ed. Thomas Arnold, vol. 3, Oxford, 1871.

Selections from English Wycliffite Writings, 2nd edn, ed. Anne Hudson, Toronto: University of Toronto Press, 1997.

Somerset, Fiona, 'A Mirror to See God in: An Edition of "Þe Wordes of Poule"', *Yearbook of Langland Studies* 31 (2017), 257–86.

[Thirty-Seven Conclusions] Remonstrance against Romish Corruptions, ed. J. Forshall, London, 1851.

Thorpe, William, *The Testimony of William Thorpe*, in *Two Wycliffite Texts*, ed. Anne Hudson, EETS o.s. 301, Oxford: Oxford University Press, 1993, 24–93.

Wyche, Richard, 'The Letter of Richard Wyche: An Interrogation Narrative', ed. and trans. Christopher G. Bradley, *Publications of the Modern Language Association* 127, 2012, 626–42.

14

SEBASTIAN SOBECKI

Lancastrian Literature

This chapter will provide an overview of how both major and lesser-known Lancastrian writers and texts engage with the law and legal contexts. Covering the period between Henry IV and Prince Edward of Westminster, this chapter will address legal aspects in Thomas Hoccleve's *Regement of Princes*, Osbern of Bokenham's *Mappula Angliae*, George Ashby's *Active Policy*, John Fortescue's *De laudibus legum Angliae* and such anonymous works as the *Libelle of Englyshe Polycye* in order to demonstrate how they intervened in and commented on shifting legal ideas and practices during the first two-thirds of the fifteenth century.

The sixty years of unbroken Lancastrian rule between Henry IV's usurpation of the crown in 1399 and the first deposition of his grandson Henry VI in 1461 'exceeded the longest prescription limit in the laws of the church applicable to secular kingdoms'.[1] The doctrine of prescription means that possessing something de facto over a certain period of time amounts to a right to this possession. This may not seem to be a particularly scintillating benchmark if viewed with 500 years' worth of hindsight, yet at the time the relatively smooth and refreshingly unchallenged royal transitions binding together three kings through the principle of primogeniture offered a sense of continuity rarely seen in medieval England's public politics. Sixty years covers three generations and spans the shared biological memory of the better part of a century. Although the Lancastrian period is now often perceived as a time of dynastic unease and repressed guilt over the manner of Henry IV's seizing of the crown (an impression fostered by Shakespeare's history plays and reinforced by New Historicist readings of the ideological aspects of Lancastrian rule), many contemporary documents betray no such institutional instability or fragility of governance. On the contrary, the continuity of Lancastrian rule created the necessary framework for an institutional consolidation and a strengthening of royal authority, while, at the same time, sustaining and developing the conciliar outlook on which the Lancastrians had founded their rule and which they used to justify their ascent to the throne. Paradoxically, the same conciliarism and consultative character that Henry IV summoned to present himself as a more competent ruler than Richard II became the touchstone of much Lancastrian communication, to the extent that it genuinely changed – for better and for good – English practices of governance. In other words, conciliar politics moved from being a utilitarian means to becoming a political principle. Consequently, one of the greatest beneficiaries of this period of institutional development was the law itself, primarily in its secular, and common, form.

The first half of the fifteenth century does not offer any engaged or complex literary interest in specific areas of the law. There are glimpses of the law in Lydgate's writings, but these instances are neither sustained throughout his oeuvre nor do they tackle specific aspects of the law. Instead, in *Saint Austin at Compton* Lydgate champions legal flexibility and interpretive mitigation. Jennifer Sisk observes that Lydgate's 'poem in fact argues against a legal practice that strictly follows the letter of the law, instead bowing to legal and affective discernment on a case-by-case basis'.[2] Royal justice is at the heart of his *Disguising at Hertford*, a work that, according to Emma Lipton, 'shows Lydgate's inability to imagine a viable model for celebrating kingly justice and perhaps his own dissatisfaction with the ending'.[3]

Thomas Hoccleve's *Regement of Princes*, on the other hand, is centrally concerned with the art of statecraft. Written for Prince Henry (the future Henry V) in the tradition of mirrors for princes,[4] Hoccleve's most ambitious work was composed in 1410–11, when Prince Henry was temporarily head of the council during Henry IV's prolonged illness.[5] Sometimes read as an attempt to profile the young prince politically,[6] the work is usually understood as delivering a critique of the king's policies by contrasting the virtues of his designated successor, Prince Henry, with those of his father's reign.[7] Surviving in twenty-six manuscripts, Hoccleve's poem appears to have been read widely and, more importantly, by publicly significant individuals.[8]

The arithmetic middle of the poem, and therefore perhaps even its central place, is reserved for the 500-line section entitled 'De justitia' (On Justice) (ll. 2,465–996).[9] Given the lofty expectations of Hoccleve's genre – the mirror for princes – the poem's understanding of justice and law is calibrated for future monarchs and their political needs. Hoccleve's passage on justice, and much of the *Regement* itself, is assembled from readily available commonplaces, while the basic definition of 'justice', as introduced in the first stanza of this chapter, conforms to orthodox views prevalent at the time: 'justice is libertee / Of wil, gevynge unto every wight / That longith to his propre dignitee' (ll. 2,465–7). 'Dignitee' is one's social rank, so that 'justice' is understood not as a form of equality before the law but as equality *within* one's tier in a stratified society. But Hoccleve is quick to adjust to the formative needs of a prince cast into the turbulent world of politics by shifting in the fourth stanza to the paramount importance of accepting counsel and working within conciliar structures:

> Of conseil and of help been we dettours,
> Eche to othir, by right of brethirheede;
> For whan a man yfalle into errour is,
> His brothir owith him conseil and rede
> To correcte and amende his wikkid dede   (ll. 2,486–90)

Conciliar rule was not only a cornerstone of late medieval political theory but also the self-declared basis of Lancastrian political thought.[10] To Hoccleve a king is a constitutional instrument, 'maad to keepen and maynteene / Justice' (ll. 2,514–15). Kings are thus 'made' to uphold justice in accordance with divine law ('The lawe of Cryst', l. 2,502) and natural law ('of the kynde and the nature / of God', ll. 2,507–8). Anticipating the conciliar and constitutional thought of the legal thinker John Fortescue, Hoccleve reiterates the late medieval maxim that kings are bound to uphold the law: 'A kyng is by covenant / Of ooth maad in his coronocioun / Bouwnde to justices sauvacioun' (ll. 2,518–20). Lexically this sentence is held in balance by 'maad' – the first instance invoking kings not as active individuals but as purposive social constructs, while the second use ('by covenant / Of ooth maad') appears to gesture at the same meaning, thus stressing the sacramental and politicised nature of the coronation, before turning 'maad' into an auxiliary part of the verbal phrase 'maad ... Bownde': kings are not only tied to justice but created as limited political actors bound by the act of their coronation. The upshot of this circumspect phrasing is that kings are never free to begin with; at the very moment of their public creation, that is, their crowning, they are already limited in the scope of their actions.

In a series of case studies, mostly drawn from antiquity, Hoccleve illustrates the basic principles of peaceful and just rule. But then, in an interpolation, he adduces the Lancastrian protoplast and father-in-law of John Gaunt as a law-maker and defender of justice: 'Of Lancastre good Duke Henri also, / Whos justice is writen and auctorysid' (ll. 2,646–7). By embedding the first duke of Lancaster in a string of Classical precedents for just and lawful rule (Gaunt was Prince Henry's grandfather), Hoccleve historicises Lancastrian principles of governance and creates a constitutional pedigree for Prince Henry.

As a next step, the poem reinforces the dynastic principle behind constitutional and just governance by invoking the tale of a Persian judge who knowingly condemned an innocent man to death (ll. 2,685–709). On hearing of this case, the king of Persia has the judge flayed alive before using his skin as upholstery for the justice's chair on which he places the judge's son – to serve as a reminder for the need to uphold justice without compromise. The gruesome punishment meted out by the king and the macabre decision that follows detract from the point (perhaps not readily noticeable for a modern audience) that in this tale the role of the judge is hereditary. This is Hoccleve's essential building brick for the ensuing analogy between kings and judges, one that turns monarchs into justices, presiding with their instruments of grace and equity over a country's legal system. And yet Hoccleve's king is not above the law: 'Prince excellent, have your lawes cheer; / Observe hem and offende hem by now weye' (ll. 2,773–4). For all his power, a king must observe the laws of his polity. And it is here that Hoccleve turns to technical speech, in admonishing the prince to combat what the narrator perceives to be a tendency to resort to vigilante justice (ll. 2,787–97). 'Armed folk' participating in unlawful 'assemblee' (ll. 2,791–2) do not wish to pursue actions at common law: 'Hem deyneth nat an accioun attame / At commun lawe' (ll. 2,795–6). Here, Hoccleve's understanding of constitutional law is fully uttered: his king is not only the head of the executive and judicial branches of government but he also presides of the legislative domain: 'Is ther no lawe this to remedie?' (l. 2,801).

But it was not until the troubled reign of Henry V's son, Henry VI, that England's waning fortunes in the Hundred Years' War triggered a renewed literary impulse to question governance and law. The first wave was formed by the political poems of the 1430s and 1440s, primarily the remarkable *Libelle of Englyshe Polycye* (henceforth: *Libelle*).[11] The *Libelle* is a combative political poem, written in response to the collapse of the Anglo-Burgundian alliance at the Congress of Arras in 1435, an event that marked a turning point in the Hundred Years' War. Burgundy's reconciliation with France could not have come at a worse time for England: the king, Henry VI, was still in his minority, and the ruling council was bitterly divided into the feuding camps of Cardinal Beaufort and the king's uncle, Humphrey, Duke of Gloucester. In the following year, Burgundy's Philip the Good turned on his former ally and swiftly laid siege to Calais. Duke Humphrey led a successful relief effort and, as a punitive measure, raided Flanders. This relief effort coincided with the end of Henry's minority, and the writer behind the anonymous *Libelle* appeared to have seen an opportunity to rally the country's elites around a unifying political project that now sounds all too familiar: xenophobia at home, isolationism abroad, all propped up by a jingoistic mercantilist regime of import taxes. The *Libelle* – which means small book or booklet – survives in two versions or editions. The first was composed after the siege of Calais but before the end of 1438. A second version circulated before June 1441 and was followed by a subsequent revision. The poem, as I have argued elsewhere,[12] probably originated in the young king's immediate circle of educators and advisors, and I believe that the *Libelle* is most closely linked with Richard Caudray, Clerk of the Council until 1435, thereafter secretary to John Holland, Admiral of England, and Dean of St Martin le Grand in London.

Although the *Libelle* is firmly situated in a clearly defined set of fifteenth-century political and economic circumstances – I like to think of it therefore as an acute political poem – this work is crucial to understanding the legal implications of England's European and global political ambitions during the Lancastrian, Tudor and even Jacobean periods. Given that the *Libelle* is an anonymous work of just over 1,100 lines, it is remarkable that we have twenty surviving manuscript copies, and we know of at least another handful of lost exemplars. More tantalising still is the list of known early owners of copies of the *Libelle* – a list that reads like a who's who of lawyers and public figures in early modern England: in the fifteenth century, John Paston, who was trained in the law, owned a copy of the poem; in the sixteenth century, Queen Elizabeth's chief advisor and secretary of state William Cecil owned a manuscript, while the travel writer Richard Hakluyt had access to two exemplars; in the seventeenth century, both Chief Justice Matthew Hale and Samuel Pepys, Clerk of the Acts to the Navy Board, owned copies. In fact, Hale's copy may have been previously owned by the leading seventeenth-century legal thinker John Selden, who quotes thirty-four lines from the poem in his influential treatise *Mare clausum* (*The Closed Sea*), a repudiation of Hugo Grotius's influential plea for open seas *Mare liberum* (*The Open Sea*).

In addition to its reception by leading lawyers in subsequent centuries, the *Libelle*'s investments in the law and legal thought are twofold. The reason why both Pepys and Selden took an interest in the poem is its remarkably sophisticated approach to the notion of territorial waters in international law. Although the notion of viewing the sea as territorial already existed in late medieval England, the law had not yet formulated the concept of territorial waters. The *Libelle* may very well have been the first work to have done so. The poem resourcefully draws on a number of legal mechanisms to stake its claim. The detailed case made by the *Libelle* is complex and has been discussed in detail,[13] but the poem relies on a number of principal arguments to advance the notion of territorial waters which include employing Emperor Sigismund's imperial *regalia* following his visit to Henry V; using precedent by adducing a list of sea-keeping kings of England; citing the need to curb piracy; and frequently restating the territorial equivalence of land and sea. While the *Libelle* may not have succeeded in effecting a shift in legal thought and policy at the time of its composition and initial circulation, the poem's subsequent use by John Selden underscores its long-lasting influence on the theory of territorial waters and on the development of international law.

The second area in which the *Libelle* stands out if viewed through the prism of the law is its ingenious use of the petitionary form of the *libellus*, the technical term for the bill of complaint submitted to the Court of Admiralty.[14] The *Libelle* is an unusual variation on the theme that Matthew Giancarlo calls the 'bill-poem'.[15] Such poems embed themselves in the complaint tradition, usually invoking complaints made by individuals. Instead, the *Libelle* advances an instance of collective complaint or clamour.[16] Essentially, the *Libelle* is a policy complaint requesting redress, basing the poem on a petitionary *libellus* employed in certain civil law courts, including the Court of Admiralty and various mercantile jurisdictions. The appropriate legal model for the *Libelle* is therefore the Latin *libellus*: 'A *libellus* is a writing in which are contained the suit which is sued, the case for the suit, and the name of the disputant and the action', as one early English jurist puts it.[17] In civil law, the *processus ordinarii*, or legal suit, opens with the presentation of the bill of complaint' (*oblatio libelli*). And this is how the *Libelle* refers to itself at the outset: '[t]he trewe processe of Englyshe polycye', followed by 'the processe of the Libelle of Englyshe polycye'.[18] Contemporary readers understood the legal allusions embedded in the poem's format, and one scribe of the *Libelle* modifies the envoi in one of the manuscripts of the second edition, replacing the word 'libelle' (l. 1,142) with the phrase 'little bylle' – a bill of complaint as used in the common law.

A few years later, in about 1440, Osbern Bokenham composed in English the prose work *Mappula Angliae*, a text designed to accompany his saints' lives.[19] Bokenham based the *Mappula* on the opening survey of England in Ranulph Higden's *Polychronicon*, one of the most widely read and authoritative medieval encyclopaedias. In his text, Bokenham engages with the technical language of the common law and its lexical complexity. He opens his section on law with an acknowledgement of the specificity of English law: 'knowlege of lawis and of suche termys as been straunge and vsyd yn lawis, is nessessary to hem þat byn vndur þe lawis & nedis muste be gouernyd & rewlyd by þe lawis'.[20] The progressive idea underlying this statement – that those to whom the law applies must understand that law – is an early forerunner of early modern attempts to disseminate the law more widely across the population. Bokenham's sentiment is his own and marks a departure from his source.

Bokenham then offers a brief history of English laws which leads him to put into practice his own belief in the need to render understandable to his audience some of the arcane laws that govern them, or, as he calls it, terms

that are 'straunge to vundurstonde'.[21] To do so, Bokenham explains a series
of Old English legal terms, but he does so simultaneously in Middle English
and in Law French, claiming both accessibility (through the use of English)
and authority (by employing the French terms):

> Mundebryche: that is to sey on frensshe blesmure de honneire, on Englyshe
> hurte of worschepe. | Borugebriche is in frensche blesmure de court ou de cloys,
> In englische hurt of Court or of cloos. Grythebriche is brekynge of pees.
> Myskennynge is variacioun or chaunge of speche in court. | Sheawynge is
> leyng forthe of marchaundise.[22]

References to the law are not frequent in the *Mappula*, but this passage is
unique in its enlightened understanding of the need to disseminate legal
education – a principle by which Bokenham himself abides.

The dynastic turmoil of the Wars of the Roses precipitated a Lancastrian
windfall of legally informed and jurisprudential works and manuscripts,
including the poetry of George Ashby, the writings of John Fortescue,
Thomas Littleton's *Tenures*, and the circulation of the *nova statuta*. In
a circumstantial way, the Wars of the Roses, the dynastic struggle in the
1460s, 1470s and 1480s that ended the Lancastrian hold on the throne, also
created the conditions necessary for political and legal reflection. The hopes
of the Lancastrians rested on Prince Edward of Westminster, Henry VI's only
son. His education and safe-keeping became the focus of the exiled party, and
two writers, drawn from Henry VI's inner circle of administrators and
bureaucrats, emerged at the helm of the project to guide the young prince:
George Ashby and John Fortescue. Ashby, for many years clerk of the
signet to Henry and Queen Margaret, is best known for *A Prisoner's
Reflections* and his mirror for princes, *The Active Policy of a Prince*.
The second text was written for Prince Edward, much in the tradition of
Hoccleve's *Regement of Princes*. Although not overtly concerned with the
law, at one point Ashby's poem urges the young prince to implement and
guard the laws of England:

> Prouide that lawe may be excercised,
> And executed in his formal cours,
> Aftur the statutes autorised
> By noble Kynges youre progenitours
> Yeving therto youre aide helpe & socour.
> So shall ye kepe folk in subieccion
> Of the lawe and trewe dispocision.   (ll. 520–6)[23]

For Ashby, laws primarily exist to be kept; they ensure that people remain 'in
subieccion'. Yet, as Rosemary McGerr has shown, this moment in Ashby's

text is significant because the narrator expects Edward to have read the statutes of the realm since he urges the prince to respect the statutory legislation enacted by his ancestors.[24]

It was Ashby's fellow Lancastrian exile, the former chief justice John Fortescue, who took it upon himself to instruct Prince Edward in legal custom and statutory legislation. Fortescue's *De laudibus legum Angliae* (*In Praise of England's Laws*) stands out among his three major legal treatises as a literary work, a mirror for princes – the other two are *On the Governance of England* and *De natura legis naturae* (*On the Nature of Natural Law*). Unlike Ashby's *Active Policy*, Fortescue's work is written in Latin, thereby assuming an authoritative quality that is denied to vernacular texts. The *De laudibus* and the English *On the Governance* establish Fortescue's celebrated theory of constitutional and political law, that of the *dominium politicum et regale* (the political and royal realm). In this model, which applies to England in Fortescue's thought, the king as sovereign is subject to the will of the people, as expressed in the institution of parliament. Addressing Edward directly, Fortescue clarifies his legal theory:

> For you doubt whether you should apply yourself to the study of the laws of the English or of the civil laws, because the civil laws are celebrated with a glorious fame throughout the world above all other human laws. Do not, O king's son, let this consideration trouble you. For the king of England is not able to change the laws of his kingdom at pleasure, for he rules his people with a government not only regal but also political.[25]

The degree to which Fortescue's king is constitutionally limited in his power has been the subject of much debate,[26] but English legal thought would hark back to Fortescue's *dominium politicum et regale* for the coming centuries. If we situate this work historically in the context of political exile and the predicament of the Lancastrian side, then it is tempting to read Fortescue's legal theory as occasional and conditioned by the needs of his losing side. Yet if read from within fifteenth-century political narratives, then the *De laudibus* emerges as a visionary, almost apolitical, work that applies equally to all rulers of England, whether Yorkist or Lancastrian, and that is marked primarily by a deep understanding of and loyalty to England's legal system rather than to any particular political faction.

In his three major treatises, Fortescue was able to articulate a legal definition of England's political structures precisely because the political stability afforded by sixty years of consecutive Lancastrian rule allowed these structures to unfold, while Thomas de Littleton's *Tenures* – a work belonging to the law proper rather than to literary discourses – emerged towards the end of this period as a first comprehensive attempt to write down the principles of the common law.

Notes

1. Paul E. Gill, 'Politics and Propaganda in Fifteenth-Century England: The Polemical Writings of Sir John Fortescue', *Speculum* 462 (1971), 344; S. B. Chrimes, *English Constitutional Ideas in the Fifteenth Century* (Cambridge: Cambridge University Press, 1936), 64–5.
2. Jennifer Sisk, '"We Must Be Tretable": Law and Affect in Lydgate's *Saint Austin at Compton*', *Modern Philology* 112:1 (2014), 93.
3. Emma Lipton, 'Law, Chaucer, and Representation in Lydgate's "Disguising at Hertford"', *JEGP* 113: 3 (2014), 364.
4. On this genre in the fifteenth century, see Matthew Giancarlo, 'Mirror, Mirror: Princely Hermeneutics, Practical Constitutionalism, and the Genres of the English *Fürstenspiegel*', *Exemplaria* 27:1–2 (2015), 35–54.
5. David Watt, 'Thomas Hoccleve's *Regiment of Princes*', in *A Companion to Fifteenth-Century English Poetry*, ed. Julia Boffey and A. S. G. Edwards (Cambridge: D. S. Brewer, 2013), 47. Hoccleve revised the poem in 1412 (Watt, 47).
6. Ethan Knapp, *The Bureaucratic Muse: Thomas Hoccleve and the Literature of Late Medieval England* (Philadelphia: Pennsylvania State University Press, 1997), 80.
7. Judith Ferster, *Fictions of Advice: The Literature and Politics of Counsel in Late Medieval England* (Philadelphia: University of Pennsylvania Press, 1996), 89–159.
8. Watt, 'Thomas Hoccleve's *Regiment of Princes*', 48–9.
9. All quotations to *The Regement of Princes* are taken from Thomas Hoccleve, *The Regiment of Princes*, ed. Charles Ramsay Blyth (Kalamazoo, MI: Western Michigan University, 1999).
10. Sebastian Sobecki, *Unwritten Verities: The Making of England's Vernacular Legal Culture, 1463–1549* (Notre Dame, IN: University of Notre Dame Press, 2015), 70–101.
11. The standard edition is George Warner, ed., *The Libelle of Englyshe Polycye: A Poem on the Use of Sea-Power, 1436* (Oxford: Clarendon Press, 1926).
12. Sebastian Sobecki, *Last Words: The Public Self and The Social Author in Late Medieval England* (Oxford: Oxford University Press), forthcoming.
13. Sebastian Sobecki, *The Sea and Medieval English Literature* (Cambridge: D. S. Brewer, 2008), 145–60.
14. Sebastian Sobecki, 'Bureaucratic Verse: William Lyndwood, the Privy Seal, and the Form of *The Libelle of Englyshe Polycye*', *New Medieval Literatures* 12:1 (July 2011), 251–88.
15. Matthew Giancarlo, *Parliament and Literature in Late Medieval England* (Cambridge: Cambridge University Press, 2007), 144–5.
16. On clamour writing, see Wendy Scase, *Literature and Complaint in England, 1272–1553* (Oxford: Oxford University Press, 2007).

17. *Select Bills in Eyre AD 1292–1333*, ed. William Craddock Bolland, *Selden Society*, 30 (London: Quaritch, 1914), xiii–xiv. The translation is from Scase, *Literature and Complaint in England, 1272–1553*.
18. See the incipit as well as ll. 1, 1049, 1078, and the English explicit.
19. Osbern Bokenham, 'Mappula Angliae', ed. Carl Horstmann, *Englische Studien* 10 (1887), 1–34.
20. Bokenham, 'Mappula Angliae', 21.
21. Bokenham, 'Mappula Angliae', 21.
22. Bokenham, 'Mappula Angliae', 21.
23. *George Ashby's Poems: From the Fifteenth-Century MSS at Cambridge*, ed. Mary Bateson, repr. 1965, EETS e.s. 76 (London: Kegan Paul, Trench and Trübner, 1899), 28.
24. Rosemarie McGerr, *A Lancastrian Mirror for Princes: The Yale Law School New Statutes of England* (Bloomington, IN: Indiana University Press, 2011), 106.
25. John Fortescue, *De laudibus legum Anglie*, ed. Stanley B. Chrimes (Cambridge: Cambridge University Press, 1949), 25.
26. For a summary, see Sobecki, *Unwritten Verities*, 70–101.

Further Reading

Giancarlo, Matthew, *Parliament and Literature in Late Medieval England*, Cambridge: Cambridge University Press, 2007.

McGerr, Rosemarie, *A Lancastrian Mirror for Princes: The Yale Law School New Statutes of England*, Bloomington, IN: Indiana University Press, 2011.

Nuttall, Jennifer, *The Creation of Lancastrian Kingship: Literature, Language and Politics in Late Medieval England*, Cambridge: Cambridge University Press, 2007.

Scase, Wendy, *Literature and Complaint in England, 1272–1553*, Oxford: Oxford University Press, 2007.

Sobecki, Sebastian, *Unwritten Verities: The Making of England's Vernacular Legal Culture, 1463–1549*, Notre Dame, IN: University of Notre Dame Press, 2015.

Staley, Lynn, *Languages of Power in the Age of Richard II*, Philadelphia, PA: Pennsylvania State University Press, 2006.

Strohm, Paul, *England's Empty Throne: Usurpation and the Language of Legitimation, 1399–1422*, New Haven, CT: Yale University Press, 1998; repr. 2006.

Politique: Languages of Statecraft between Chaucer and Shakespeare, Notre Dame, IN: University of Notre Dame Press, 2005.

15

CORINNE SAUNDERS

Middle English Romance and Malory's *Morte Darthur*

> It was a king bi are dawes [former days]
> That in his time were gode lawes
> He dede maken and ful wel holden.
> *(Havelok the Dane, 27–9)*

Romance has most often been viewed as an escapist mode, comparable to contemporary fantasy and romantic fiction. Northrop Frye characterises romance as 'secular scripture', built on universal human desires and archetypal patterns – a genre, one might suppose, with little space for the law. Yet medieval romance is fluid and various: writing in 'romanz', the vernacular, only gradually came to have generic associations. Subjects range from classical to historical to legendary, linked most of all by recurring motifs: love, adventure, the supernatural. Often exotic and fantastical, romance is also profoundly concerned with social contexts, and this balance between mimetic and non-mimetic is acutely evident in its engagement with law. Middle English romances reflect a growing 'legal consciousness' that shapes 'values, beliefs and aspirations' and 'provid[es] a reserve of knowledge, memory and reflective thought'.[1] Their treatment of legal concepts and processes can be remarkably specific, while the idea of 'good laws' also informs their deep structures, founded on notions of order, honour and right. Romances repeatedly dramatise issues of inheritance and outlawry, accusations of felony and treason, trials by combat and ordeal, oaths and contracts, and debates over property and marriage. In Malory's *Morte Darthur*, these motifs are woven into a tragic disquisition on the need for social order founded on good laws.

Exile and Return

The motif of exile and return of the rightful heir forms a cornerstone of romance. Two early 'matter of England' romances, *King Horn* (*c.* 1225) and *Havelok the Dane* (*c.* 1275), adapt Anglo-Norman sources to relate in contrasting ways a lost heir's return to the throne. *King Horn* is founded on folkloric patterns and repetitions, located in the symbolic kingdoms of Westernesse and Sudenesse and structured by Horn's battles against the Saracens and journeys over the sea, yet its broad movement from disorder to order affirms the need to uphold just law. The work centres on the reward of right and punishment of wrong: Fikenhild (a wicked steward) misleads Aylmar ('the gode Kyng'), his falseness set against the troth of Rymenhild and Horn; Horn, disguised as a 'thralle', is rewarded for his prowess by being dubbed knight; and later, falsely accused, made 'fleme' (outlaw), returning to gain his 'heritage' and 'baronage'; finally, the villain is 'todraghe' (torn apart or quartered) as a public mark of his crime.[2]

Havelok traces a similar pattern of exile, return and establishment of just rule, but with remarkable realism that balances out fairy-tale aspects such as the king-light that shines from Havelok's mouth. The narrative opens with an extended account of the laws of the holy Anglo-Saxon king Athelwold: he rewards righteous men and has traitors, informers, outlaws and thieves bound '[a]nd heye hengen on galwe-tre'. Bribes are resisted, merchants travel safely, victims receive justice, those who harm widows are 'kesten / In feteres and ful faste festen', and those who shame maidens 'He made him sone of limes spille'.[3] Like the laws of William I and Henry I in early chronicles, Athelwold's laws prove his excellence. The penalty for rape resembles early post-Conquest law, while details echoing Anglo-Saxon laws suggest the poet was familiar with Ælfred's law-code.

The narrative is saturated with legal vocabulary, processes and oaths. The dying Athelwold summons his earls and barons by writs (136), while the earl Godrich swears on the missal and implements of the Mass to protect the king's daughter and heir, Goldeboru (185–8). This ideal legal order (echoed by the Danish king Birkabein's rule) is contrasted to the disordered present, where Godrich and his Danish counterpart Godard (protector of Prince Havelok) betray their oaths, and are condemned for treason and felony. Treason is characterised by misappropriation of law: Goldeboru is threatened with exile, gallows and fire if she does not marry the supposed thrall Havelok and the marriage is endorsed to 'parlement' by the archbishop of York (1180). Loyalty too is presented in legal terms: the Danish Ubbe pledges himself as 'borw' (guarantor, 1667) for Havelok, summoning all men by writ; the Danes take 'man-rede' (oaths of fealty, 2265); Havelok swears loyalty and takes an oath of vengeance 'on the bok' (2311, 2373). Godard's graphically recounted death enacts legal penalties for treason: he is flayed, bound backwards on a mean horse, dragged and hanged, while Godrich, defeated in a duel by Havelok, is submitted to the English for judgement and drawn and burnt at the stake, a warning to traitors. All swear 'after law of londe' 'manrede ... on the bok' (2817, 2850–1) to Havelok, the rightful king who liberates and unites England and Denmark, engendering a line of kings. *Havelok* both endorses and exemplifies English law, placing it as essential to social order and just rule.

Romance outlaws were not always lost heirs to the throne. The Anglo-Norman *Fouke le Fitz Waryn* (a prose redaction (*c*. 1325–40) of a lost French verse romance) treats the loss of feudal inheritance, combining the historical outlaw's pursuit of his rightful inheritance with a narrative of chivalrous exploits; a sixteenth-century summary signals a lost Middle English version. In the English romance of *Gamelyn* (*c*. 1350), the forest rather than foreign lands is the place of exile; the work may underlie the Robin Hood ballads and was a source for Thomas Lodge's *Rosalynde* (1590), in turn Shakespeare's source for *As You Like It*. Like *Havelok*, *Gamelyn* engages vividly with detailed legal processes, perhaps reflecting the gentry's concerns. It focuses on a struggle over inheritance between Sir John of Boundis's three sons. Although Sir John divides his property equally, Gamelyn's share is taken by his elder brother, whose power is endorsed by a corrupt sherriff and company of clerics. When Gamelyn and his companion Adam retaliate with violence, they are accused of contravening 'the kinges pees' and flee to the forest, the traditional place of exile ('He most needes walke in woode / that may not walke in toune'), but also of liberty ('Better is us ther loos / than in town y-bounde').[4] Here Gamelyn encounters the king of the outlaws and his men, and eventually becomes their king. While the designation of the forest as a separate legal space, connected with hunting, game and play, colours the narrative, the work also treats seriously the process of outlawry, which removed the protection of the law and necessitated flight; the outlaw was seen as bearing the wolf's head and was to be killed if caught. When his brother becomes sheriff and bailiff, Gamelyn is cried 'wolves-heed' and thrown into the 'kinges prisoun' on return to await judgement (710, 741). Like Robin Hood later, Gamelyn and his men challenge false justice, enacting a rough and ready form of right rooted in force. Gamelyn saves from hanging his second brother, Ote, who has stood 'borwe' (795) for him, and takes the role of judge in a comic courtroom scene. In the judge's seat, Gamelyn fetters his brother and the judge, brings the jury to the bar and orders 'a quest' (inquest, 840), in which his men condemn jury, sheriff and judge to be hanged. The legal detail inflects comedy and folktale with realism and provides a strong – if brutal – critique of corruption. In its focus on individual wit and strength, depiction of outlaw society and opposition to established authority, *Gamelyn* asserts robust notions of justice and rights enforced by physical strength.

Ordeals and Oaths

The movement from disorder to order inherent in exile-and-return narratives is also integral to works that turn on ideals, oaths and testing. A third romance set in an English past, *Athelston* (*c.* 1355–80), returns to the subject of corruption. Despite this work's hagiographic structures, legal concepts and practices pervade it from the start, when King Athelston and his three brothers take an oath of loyalty.[5] The eldest brother, Wymond, swears a second, false oath, 'be masse-book and belle' (150), that his brother Egelond is a traitor – and Athelston in turn swears vengeance. When the king furiously kicks the queen, who intercedes on Egelond's behalf, her child is stillborn, chilling evidence of the effects of injustice: 'Thus may a traytour baret [strife] rayse' (294). Legal vocabulary colours the narrative: the fourth brother, the archbishop of Canterbury, stands 'borewe' (305) until there has been an enquiry and 'comoun asent / In the pleyne parlement' (447–8); the queen offers her 'moregeve' (dowry, 315) and the bishop 'warysoun' (a reward, perhaps of lands or an annuity, 402) to the messenger. Athelston's rashness is affirmed by his rejection of law: when he strips the archbishop of his powers, England is 'entyrdytyd' (excommunicated, 513). When the king repents, the Archbishop invokes divine justice through trial by ordeal. In contrast to the unjust kick, the fire, ritually consecrated by the Archbishop, preserves rather than destroys bodies: Egelond emerges 'unblemeschyd' (588); his children laugh, finding the fire 'cold onowgh' (610); and his wife stands still 'amydde, / And callyd it merye and bryght' (634–5). The loss of the king's son is answered in the birth of Egelond's son, Saint Edmund. Alongside this hagiographic emphasis, the law continues to be evoked: men withdraw at childbirth 'As it was the landys lawe' (646); the bishop swears 'be book and belle' to exact the 'ryght doom' (681, 683) of ordeal on the king if he does not identify the traitor, who, failing the trial of fire, is drawn through the streets and hanged. The concluding moral is one of legal judgement: 'Leve nevere traytour have betere endyng, / But swych dome for to dye' (811–12).

Many other romances turn on oath and ordeal, though not always with such detail. Most celebrated is the exploration of *trouthe* and treason found in the late fourteenth-century Arthurian romance *Sir Gawain and the Green Knight*, in which a series of covenants calls into question Gawain's contract of chivalry, symbolised by the Pentangle or 'endeles knot' on his shield.[6] The Green Knight's 'couenaunt' (393) with Gawain is rehearsed with sinister legal seriousness: the Green Knight will 'quit-clayme' his axe (292); Gawain carefully restates the 'forwardes' (378) and gives his own binding oath, 'I swere þe for soþe, and by my seker traweþ' (403). At Hautdesert, he enters into a second 'gomen' (273), the covenant of exchanging winnings with Sir Bertilak. The 'forwarde' (1105) sworn each evening is clearly set out 'bi lawe' (1643): 'Swete, swap we so: sware with trawþe' (1108). The terms 'covenant', 'forward' and 'trawþe' are repeated, and the bargains sealed with drink. Gawain uses legal terminology in presenting his winnings, 'I wowche hit saf fynly' (1391), invoking the covenant when refusing to reveal the source of the kisses he returns, 'Þat watz not forward' (1395). On the third evening, having concealed the supposedly magical girdle, he speaks first to 'fylle ... oure forwardez' (1934). The language of 'trawþe' similarly colours the denouement at the Green Chapel: the Green Knight rehearses the first covenant, and after the two feinted blows, Gawain reminds him of its terms, 'Bot on stroke here me fallez' (2328). This 'trawþe' is kept, but the higher 'trawþe' of the Pentangle has been broken: concealing the girdle, placing love of life over trust in the virtues of the Pentangle, jeopardises the interlinked whole – an act of treachery, falsehood, covetousness and cowardice. In contravening his covenant, Gawain contravenes Christian *trouthe* – but from this fault, learns to put on greater humility. This romance aligns earthly and spiritual oaths, but demonstrates the need for grace as well as justice.

Love and Chivalry

Legal concerns are integral to narratives of exile and return, ordeal and oath. Yet even romances more focused on secular love and chivalry prove surprisingly conscious of legal concepts and terminology. Thomas Chestre's *Sir Launfal*, a late fourteenth-century reworking of Marie de France's *Lanval* (c. 1160–80), demonstrates how deeply legal concepts and processes penetrate the literary imagination. The *lai* recounts the eponymous hero's alienation from the court, his encounter with a faery mistress and his trial for treachery when he claims that his beloved's beauty exceeds that of the queen. Both Chestre and Marie portray the trial in realistic detail, elaborated in the English: Launfal is threatened with hanging 'as a thef'; the queen makes a 'waiowr' (condition) that her eyes may be put out (itself a legal penalty) if Launfal is proven true; Perceval and Gawain stand as 'borwes'; and the barons gather to 'yeve jugement' on Launfal on the appointed day, urging a mitigation of the penalty to exile. With the appearance of his lady, Launfal is 'quyt', leaving the court for Avalon.[7] The grounding of marvel in such careful legal process enhances the effect of magic realism, but also renders the work a sharp social critique.

Ywain and Gawain, a late fourteenth-century English adaptation of Chrétien de Troyes's *Le Chevalier au Lion* (c. 1170), similarly balances marvellous adventure with legal realism, explicitly probing the female predicament:

Alundyne must accept Ywain, her lord's killer, in marriage to 'maintene [her] rightes'.[8] The second part of the romance relates Ywain's quest to regain Aundyne after breaking his promise to return. To refute the charge of 'treson and treachery' (1609), he fights a series of battles to defend ladies, which repeatedly involve legal issues, from ravishment to calumny to exploitation. Legal terminology is prominent: Ywain rescues a besieged lady and receives the 'trowth' of her attacker (1925), who promises to mend his 'trispase' (1930); defends the 'right' (2170) of Lunete, imprisoned for 'tresown' (2133); defeats a giant who demands a man's daughter as 'warisowne' (payment; reward, 2399); and opposes the 'unsely [unhappy; evil] law' (3129) of two giants who keep women in 'trowage' (servitude, 3035). The work explicitly states the need for justice: 'Wha juges men with wrang / The same jugement sal thai fang' (2641-2). The final episode revolves around a quarrel of property between two sisters. Ywain defends the younger, who demands her 'right' (3424) of inheritance, and Gawain the older, who seeks 'dome' from Arthur (3428). Arthur resolves the battle by legally dividing the land, using the model of tenantry: 'In hir land I sal hir sese, / And sho sal hald hir land of the / And to the tharfore mak fewté ... / And sho sal be to the tenant' (3760-6). This, the narrator tells us, is the first division of lands in England (3767-8). While the male quest for maturity and self-realisation is the ostensible focus, this is closely related to issues of land, feudal loyalty and protection of women. Romance, then, explores in realistic detail the need for good laws, fair judgement and just consequences, particularly in relation to property, inheritance and marriage.

Malory's *Morte Darthur*

A century later, Malory's *Morte Darthur* draws together many of the legal concerns of romance, weaving them into a narrative of fellowship and chivalry and their inverse, felony and treason. The *Morte* explicitly identifies its author as 'a knyght presoner sir Thomas Malleorré'.[9] If, as seems likely, he can be identified with Sir Thomas Malory of Newbold Revell, he had a unique personal knowledge of the law, accused of a series of crimes, many connected to an alleged attempt to murder the Duke of Buckingham, including rape, theft, church-robbery, extortion, cattle-rustling and damage to property. Although Malory was twice charged with felony, he was never tried; he spent eight years in London prisons before being freed when Yorkist forces defeated the Lancastrians in 1460. Without the evidence of a trial, the truth is impossible to gauge: the accusations may be linked to other attacks intended to damage public figures. Malory's apparent contravention of the law continued. Allegedly involved in a plot against the king in 1468, he was again imprisoned, though not formally charged, and during this period wrote the *Morte*. Excluded from two general pardons (a mark of the seriousness of his alleged crimes), he was freed with the Lancastrian return in 1470, dying in 1471. Although this biography may seem at odds with the *Morte*'s focus on chivalry, the book is also deeply engaged with its inverse, lawlessness.

Malory's reworking of his 'Frensshe booke' (I.5, 12), in reality a series of sources including parts of the thirteenth-century Old French Vulgate, Post-Vulgate and Prose Tristan cycles, and the English Alliterative and Stanzaic *Morte Arthure* poems, was marked by heightened realism, evident in his concern with legality and justice. From the start, Arthur's legitimacy as king and authorisation by the Commons are emphasised: 'We wille have Arthur unto our kyng!' (I.7, 16). His war against Rome is carefully justified as a response to the demand for 'trewage', decided by a 'counceyle' of nobles, and Arthur states the 'evydence' of his claim to the Roman Empire based on lineage (V.1, 185–8). Malory's most striking legal addition to his sources, the chivalric oath sworn each year by all knights at Pentecost, establishes a system of law. The oath requires them

> never to do outerage nothir mourthir, and allwayes to fle treson, and to gyff mercy unto hym that askith mercy ... allwayes to do ladyes, damesels, and jantilwomen and wydowes [socour:] strengthe hem in hir ryghtes, and never to enforce them, uppon payne of dethe. Also, that no man take no batayles in a wrongefull quarell for no love ne for no worldis goodis. (III.15, 120)

While the oath echoes chivalric treatises, the clause concerning violence against women is unusual and seems to engage with contemporaneous (though not generally enforced) English legal penalties of death for rape. As upholders of justice, knights are bound to defend women, who are vulnerable in a world where law depends on single combat.

The rest of the *Morte* explores the enactment – and failure – of the oath. Thus Launcelot's adventures typically centre on encounters with transgressive knights, who, rather than taking up righteous quarrels, assert power over knights and ladies through unfair means. Sir Tarquin has imprisoned 'good knyghtes three score and foure' (VI.7, 264), while Sir Peris de Forest Savage is specifically condemned as a rapist: 'here by this way hauntys a knyght that dystressis all ladyes and jantylwomen, and at the leste he robbyth them other lyeth by hem' (VI.10, 269; the detail of rape is not in the French source). Through the appellation 'de Foreste Savage' (VI.10, 270), also not in the French, Malory places Peris as an outlaw figure, his contravention of chivalry explicitly condemned by Launcelot: 'He doth shame unto the Order of Knyghthode, and contrary to his oth' (VI.10, 269). In beheading

Peris, Launcelot exacts the legal penalty of death for rape allowed in Malory's time.

As the *Morte* unfolds, failures of the oath become more visible. The final books turn from enemies without to those within, centring on three episodes where the queen is accused of felony or treason. When the knight Sir Patrise dies after eating a poisoned apple intended for Gawain, the readiness of the court to condemn her is striking; the impression of warring factions evokes fifteenth-century court politics. The accusation and process of trial are carefully contextualised. When Guinevere is 'appeled' by Sir Mador (an oral practice largely replaced by writs), Malory adds that 'the custom was such at that tyme that all maner of shamefull deth was called treson' (XVIII.4, 1050). The clause suggests his knowledge of the legal definition of treason as concerning the person of the king or queen, and his familiarity with the term's widening use. Careful distinctions are made between defence and judgement: Arthur as judge cannot fight for the Queen. The principle of trial by combat is clearly stated: God will 'spede the ryght' (XVIII.4, 1051); if Guinevere's defender does not win, she will be burned. The episode illustrates Guinevere's vulnerability but also the law's rightful reach:

> for such custom was used in tho dayes: for favoure, love, nother affinité there sholde be none other but ryghtuous jugemente, as well uppon a kynge as uppon a knyght, and as well uppon a quene as uppon another poure lady.
>
> (XVIII.6, 1055)

Both accuser and defender take oaths before the battle, and the outcome is stated in legal terms: Launcelot arrives to fulfil his 'covenaunte' as Guinevere's defender and Sir Mador 'releace[s] the quene of hys quarell' (XVIII.6-7, 1056-7); the real murderer's identity is discovered. But the scene also hints at the complexities of Launcelot's responsibility, as he reiterates his oath to Arthur:

> y ought of ryght ever [to be] in youre quarell and in my ladyes the quenys quarell to do batayle; for ye ar the man that gaff me the hygh Order of Knyghthode, and that day my lady, youre quen, ded me worshyp ... I promysed her at that day ever to be her knyght in ryght othir in wronge.
>
> (XVIII.7, 1058)

Increasingly, Launcelot will be positioned as Guinevere's knight 'in wronge' and consequently, in opposition to his king.

Malory borrows the second episode of treason, the abduction of the queen by Sir Meliagaunt, from the Lancelot section of the Prose Vulgate, but moves it from the start of Launcelot's career to near its end. The celebrated defence of virtuous love that opens the episode also restates the legal duty of the knight, 'firste reserve the honoure to God and secundely thy quarrell muste com of thy lady' (XVIII.25, 1119). Malory emphasises Meliagaunt's unlawful violation of a peaceable Maying excursion when the Queen's Knights (her customary group of defenders) are unarmed. According to the Statute of Treasons of 1352, which explicitly mentions 'violation' (rape or abduction) of the king's wife, Meliagaunt's crime is one of high treason. Launcelot arraigns him as 'false traytoure' (XIX.4, 1127), an accusation enhanced by his cowardly refusal to fight. This avoidance of legal resolution through battle leads to further disorder when Launcelot, cut by the bars of the window on entering the Queen's chamber, leaves blood in the bed. When Meliagaunt accuses the Queen of adultery with her knights, Launcelot's defence is equivocal: she is innocent of this appeal 'of hyghe treson' (XIX.7, 1135) but not more generally. Meliagaunt's warning, 'yet shulde ye be avysed to do batayle in a wronge quarell, for God woll have a stroke in every batayle', reiterates the rationale for trial by ordeal, and Launcelot's response is carefully phrased ('thys nyght there lay none of thes ten knyghtes wounded with my lady, quene Gwenyver, and that woll I prove with myne hondys' (XIX.7, 1133). The battle itself is carefully detailed: the queen is 'brought tyll a fyre to be brente', the heralds cry 'Lechés les alere!' (Let them begin!), Launcelot escapes to fight as the Queen's champion (XIX.9, 1137–8). Again, Meliagaunt is presented as cowardly, seeking to yield as 'recreaunte' (XIX.9, 1139), and his beheading is fitting to a traitor, yet the episode also suggests that Launcelot wins through might rather than divine intervention.

In the final accusation of treachery, when Launcelot is apprehended in her chamber, Guinevere is guilty. While Malory displaces blame onto the slander and strife created by Agravain and his brothers, and avoids the charge of adultery ('love that tyme was nat as love ys nowadayes', XX.3, 1165), for Arthur to ignore a public accusation is impossible. The focus is the queen's person: Guinevere is accused of treason: 'I may nat with my worshyp but my quene must suffir dethe' (XX.7, 1174). Again, the process of law is emphasised: 'So than there was made grete ordynaunce in this ire, and the quene muste nedis be jouged to the deth'. Malory elaborates:

> the law was such in tho dayes that whatsomever they were, of what astate or degré, if they were founden gylty of treson there shuld be none other remedy but deth, and othir the menour [incriminating circumstances] other the takynge wyth the dede shulde be causer of their hasty jougement. (XX.7, 1174)

Now Arthur refuses Launcelot his role as defender, presenting it as contravening rather than enacting law: 'for he trustyth so much uppon hys hondis and hys myght that he doutyth no man. And therefore for my quene he shall nevermore fyght, for she shall have the law' (XX.7, 1175). She is to suffer trial by fire, brought 'to have her jougement' by armed knights, 'despoyled [stripped] into her smokke' (XX.8, 1176–7). While Launcelot's kinsmen urge him to rescue her, he recognises the destructive force of such an action: 'I woll feyght for the quene, that she ys a trew lady untyll her lorde. But the kynge in hys hete, I drede, woll nat take me as I ought to be takyn' (XX.5, 1171). By keeping his oath to the queen Launcelot betrays his overlord, and has committed the high treason of violating the king's wife. Only his prowess allows him to rescue Guinevere from the fire, the action not a legal trial by combat but a battle with disastrous consequences: he unwittingly kills Gawain's two best-loved brothers, Gareth and Gaheris. Now, Sir Gawain is irrevocably set against him, and Arthur summons his knights through 'lettirs and wryttis' (XX.10, 1186) to besiege Launcelot's castle of Joyous Gard.

Malory contrasts Gawain's implacability with Launcelot's penitence and Arthur's wish for reconciliation, again emphasising legal process. Launcelot defends himself against the charge of treason, arguing that he killed Arthur's knights to preserve his own life, and treated the queen honourably: 'there nys no knyght undir hevyn that dare make hit good uppon me that ever I was traytour unto [the king's] person' (XX.11, 1188). This is enhanced by Launcelot's ceremonious return of Guinevere to Arthur at the decree of the pope, who sends 'bulles undir leade' and, as in *Athelston*, threatens interdictment of the kingdom (XX.13, 1194). Described in extravagant material terms, the ceremony echoes the grandest courtly processions of Malory's time. Launcelot again publicly states his honourable protection of the queen: 'I here myselff . . . woll make hit good uppon hys body that she ys a trew lady unto you' (XX.15, 1197). Gawain's implacability is underscored by his refusal to allow Arthur to accede. Gawain's insistence on Launcelot's treachery, 'evermore callyng hym "traytoure knyght"' (XX.22, 1221), leads to the final fateful configuration of events when the absence of Arthur and Gawain allows Mordred to seize the English throne, and Guinevere's honourable sojourn at Joyous Gard finds a sinister counterpart in her incestuous abduction by Mordred. Discord on the highest level, amongst the fellowship, also leads to discord amongst the people, who support Mordred against their king. Malory sees in their instability echoes of the civil war of his own time ('Lo thus was the olde custom and usayges of thys londe; and men say that we of thys londe have nat yet loste that custom', XXI.1, 1229).

Mordred's treason illuminates Launcelot's virtue: dying, Gawain writes for forgiveness, summoning him back to defend Arthur. The forces of the supernatural, law and chance interweave strangely in the ensuing battle: Gawain's ghost warns Arthur in a dream not to fight and a treaty is carefully set out by the distrustful Mordred and Arthur, but betrayed when a solider draws his sword to kill an adder. In the 'unhappy day' of the final battle, closely modelled on chronicle descriptions of the battle of Towton, Malory depicts the fitting vengeance taken by Arthur on Mordred as 'Traytoure', his treason furthered by his death-blow against his father (XXI.4, 1235–7). The great army raised by Launcelot arrives too late to take vengeance on the 'double traytoure' (XXI.8, 1249). While Constantine takes up the office of king to 'worshypfully' rule the realm (XXI.13, 1259), it is appropriate to the re-establishment of rightful law and order that Launcelot remain to carry out funeral rites for Gawain, to assume a penitential life, and eventually, to give Guinevere a noble burial next to Arthur. Such observances are a crucial response to the devastation of the ending, allowing the book, for all its tragedy, to stand as 'doctryne' for its readers: 'For herein may be seen noble chyvalrye, courtosye, humanyté, frendlynesse, hardynesse, love, frendshyp, cowardyse, murdre, hate, vertue, and synne. Doo after the good and leve the evyl, and it shall brynge you to good fame and renomme' (Caxton's Preface, cxlvi). Like the Middle English romances, the *Morte* commemorates and advocates stable kingship and 'gode lawes' that are 'ful wel holden'.

Notes

1. Anthony Musson, *Medieval Law in Context: The Growth of Legal Consciousness from Magna Carta to the Peasants' Revolt*, Manchester Medieval Studies (Manchester: Manchester University Press, 2001), 1–2.
2. *King Horn*, in *Four Romances of England: 'King Horn', 'Havelok the Dane', 'Bevis of Hampton', 'Athelston'*, ed. Ronald B. Herzman, Graham Drake and Eve Salisbury, TEAMS: Middle English Texts Series (Kalamazoo, MI: Medieval Institute Publications, Western Michigan University, 1999), 11–70, ll. 345, 423, 1283, 1293–94, 1506.
3. *Havelok the Dane*, in *Four Romances of England*, ed. Herzman et al., 73–185, ll. 43, 81–2, 86. Subsequent references to this edition, by line number.
4. *Gamelyn*, in *Middle English Verse Romances*, ed. Donald B. Sands, Exeter Medieval English Texts and Studies (1966; Exeter: Exeter University Press, 1986), 154–81, ll. 548, 672, 606. Subsequent references to this edition, by line number.
5. *Athelston*, in *Four Romances of England*, 341–84, ll. 23–4. Subsequent references to this edition, by line number.
6. *Sir Gawain and the Green Knight*, in *The Poems of the Pearl Manuscript: 'Pearl', 'Cleanness', 'Patience', 'Sir Gawain and the Green Knight'*, ed. Malcolm Andrew and Ronald Waldron, 5th edn, Exeter Medieval Texts and Studies (Exeter: Exeter University Press, 2007), 207–300, l. 630. Subsequent references to this edition, by line number.

7. *Sir Launfal*, in *Of Love and Chivalry: An Anthology of Middle English Romance*, ed. Jennifer Fellows, Everyman's Library (London: Dent, 1993), 199–229, ll. 803, 811, 812, 836, 846, 915.
8. *Ywain and Gawain*, in *'Ywain and Gawain', 'Sir Percyvell of Gales', 'The Anturs of Arther'*, ed. Maldwyn Mills, Everyman's Library (London: Dent, 1992), 1–102, ll. 1171, 1181. Subsequent references to this edition, by line number.
9. Sir Thomas Malory, *The Works of Sir Thomas Malory*, ed. Eugène Vinaver, rev. P. J. C. Field, 3rd edn, 3 vols. (Oxford: Clarendon Press, 1990), IV.29, 180. Subsequent references to this edition, by Caxton's book and chapter numbers, and page number.

Further Reading

Appleby, John C. and Paul Dalton, *Outlaws in Medieval and Early Modern England: Crime, Government and Society, c.1066–c.1600*, Farnham: Ashgate, 2009.
Archibald, Elizabeth and A. S. G. Edwards, eds., *A Companion to Malory*, Arthurian Studies 37, Cambridge: D. S. Brewer, 1996.
Archibald, Elizabeth and Ad Putter, eds., *The Cambridge Companion to Arthurian Legend*, Cambridge Companions to Literature, Cambridge: Cambridge University Press, 2009.
Bellamy, J. G., *The Law of Treason in England in the Later Middle Ages*, Cambridge Studies in Legal History, Cambridge: Cambridge University Press, 1970.
Cartlidge, Neil, ed., *Boundaries in Medieval Romance*, Studies in Medieval Romance, Cambridge: D. S. Brewer, 2008.
    ed., *Heroes and Anti-Heroes in Medieval Romance*, Studies in Medieval Romance, Cambridge: D. S. Brewer, 2012.
Cherewatuk, Karen, *Marriage, Adultery and Inheritance in Malory's 'Morte Darthur'*, Arthurian Studies 68, Cambridge: D. S. Brewer, 2006.
Clanchy, M. T., *From Memory to Written Record: England 1066–1307*, 2nd edn, Oxford: Blackwell, 1993.
Cooper, Helen, *The English Romance in Time: Transforming Motifs from Geoffrey of Monmouth to the Death of Shakespeare*, Oxford: Oxford University Press, 2004.
Crane, Susan, *Insular Romance: Politics, Faith, and Culture in Anglo-Norman and Middle English Literature*, Berkeley: University of California Press, 1986.
Field, P. J. C., *The Life and Times of Sir Thomas Malory*, Arthurian Studies 29, Cambridge: D. S. Brewer, 1993.
Furrow, Melissa, *Expectations of Romance: The Reception of a Genre in Medieval England*, Studies in Medieval Romance, Cambridge: D. S. Brewer, 2009.
Green, Richard Firth, *A Crisis of Truth: Literature and Law in Ricardian England*, The Middle Ages Series, Philadelphia: University of Pennsylvania Press, 1999.
Harding, Alan, *Medieval Law and the Foundations of the State*, Oxford: Oxford University Press, 2002.

Hudson, John, *The Formation of the English Common Law: Law and Society in England from the Norman Conquest to Magna Carta*, The Medieval World, London: Longman, 1996.

Jones, Timothy S., *Outlawry in Medieval Literature*, The New Middle Ages, New York: Palgrave Macmillan, 2010.

Keen, Maurice, *Chivalry*, New Haven, CT: Yale University Press, 1993.

Kennedy, Beverly, *Knighthood in the 'Morte Darthur'*, 2nd edn, Arthurian Studies 11, Cambridge: D. S. Brewer, 1992.

Knight, Stephen, *Robin Hood: A Complete Study of the English Outlaw*, Oxford: Blackwell, 1994.

Krueger, Roberta L., ed., *The Cambridge Companion to Medieval Romance*, Cambridge Companions to Literature, Cambridge: Cambridge University Press, 2000.

Leitch, Megan G., *Romancing Treason: The Literature of the Wars of the Roses*, Oxford: Oxford University Press, 2015.

Lynch, Andrew, *Malory's Book of Arms: The Narrative of Combat in 'Le Morte Darthur'*, Arthurian Studies 39, Cambridge: D. S. Brewer, 1997.

Meale, Carol M., ed., *Readings in Medieval English Romance*, Cambridge: D. S. Brewer, 1994.

Menuge, Noël James, *Medieval English Wardship in Romance and Law*, Cambridge: D. S. Brewer, 2001.

Musson, Anthony, *Medieval Law in Context: The Growth of Legal Consciousness from Magna Carta to the Peasants' Revolt*, Manchester Medieval Studies, Manchester: Manchester University Press, 2001.

Purdie, Rhiannon and Michael Cichon, eds., *Medieval Romance, Medieval Contexts*, Studies in Medieval Romance, Cambridge: D. S. Brewer, 2011.

Putter, Ad and Jane Gilbert, ed., *The Spirit of Medieval English Popular Romance*, Longman Medieval and Renaissance Library, Harlow: Longman-Pearson Education, 2002.

Radulescu, Raluca, *The Gentry Context for Malory's 'Morte Darthur'*, Arthurian Studies 55, Cambridge: D. S. Brewer, 2003.

Radulescu, Raluca and Cory Rushton, eds., *A Companion to Medieval Popular Romance*, Studies in Medieval Romance, Cambridge: D. S. Brewer, 2009.

Riddy, Felicity, *Sir Thomas Malory*, Medieval and Renaissance Authors, Leiden: E. J. Brill, 1987.

Ross, Charles, *The Custom of the Castle: From Malory to Macbeth*, Berkeley: University of California Press, 1997.

Rouse, Robert, *The Idea of Anglo-Saxon England in Middle English Romance*, Studies in Medieval Romance, Cambridge: D. S. Brewer, 2005.

Saunders, Corinne, ed., *A Companion to Romance: From Classical to Contemporary*, Blackwell Companions to Literature and Culture, Oxford: Blackwell, 2004.

Cultural Encounters in the Romance of Medieval England, Studies in Medieval Romance, Cambridge: D. S. Brewer, 2005.

Saunders, Corinne, *The Forest of Medieval Romance: Avernus, Broceliande, Arden*, Cambridge: D. S. Brewer, 1993.

Magic and the Supernatural in Medieval English Romance, Cambridge: D. S. Brewer, 2010.

Rape and Ravishment in the Literature of Medieval England, Cambridge: D. S. Brewer, 2001.

Weiss, Judith, Jennifer Fellows and Morgan Dickson, eds., *Medieval Insular Romance: Translation and Innovation*, Cambridge: D. S. Brewer, 2000.

York, Ernest C., 'Legal Punishment in Malory's *Le Morte Darthur*', *English Language Notes* 11 (1973–4), 14–21.

16

EMMA LIPTON

Marriage and the Legal Culture of Witnessing

To understand the origins of the legal culture of witnessing, we will begin with institutional church history, specifically the Fourth Lateran Council of 1215. Better known in recent scholarship as a watershed in the history of confession, the Fourth Lateran Council catalysed a major shift in legal practice by promoting the witness trial and effectively outlawing the ordeal and trial by battle.[1] In its aftermath, witness depositions became, in practice, the most common form of proof in late medieval English church courts.[2] In contrast to the ordeal and trial by battle which relied on direct divine intervention to determine the outcome, the trial gave new power to ordinary people to act as witnesses in court. This emphasis on testimony in both ecclesiatical and secular courts led to the wide participation of the community in legal culture as victims, neighbours and jurors, ensuring that legal concepts of evidence were not, in Lorna Hutson's words, 'esoteric professional doctrine', but widely diffused through society.[3]

Medieval literature draws on the law of witnessing to theorise the relationship between acts of speaking and their audience; in turn, literature shows that concepts of speaking were shaped by the culture of witnessing in the period. Late medieval literary texts, both dramatic and narrative, frequently depict trials, exploring the legal nature of speech and the role of the audience in bearing witness. These texts depict the role of the witness in court, and also the ways that the prevalence of trials operated more broadly to make acts of seeing and overhearing one's neighbours understood in legal terms as potentially relevant to future litigation. Despite the popular association of the medieval period with spectacles of punishment or torture, late medieval representations of law were shaped more by a legal culture of witnessing centred on public acts of speaking.

This chapter explores this culture of witnessing in the context of weddings and marriage trials, common social practices that shaped medieval ideas of law and performance. Marriage contracts were enforced in the ecclesiastical courts of medieval England, providing representative examples of the participation in the legal system by a broad range of medieval society as witnesses, defendants and plaintiffs. Marriages were often themselves public performances before witnesses who could and sometimes did provide subsequent testimony in court, since the legal enforcement of marriage contracts relied on witness testimony.[4] Marriage cases add another layer to the consideration of the power of legal language since the couple's act of speaking itself made a legal contract. Taking as case studies the depiction of marriage in two texts from East Anglia, the N-Town plays and *The Book of Margery Kempe*, this chapter demonstrates the ways that the culture of witnessing and the literary theorisation of the relationship between speaking and action shaped each other.

Both of these texts point to the social and political implications of the performative quality of legal language in marriages and trials, showing that it had the potential to undermine the linked hierarchies of gender and religious status by giving equal roles to men and women, and by allowing lay people to act like priests. Although it is well known that women's legal status was limited by marriage, the legal definition of marriage contracts gave relative equality to women. According to the legal definition of a marriage contract upheld in the church courts of late medieval England, a marriage contract was made by the exchange of words of present consent ('I take you, X, to be my wedded wife' or 'I take you Y to be my wedded husband') or a promise in the future tense followed by sexual consummation. Technically, the approval of family was not necessary to make a marriage, nor was the presence of a priest essential, although the church promoted clerical participation. According to medieval marriage law, the words of the couple were performative in the sense that J. L. Austin made famous when he defined the performative as the kind of speech in which 'the issuing of the utterance is the performing of the action'.[5] Indeed, the wedding vows were one of Austin's defining examples of 'performative utterances'. Since the promises of both partners made a legally binding contract, marriage could be accomplished entirely by lay people; women's and men's vows were equally effective under the law.

Although technically only the couple's exchange of vows was necessary to make a marriage, witnesses were essential to make the marriage contract enforceable in court. Court records indicate that medieval people were aware of the importance of witnesses to marriage contracts and often invited friends and neighbours to the event.[6] This meant that marriages were performative in the additional sense of having an audience. Although men were summoned more often to serve in this role in court, both women and men were eligible to serve as witnesses in the courtroom and both are recorded as being present at medieval marriages. The fact that marriages were created by the couple and witnessed by neighbours and friends gave power to lay people, in contrast to the institutional moral authority granted to priests when, for example, hearing confession or performing other sanctified offices.

The N-Town 'Marriage of Mary and Joseph' draws attention to two aspects of the performative nature of legal marriage practised in the late medieval ecclesiastical courts: the fact that an act of speaking made a marriage contract, and the fact that the marriage contract required an audience to be enforceable. The N-Town compilation, like other religious play texts, depicts Christian history from Creation to Doomsday in a series of episodic pageants. This collection contains an unusual number of plays about the Virgin Mary, including the marriage play, and is believed to have incorporated material from a separate 'Mary Play' that is no longer extant.[7] At the heart of the marriage play is the holy couple's exchange of vows. When Joseph says, 'I take the, Mary, to wyff' (l. 310) and 'with this rynge, I wedde her ryff' (l. 320), his words are in the present tense, and (when reciprocated by Mary) make a legal contract of the sort enforceable in the courts of late medieval England.[8] Although Austin famously claimed that performatives were 'void' if performed on stage, the play nonetheless calls our attention to the performativity of the legal language of the marriage contract.[9] Furthermore, staging a marriage creates a parallel between those watching a marriage and the audience of the plays, highlighting the theatricality of marriage. This parallel would have been particularly forceful in the case of medieval religious plays which were performed by lay amateurs on the city streets, and were likely to be seen by neighbours like those called on to witness marriage contracts.[10] By making the play's audience communal witnesses to the marriage of Mary and Joseph, the play reminds us that medieval marriages were often public performances.

The N-Town marriage play shows the relationship of legal marriage to lay authority by teaching the theology behind the definition of marriage as an exchange of vows rather than as a sexual union. The grounding of legal court practice in marriage theology is not surprising, since both ecclesiastical and common law, when just, were seen as an expression of divine law.[11] The play features the holy couple and emphasises the fact that a verbal contract rather than sex defined the sacrament of marriage. The play comically emphasises Joseph's reluctance to marry, based on his false assumption that marriage requires sexual activity. He says, 'What? shuld I wedde? God forbede! . . . An old man may never thryff / With a yonge wyf' (ll. 268, 278). Similarly, Mary resists on the grounds she is already dedicated to chastity, being committed to a 'clene lyff . . . in the servyse of God' (ll. 72, 77) instead of an earthly spouse. The couple eventually agree to a chaste marriage, with Joseph vowing that 'in bedde we shul nevyr mete' (l. 295). By drawing attention to the chastity of the couple's marriage, the play highlights the fact that consummation is not required to make a marriage. The play reminds viewers that the definition of marriage as love developed from exegesis of the biblical story of Mary and Joseph's chaste marriage which precluded making intercourse essential to marriage. In the twelfth century Hugh of St Victor cited Saint Augustine's exegesis of the holy couple in his influential codification of the marriage sacrament. He asserts that 'the sacrament of marriage is accomplished in marital consent' and that 'the true sacrament of marriage can exist, even if carnal commerce has not followed'.[12] In the N-Town play, when Joseph vows to take Mary as his wife, he promises, 'To love yow as myselff, my trewth I yow take' (l. 313). The staging of vows reminds viewers that the words of consent that make a marriage contract are also the sign of love that constitutes the sacrament. In sacramental theory, the couple's vows were the sign of their mutual love which, in turn, was the sign of God's grace. Although the Bishop participates in the marriage of the holy couple in the play, as we have seen, the presence of clergy was not essential to making a marriage either legal or sacramental. The lay nature of marriage is amplified in the play by the fact that all the roles, even that of the Bishop, would have been played by lay people on the city streets, outside of church jurisdiction. Furthermore, by showing the Virgin participating in a chaste marriage that would have been upheld in the courts of late medieval England, the play dignifies legal marriage as a lay spiritual practice.

Although legal marriage contracts did not require the presence of clergy to be upheld as valid in the church courts of medieval England, the nature of the marriage as a sacrament that could be performed without clergy was litigated in the heresy trials of late medieval England. Court records from the trials held by Bishop Alnwich in the East Anglian city of Norwich from 1428 to 1431, for example, show that the accused denied the need for clerical participation in the marriage sacrament in the same language as they denied the validity of other sacraments. One defendant allegedly claimed that 'only consent of love in Jhu' Christ' between a man and woman of Christian belief is 'sifficiant for the sacrament of matrimony'.[13] Although this passage accurately defines legal marriage and fulfils the sacramental theory articulated by twelfth-century theologians, the court records link the denial of the necessity of clerical participation in marriage to a broader denial of the validity of the sacraments and priestly authority. These records, and others like them, indicate that in both theory and practice, the legal definition of marriage as the performance of vows by the couple was seen to promote lay authority potentially at the expense of clerical power.

Like the N-Town compilation, *The Book of Margery Kempe*, which records the life of a lay woman who aspired to sainthood, also explores the

implications of the performative definition of legal marriage for lay authority. *The Book* describes Margery's struggles with her earthly husband to
maintain marital chastity, while also showing her intimate relationship to
Christ in a series of visions. For Margery, like the other medieval holy women
she imitates, having visions was a way to claim spiritual authority through
a direct relationship to Christ unmediated by clerical authority or the institution of the church. Emulating saints and nuns who depicted their closeness to
God as a marriage to Christ, Margery puts marriage at the centre of her
relationship with God. *The Book* includes a vision of a marriage ceremony
rendered in terms that are both legal and performative. Margery's God says
'to hir sowle': 'I take the, Margery, for my weddyd wyfe, for fayrar, for
fowelar, for richar, for powerar ... I make the suyrté'.[14] God's words of
present consent in this passage are performative in that His act of speaking
would make an enforceable marriage contract according to the practices of
contemporary ecclesiastical courts. Margery's God takes the role of an
ordinary lay person, reminding the reader that the performative nature of
the legal marriage contract relies on a theology that dignifies marriage as an
expression of love. The passage includes witnesses, who are not technically
needed to make a marriage, but necessary to enforce a marriage contract in
a court of law. The visionary vow takes place 'befor the Sone and the Holy
Gost and the Modyr of Jhesu, and alle the twelve apostelys, and Seynt
Kateryn and Seynt Margarete and many other seyntys and holy virgynes,
wyth gret multitude of awngelys' (l. 92). The saints named in the passage
were lay women, reminding the reader not only that lay women could
become saints, but also that women as well as men could be legal witnesses
to the marriage contract. In addition, the presence of multiple witnesses in
this passage highlights the nature of the marriage contract as public
performance.

Another marriage play from the N-Town compilation, 'The Trial of Mary
and Joseph', shows how the theatricality of witnessing creates collective
identity. The play establishes a parallel between trial and theatre at the
beginning of the play when the Summoner calls audience and court to
order. Possibly addressing the audience directly, he says 'I warne yow here
all abowte / That I somown yow, all the rowte! (ll. 5–6), and a few lines later,
'Fast com away ... The courte shal be this day!' (ll. 29, 33). He lists a cross-
section of the urban community corresponding both to those who might have
been called to witness in the lower ecclesiastical courts of late medieval
England and to the audience for the drama performed in late medieval
towns. His list includes both male and female names, such as 'Thom
Tyndere and Betrys Belle' (l. 13), 'Johan Jurdon and Geffrey Gyle, Malkyn
Mylkedoke and fayr Mabyle' (ll. 9–10, 13), suggesting that the audience

includes both genders. This mapping of audience of play and trial together engages two legal paradigms of medieval witnessing. By the late Middle Ages, witnessing was defined as first-hand experience, a report of what an individual had personally seen and heard. On the other hand, more traditional modes of proof persisted that relied on common knowledge rather than sensory perception such as testifying to a person's public reputation. In late medieval court practice, the witness was defined as someone from the neighbourhood, and collective knowledge was widely accepted, especially in difficult cases.[15] For example, in a marriage case from York, the deposition includes the following statement: 'The whole neighbourhood testifies to this, and it is well known to all.'[16] In this way, both court and play demonstrate that legal and dramatic practices of witnessing helped to construct collective identity.

The N-Town trial play shows the operation of both empirical and collective paradigms of legal witnessing. In the play, two men accuse Mary of adultery, claiming to speak from direct visual evidence. One (presumably portly) man reports to the other having seen Mary conspicuously pregnant: 'her wombe doth swelle / And is as gret as thinne or myne' (ll. 80–1) and later accuses her directly: 'Thu art with chylde, we se in syght!' (l. 302). On the other hand, following the speech of the Summoner, the opening dialogue of the play shows that the charges against Mary and Joseph originate in gossip between her two accusers, rather than any direct observation of her adultery. The second accuser asks the first, 'canst thu owth telle / Of any newe thynge that wrought was late?' (ll. 66–7). In this way, Mary's accusers testify both to their direct experience and to neighbourhood gossip, ostensibly based in common knowledge of her affairs.

Mary's accusers specifically depict the requirements of accusation by public voice, which allowed two reputable citizens to accuse in a court of law solely on the basis of a person's reputation. Typically two well-respected male leaders of the community would have brought the rumour to the attention of the Bishop who then prosecuted the case 'from the office'.[17] Aside from raising suspicions of their integrity, the names of the two characters in the play, 'Reysesclaundyr' (Raise-Slander) and 'Bakbytere' (Backbiter), represent the simultaneously public and impersonal nature of these kinds of accusations, which did not require an individual eyewitness litigant. 'Reysesclaundyr' refers to 'slander' (also known as 'defamation'), a legal crime. By suing their accusers for slander or defamation, people could protect themselves and their reputations from false accusations. Defamation cases were the natural corollary of a system of justice which allowed suits to be brought on charges of bad reputation. The intimacy between legal defamation and witnessing is clear in the fact that no one tainted by defamation could testify in a criminal trial.[18] The crime of defamation was formalised by the Council of Oxford in 1222, which made it actionable in the church courts to 'maliciously impute a crime to any person who is not of ill fame among good and serious men'.[19] The N-Town Bishop uses this legal term when he addresses Mary's accusers: 'Ye be acursyd so hir for to defame!' (l. 108). The name of the other detractor, 'Bakbytere' (Backbiter), refers to a term often used in confessional texts to connect the sin of envy to the crime of defamation. Both the moral category of 'backbiting' and the legal category of 'slander' were defined by evil intention. One confessional manual's section on envy describes those who secretly watch their neighbour's deeds and then exaggerate their faults behind their backs: 'backbiters ... tear their neighbour's good name to pieces and make themselves partners in the crime of detraction with them'.[20] The discussion of the crime of defamation in a broad range of texts indicates a cultural preoccupation with the risks of testimony based on collective knowledge rather than direct personal experience.

The characters 'Reysesclaundyr' (Raise-Slander) and 'Bakbytere' (Backbiter) are personifications of speech-acts who raise questions about the performativity of legal witnessing. The first detractor boasts, for example, that, together with his brother, Backbiter, 'More slawndyr we to shal arere / Within an howre thorweouth this town / Than evyr ther was this thowand yere' (ll. 46–8). He articulates a model of language detached from its referent, in which slander grows through repetition. While not strictly performative in the Austinian sense, the detractors' words are inherently powerful because the act of pronouncing them within an institutional framework causes Mary and Joseph to be hauled into court, despite the fact that they are detached from provable events.[21] The play's focus on the potential performativity of the language of witnessing should be seen in the context of a broader cultural concern with the vulnerability of the trial to acts of false witnessing. Another confessional manual described the evil consequences of false witnessing in practical legal terms: 'wyl men swere falsely a sawe, /And bere wytnes of swyche a fals / To make a man hang in þe hals'.[22] In this passage the false words of men lead to severe legal punishment, suggesting the power of language to cause injustice to happen. Similarly, the same text depicts the fifth commandment against false witnessing in legalistic terms: 'false traitours and feloune, – that falslyche, for enuye, / On here neghburs wyl gladly lye'.[23] 'Traitours' and 'feloune' allude to crimes, while 'neghburs' invokes the legal definition of witness in the period. All these instances provide a broader context for the play's concern with the power of words in cases of false witnessing, condemning it as an immoral practice. Furthermore, the detractors function as embodiments of community and figures for the audience of the plays.

The N-Town trial play links false witnessing with transgressive male speech and desire. The detractors comment repeatedly on the Virgin's attractive appearance and speculate on how and with whom she may have gotten pregnant. One of them says 'Sum fresch younge galaunt she loveth wel more / That his leggys to her hath leyd' (ll. 87–8) and the other comments, 'For fresch and fayr she is to syght, / And such a mursel – as semyth me– / Wolde cause a younge man to have delight!' (ll. 91–3). The depiction of Mary's accusers in the play corresponds to the pattern demonstrated by medieval legal records, which show that women were more likely than men to be victims of rumour, and that women were more often accused of transgressive sexuality.[24] Through unflattering portraits of Mary's accusers, the play ascribes the reason for this to male desire rather than female culpability. This gendering of false witnessing corresponds to the fact that men typically functioned as the representatives of community in instances of accusation by public reputation. While women could be witnesses, men were more often summoned to court. Like the N-Town trial play, conduct books, which taught manners and were popular with urban elites, link the problems of false witnessing to a broader discourse on men's need to regulate their speech. For example, the gendered advice poem, 'How the Wise Man Taught His Son' instructs, 'Neiþer fals witness þou noon bere / On no mannys matere ... Þou were betere be deef & dombe / Þan falseli to go upon a qweste'.[25] This poem teaches boys that regulating their speech is essential to masculine virtue and that failure to do so can have material legal consequences. By contrast, the gendered poem 'How the Good Wife Taught Her Daughter' teaches the importance of proper speech, advising against gossiping, cursing and scolding, but does not tie female speech to legal witnessing.[26] Although witnessing could be legally performed by both men and women, witnessing was often linked to male identity, and false witnessing to male desire and undesirable male loquaciousness.

Although the N-Town trial play associates false witnessing with men, it also makes a case for the potential of female testimony in court to be a source of power and relative equality for women. When Mary denies her adultery, she invokes the standard vow of witnesses in court: 'God to wyttnes, I am a mayd! / Of fleschly lust and gostly wownde / In dede nere thought I nevyr asayd' (ll.211–13). God's validation of her testimony is subsequently literalised in the play when Joseph, Mary and their accusers drink a miraculous potion that reveals the truth of people's words on their faces. Whereas Mary and Joseph maintain their story, their accusers change theirs. One exclaims: 'I do me repent / Of my cursyd and fals langage!' (ll. 366–7), while the Bishop declares, 'All cursyd langage and schame onsownd, / Good Mary, forgeve us here in this place!' (ll. 372–3); the play ends with Mary forgiving the acts of false witnessing. Despite its reliance on divine intervention, the play implies that the testimony of women in court can be effective and perhaps even more honest than the testimony of men, thus making a case for witnessing as a source for female authority.

This chapter has shown that legal and literary notions of performance built on a culture of witnessing to influence each other. Despite limited legal rights for married women, the N-Town plays and *The Book of Margery Kempe* were clearly aware of the potential for gender equality in the legal definition of the marriage contract as an exchange of vows. Although men more often served as witnesses in the courts of medieval England and warnings against false witnessing were more often directed at men, both the N-Town plays and the *Book of Margery Kempe* suggest that witnessing could be an area of gender equality. Late medieval representations of witnessing drew attention to the performative nature of legal language, which was empowering for lay people and women, but also vulnerable to false witnessing. The theatricality of both trials and plays demonstrated the ways that medieval community was created in acts of public performance. Trials and plays provided an alternative and supplement to the institutionalised rituals of the church, suggesting they might have shaped ideas and practices of morality in late medieval England.

Notes

1. See *Decrees of the Ecumenical Councils*, vol. 1, ed. Norman P. Tanner (Washington, DC: Georgetown University Press, 1990), 244.
2. R. H. Helmholz, The *Oxford History of the Laws of England* (New York: Oxford University Press) I, 328.
3. Lorna Hutson, *The Invention of Suspicion: Law and Mimesis in Shakespeare and Renaissance Drama* (Oxford: Oxford University Press, 2007), 3.
4. Shannon McSheffrey, *Love and Marriage in Late Medieval London*, TEAMS (Kalamazoo, MI: Medieval Institute Publications, 1995); R. H. Helmholz, *Marriage Litigation in Medieval England* (New York: Cambridge University Press, 1974); Charles Donahue, Jr, *Law, Marriage, and Society in the Later Middle Ages: Argument about Marriage in Five Courts* (New York: Cambridge University Press, 2007).
5. J. L. Austin, *How to Do Things with Words* (Cambridge, MA: Harvard University Press, 1962), 6.
6. McSheffrey, *Love and Marriage*, 12.
7. *The Mary Play from the N.Town Manuscript*, ed. Peter Meredith (New York: Longman, 1987), 1–3 and *The N-Town Plays: A Facsimile of British Library MS Cotton Vespasian D. VII*, ed. Peter Meredith and Stanley J. Kahrl (Leeds: University of Leeds, School of English, 1976), esp. xvii.

8. *The N-Town Plays*, ed. Douglas Sugano (Kalamazoo, MI: Medieval Institute Publications, 2007), 98. All other citations are to this edition.

9. Austin, *How to Do Things with Words*, 22.

10. Meg Twycross, 'The Theatricality of Medieval English Plays', in *The Cambridge Companion to Medieval English Theatre*, ed. Richard Beadle and Alan J. Fletcher, 2nd edn (New York: Cambridge University Press, 2008), 26–74.

11. For an influential theorisation of this idea, see St Thomas Aquinas, *Summa Theologiae*, ed. and trans. Thomas Gilby (New York: Cambridge University Press, 1966), XXVIII, 90–100.

12. *Hugh of Saint Victor on the Sacraments of the Christian Faith*, ed. Roy J. Deferrari (Cambridge, MA: The Medieval Academy of America, 1951), 332 and 326.

13. *Heresy Trials in the Diocese of Norwich 1428–31*, ed. Norman P. Tanner, Camden 4th series 20 (London: Royal Historical Society, 1977), 153.

14. *The Book of Margery Kempe*, ed. Lynn Staley, TEAMS (Kalamazoo, MI: Medieval Institute Publications, 1996), 92. All other citations will be to this edition.

15. Charles Donahue, Jr, 'Proof by Witnesses in the Church Courts of Medieval England: An Imperfect Reception of the Learned Law', in *On the Laws and Customs of England: Essays in Honor of Samuel E. Thorne*, ed. Morris S. Arnold, Thomas A. Green, Sally A. Scully and Stephen D. White (Chapel Hill, NC: University of North Carolina Press, 1981), 136, n. 49; and R. H. Helmholz, *The Oxford History of the Laws of England* (Oxford and New York: Oxford University Press, 2004), I, 316.

16. Norma Adams and Charles Donahue Jr., eds., *Select Cases from the Ecclesiastical Courts of the Province of Canterbury, c. 1200–1301*, Selden Society vol. 95 (London: The Selden Society 1980), 29. Cited in Donahue, 'Proof by Witnesses', 140.

17. Richard M. Wunderli, *London Church Courts on the Eve of the Reformation* (Cambridge, MA: Medieval Academy of America, 1981), 32; and *Select Cases on Defamation to 1600*, ed. R. H. Helmholz, Selden Society vol. 101 (London: Selden Society, 1985).

18. *Select Cases on Defamation to 1600*, ed. Helmholz, xxi.

19. C. R. Cheney, ed., *Councils and Synods: With Other Documents Relating to the English Church* (Oxford: Clarendon Press, 1964) II, part 1, 107. Cited in Wunderli, *London Church Courts*, 64–5.

20. *Fasciculus Morum: A Fourteenth-Century Preacher's Handbook*, ed. and trans. Siegfried Wenzel (University Park, PA, and London: Pennsylvania State University Press, 1989), 161.

21. Pierre Bourdieu argues that Austin's 'performative utterances' are only effective in certain institutional contexts. See *Language and Symbolic Power*, ed. John B. Thompson, trans. Gino Raymond and Matthew Adamson (Cambridge, MA: Harvard University Press, 1991), 111.

22. *Robert of Brunne's Handlyng Synne*, ed. Frederick J. Furnivall, Part I, EETS, o.s. 119 (London: Kegan Paul, Trench, Trübner, 1901), 95.

23. *Handlyng Synne*, ed. Furnivall, 49.

24. L. R. Poos, 'Sex, Lies and the Church Courts of Pre-Reformation England', *Journal of Interdisciplinary History* 25:4 (1995), 585–607.

25. *The Babees Book*, ed. Frederick J. Furnivall, EETS, o.s. 32 (New York: Greenwood Press, 1969; London: Trübner, 1868), 49.
26. *Babees Book*, 36–47.

Further Reading

Arnold, John H., 'Margery's Trials: Heresy, Lollardy and Dissent' in *A Companion to The Book of Margery Kempe*, ed. John H. Arnold and Katherine J. Lewis, Cambridge: D. S. Brewer, 2004, 75–93.

Cannon, Christopher, 'The Rights of Medieval English Women: Crime and the Issue of Representation', in *Medieval Crime and Social Control*, ed. Barbara A. Hanawalt and David Wallace, Minneapolis: University of Minnesota Press, 1999, 156–85.

Enders, Jody, *Rhetoric and the Origins of Medieval Drama*, Ithaca: Cornell University Press, 1992.

Gold, Penny, 'The Marriage of Mary and Joseph in the Twelfth-Century Ideology of Marriage', in *Sexual Practices and the Medieval Church*, ed. Vern Bullough and James Brundage, Buffalo, NY: Prometheus Books, 1982, 102–17.

Horner, Olga, '"Us Make Lies": Witness, Evidence and Proof in the York Resurrection', *Medieval English Theatre* (1998), 24–76.

Hunt, Alison M, 'Maculating Mary: The Detractors of the N-Town Cycle's "Trial of Joseph and Mary"', *Philological Quarterly* 73 (1994), 11–29.

King, Pamela M., 'Contemporary Cultural Models for the Trial Plays in the York Cycle', in *Drama and Community: People and Plays in Medieval Europe*, ed. Alan Hindley, Turnhout, Belgium: Brepols, 1999, 200–16.

Lipton, Emma, *Affections of the Mind: The Politics of Sacramental Marriage in Late Medieval English Literature*, Notre Dame, IN: Notre Dame University Press, 2007.

'Language on Trial: Performing the Law in the N-Town Trial Play', in *The Letter of the Law: Legal Practice and Literary Production in Medieval England*, ed. Emily Steiner and Candace Barrington, Ithaca, NY: Cornell University Press, 2002, 115–35.

McCarthy, Conor, *Marriage in Medieval England: Law, Literature and Practice*, Woodbridge, UK, and Rochester, NY: Boydell, 2004.

McSheffrey, Shannon, *Marriage, Sex and Civic Culture in Late Medieval London*, Philadelphia: University of Pennsylvania Press, 2006.

Sheehan, Michael M., *Marriage, Family and Law in Medieval Europe: Collected Studies*, ed. James K. Farge, Toronto: University of Toronto Press, 1996.

Taylor, Jamie K., *Fictions of Evidence: Witnessing, Literature and Community in the Late Middle Ages*, Columbus, OH: Ohio State University Press, 2013.

INDEX

Index

Index

Einhard, 3
  Vita Karoli Magni, 3
Elyot, Sir Thomas, 50
  The boke named the Governour, 50
English (as a language of the law), 20–2,
  27, 70
equity law, 25, 26, 50, 96, 155, 157–58, 181
Exceptiones ad cassandum brevia, 69
Expositio vocabulorum, 14, 70
Exton, Nicholas, 151

Fet asaver, 69
Fisher, J.H., 159, 160, 161, 163, 164
Fitz Neal, Richard
  Dialogus de scaccario, 67
Fitzherbert, Anthony, 76
  Graunde Abridgement, 76
Fitzralph, Richard
  Defensio Curatorum, 169
FitzWarin, Fulk, 86
Flanders, 181
Fleta, 68
Forester, Richard, 149, 153
Forfeiture Act of 1870, 91
forms, literary
  bob-and-wheel, 109
  drama, 204–5
  political satire, 110
Forrest, Ian, 168
Fortescue, Sir John, xii, 24, 42–3, 46, 47, 48,
  49, 50, 51, 69, 72, 178, 180, 184, 185,
  186, 187
  De laudibus legum Angliae, 42, 46, 47, 48,
    50, 69, 178, 185, 187
  De natura legis naturae, 185
  On the Governance of England, 48, 49, 50,
    52, 185
Foucault, Michel, 84
Fouke le Fitz Waryn, 190
Fourth Lateran Council (1215), 6, 168,
  202
France, 48, 181
Francia, 3
Franks. *See* Francia
Fraser, Simon, 89–91
French (law French), 18–26, 27, 66, 75,
  184
Frye, Northrop, 188
Fyve Wyttes, The, 170

Galloway, Andrew, 160, 164
Gamelyn, 190
Gaunt, John of, duke of Lancaster, 122, 180

General Eyre, 18, 21, 67
Geoffrey of Monmouth, 49
  *Historia Regum Britanniae (History of the
    Kings of Britain)*, 49, 50
Giancarlo, Matthew, 163, 165, 183
Gilbert de Thornton
  Summa, 69
Giles of Rome
  De regimine principum, 105, 112
  Li Livres du Gouvernement des Rois. See
    Giles of Rome: *De regimine principum*
Glanvill, Ranulf de, 31, 42, 44, 45, 47, 53, 55,
  67, 109, 112
  *The Treatise on the Laws and Customs
    of the Kingdom of England*, 17,
    67, 111
Good Parliament (1376), 115
Gower, Agnes (née Groundolf), 151
Gower, John, 116, 123, 136, 148–59
  'Eneidos bucolis', 151, 152
  In Praise of Peace, 151, 162
  *Carmen super multiplici viciorum
    pestilencia*, 163
  Cinkante Balades, 151
  Confessio Amantis, 119, 146, 151, 154–6,
    158, 159, 162–5
    Apollonius of Tyre, 159
    Lycurgus, 159
  Cronica Tripertita, 148, 151, 156–8,
    165
  Mirour de l'Omme, 122, 148–9, 151–3,
    160–3, 165–6
  Traitié pour essampler les amantz marietz,
    151, 162
  Vox Clamantis, 148, 151, 153, 161, 163,
    165, 166
  will, 150–1
Gower, Sir Robert, 148
Gratian, Roman emperor
  Decretum, 30, 31, 32, 35, 36, 109, 169,
    172–6
Great Statute of Treasons. *See* Statute on
    Treason (1351)
Green, Richard Firth, 162
Gregory IX, pope, 36
Gregory the Great, pope
  Pastoral Care, 4
Grete Sentence of Curs, 174
Grimm, Jakob, 4, 7, 8
Grotius, Hugo, 182
  Mare liberum, 182
Gruffydd, Dafydd ap, 90
Guillaume Le Talleur, 75

Index

Index

St German, Christopher, 42, 50, 51
  conscience, 50
  Doctor and Student, 42, 50
St Paul's Cathedral, 12, 103
Stanton, John, 26
Staplegate, Edmund, 137
Statham, Nicholas
  Abridgement of Cases, 75, 76, 78
Statuta Angliae, 69
Statute of Gloucester (1278), 70
Statute of Laborers (1351), 123
Statute of Marlborough (1267), 55, 70
Statute of Pleading (1362), 22–5
Statute of Rapes (1382), 138
Statute of Westminster (1275), 54, 70
Statute of Westminster (1285), 70
Statute of Winchester (1285), 56, 59, 113
Statute on Treason (1351), 84–6, 130,
  174, 196
statutory law, 54–62, 69–73
Stockton, Eric W., 164
Strohm, Paul, 164
Suffolk, Sir Michael de la Pole, 1st earl of, 103
Sywell, Simon, 35

Textus Roffensis, 7, 12
Thirty-Seven Conclusions, 173–4
Thomas of Lancaster, 85
Thorpe, Benjamin, 5
Thorpe, William
  Testimony of William Thorpe, 172,
  173
Thynne, William, 159
Tottel, Richard, 76
Tower of London, 70
Townsend, Roger, 73
Tresilian, Robert, chief justice, 115
Trevisa, John, 112, 169
trial by battle, 202
trial by ordeal, 202
trouthe. See depictions of: oaths
Tyler, Wat, 61

unwritten law, 9
Usk, Adam, 26
Usk, Thomas, 104

Vacarius, 35
  Liber pauperum, 35
van Dijk, Conrad, 163, 165
vetera statuta, 70

Virgil, 152
Vita Karoli Magni. See Einhard

Wales, 38, 90–1
Wallace, William, 89–91
Walshman, William, 130
Walter of Henley
  Le Dite de Hosebondrie, 72
Walter, Hubert, 67
Walworth, William, 151
wards, 137
Wars of the Roses, 49, 72, 184–6, 193
Westminster, 21, 22, 23, 24, 43, 45, 46, 67,
  74, 121, 122, 123, 126
Wheelocke, Abraham, 4
widows. *See* Personhood, legal: women:
  widows
Wifmannes beweddung, 6
Wihtred, 8
Wilkins, David, 4
William of Pagula
  Oculus sacerdotum, 114
  Speculum Edwardi Tertii, 114–15
William of Wykeham, bishop of Winchester
  and chancellor of England, 151
William the Conqueror, king of England and
  duke of Normandy, 10, 12, 31, 61
witan, 9
Wolsey, Thomas, archbishop of York and
  chancellor of England, 39
Woodbine, George, 19
Worcester Cathedral Library MS F. 87, 68
Wordes of Poule, 171
Wormald, Patrick, 5, 8, 10,
  12
writs, 7, 67, 73–4
Wulfstan7, 8, 9
Wyche, Richard
  Letter of Richard Wyche, 172
Wyclif, John (*c.* 1330–64), 167
Wycliffites. *See* lollardy
Wynkeburn, Walter, 130

Yale Law School Library, MS G St11/ 1, 72
Yeager, R.F., 163
Year Books, 46, 74–6
York Minster Library and Archives, MS
  XVI.D. 6, 68
York, Richard of, 3rd duke of, 103
Yorkshire, 148
Ywain and Gawain, 192–3